# MODEL BRITAIN

Throughout the twentieth century architectural models served as the miniature playgrounds in which the future of Britain's built environment was imagined, and in drawing from the evidence provided by those models today, this book considers how architects, planners, and civil engineers thought about that future by presenting a history of yesterday's dreams of tomorrow, told through architectural models.

Focused not on the making of architectural models but rather the optimistic and utopian visions they were made to communicate, this book examines the possible futures put forward by 120 models made by Thorp, the oldest and most prolific firm of architectural modelmakers in Britain, in order to reveal a century of evolving ideas about how we might live, work, relax, and move. From depictions of unbuilt city masterplans to those of seemingly ordinary shopping centres and motorways, the models featured trace a progression of the architectural, social, political, technological, and economic influences that shaped the design of Britain's buildings, transport infrastructure, and its towns and cities during a century of relentless change.

Illustrated with over 130 photographs, this book will appeal to academics and historians, as well as anyone with an interest in architectural models and the history of Britain's twentieth century built environment.

**David Lund** is Senior Lecturer in Modelmaking at Arts University Bournemouth, UK.

# MODEL BRITAIN

The Architectural Models of Twentieth Century Dreams

*David Lund*

Routledge
Taylor & Francis Group

LONDON AND NEW YORK

Designed cover image: Courtesy Thorp Archive, AUB.

First published 2025
by Routledge
4 Park Square, Milton Park, Abingdon, Oxon OX14 4RN

and by Routledge
605 Third Avenue, New York, NY 10158

*Routledge is an imprint of the Taylor & Francis Group, an informa business*

*British Library Cataloguing-in-Publication Data*
A catalogue record for this book is available from the British Library

*Library of Congress Cataloging-in-Publication Data*
Names: Lund, David, 1980– author.
Title: Model Britain : the architectural models of twentieth century dreams / David Lund.
Description: Abingdon, Oxon : Routledge, 2025. | Includes bibliographical references and index.
Identifiers: LCCN 2024025962 (print) | LCCN 2024025963 (ebook) | ISBN 9781032715711 (hardback) | ISBN 9781032715094 (paperback) | ISBN 9781032715728 (ebook)
Subjects: LCSH: Architectural models—Great Britain—History—20th century. | Architecture and society—Great Britain—History—20th century. | Built environment—Great Britain—Forecasting.
Classification: LCC NA2790 .L864 2025 (print) | LCC NA2790 (ebook) | DDC 720.22—dc23/eng/20240821
LC record available at https://lccn.loc.gov/2024025962
LC ebook record available at https://lccn.loc.gov/2024025963

ISBN: 9781032715711 (hbk)
ISBN: 9781032715094 (pbk)
ISBN: 9781032715728 (ebk)

DOI: 10.4324/9781032715728

Typeset in Sabon
by codeMantra

# CONTENTS

# FIGURES

# ACKNOWLEDGEMENTS

This book would not have been possible without the kindness and enthusiasm of the many people who have supported my research in various different ways over the past three years. First, enormous thanks must be extended to Alec Saunders and Nick Mines at Atom, Tim O'Reilly-Bennett and Valerie Lodge at Arts University Bournemouth, Cassandra Pickavance, and the Business Archives Council, all of whom have been instrumental in supporting the preservation and cataloguing of the Thorp Archive. At Arts University Bournemouth, I must also thank my colleagues Paul Johnson, Claire Holman, Will Strange, Graham Wood, Jonathan Hoyle, Lydia Miles, and Phil Anderson.

Further thanks are due to Samantha Barnes-Knight at Historic England, Sally Scagell, Jacob Paskins, Angharad Fortgang at the Duchy of Cornwall Archive, Max Batten, Fabian Hiscock, Kate Rose at Cornwall Archives, Alison Duke at the Foundling Museum, David Leboff at Transport for London, Simon Murphy at the London Transport Museum, Patrick Collins at the National Motor Museum, Ewan Harrison and Scott Miller at the Manchester School of Architecture, and Catherine Croft and Penny Loughton at the Twentieth Century Society. I must also thank the many followers of the Thorp Archive on social media who provided vital information about whether certain projects were built as the models showed, and to Francesca Ford and the editorial and production teams at Routledge for such a beautifully organised publication. Finally, thanks are due to Edward and my family as always, and to all the modelmakers who worked at Thorp for applying their incredible skills in bringing so many twentieth century dreams into miniature reality.

This book is dedicated to my father who not only helped shape the future of Britain's built environment as a civil engineer but also, and perhaps more importantly, instilled a love of models in his son.

# INTRODUCTION

Twentieth century Britain was a time and a place that overflowed with dreams. Against a backdrop of the arrival of modernity, two costly World Wars, and the long run of social and economic upheaval that followed, Britain's architects, planners, and civil engineers were relentless in their pursuit of countless visions of how tomorrow might be better than today. Accompanying those visions were thousands of architectural models and it was in these miniature playgrounds that generations of dreamers were able to freely put forward their ideas of how the future of Britain's built environment should unfold. As representations of ideas, architectural models have long served to open up conversations by providing an almost universally accessible means by which different proposals can be debated and explored.[1] Acknowledged as the 'natural territory of vision,'[2] models act as the 'architecture of the imaginary,'[3] and through the creation of captivating scale worlds, they can convince us that their bright and optimistic depictions of the future have already arrived. It was these capabilities that made architectural models such effective tools for communicating the many different futures that were proposed during the twentieth century, standing as utopian manifestations of their respective visions, forever frozen in the moments of their unveiling. Those futures are now our past, and it is precisely because architectural models were used in this way that they today provide important insights into what people were thinking at the time, serving as evidence of not just what was built, but what was dreamed.

In just the single year of 1969, for example, Thorp Modelmakers, based at 98 Gray's Inn Road in London, made 224 architectural models, working for clients such as Taylor Woodrow, T.P. Bennett, Foster Associates, and Richard Seifert and Partners – for whom Thorp completed twenty-one commissions in that year alone. Projects included models of the Slough Holiday Inn, the A10 Stockford Interchange, an early proposal for the Channel Tunnel, and two particularly notable models: one of the NatWest Tower (Figure 0.1) and another of Owen Luder's proposal for the redevelopment of St. Katherine's Dock (Figure 0.2). Following the unveiling of these models to the public the NatWest Tower was constructed as planned, opening in 1980, while Owen Luder's proposal for St. Katherine's Dock remained just a dream. In its place, RHWL's Tower Hotel was built at the western end of the plot in 1973, while the remaining warehouses were gradually

DOI: 10.4324/9781032715728-1

**FIGURE 0.1**    Model of the NatWest Tower. Architect: Richard Seifert and Partners. Made by Thorp, 1969. Courtesy Thorp Archive, AUB.

redeveloped over the next twenty years. At the time when these models were made, however, the futures of both projects were equally uncertain as there was no guarantee that either proposal would be built. The same can be said of every model Thorp made in 1969, and indeed of almost every architectural model made during the twentieth century and beyond, all of which acted as hopeful projections of future buildings, structures, and even entire towns and cities, some of which were constructed while others existed only in model form. Regardless of the outcome, however, at the time of their making, they all shared the same optimism and potential, confidently predicting idealised visions of tomorrows that had yet to be determined.

FIGURE 0.2    Model of an unbuilt proposal for St. Katherine's Dock. Architect: Owen Luder. Made by Thorp, 1969. Courtesy Thorp Archive, AUB.

The aim of this book is to examine the rich seam of evidence that such architectural models provide to understand how the future of Britain's built environment was imagined during the twentieth century by exploring some of the different ideas relating to place, home, work, leisure, citizenship, and transport that were projected through utopian scale worlds. In doing so, this study draws from the remarkable archive of Thorp Modelmakers, which in addition to the models described above made more than 10,000 architectural models during the twentieth century. Founded by John Thorp in 1883, as Britain's oldest and most prolific maker of architectural models, the extensive photographic record of the company's work offers a unique lens through which a century of shifting visions of Britain's future houses, offices, schools, hospitals, roads, shopping centres, and more can be traced. By examining the individual dreams behind 120 architectural models that Thorp made during the twentieth century, this book reveals the broader influences that shaped those dreams, and with the emphasis placed firmly on how the past thought about tomorrow, each project is considered as it was first proposed.

The historian David Edgerton has observed that while a history of the British future has yet to be written, notions of the future became particularly important in the twentieth century as its 'possibilities became clearer,'[4] and that its imagining was not just an ideological endeavour, but a material one.[5] That materiality manifested itself in many different ways, and in seeking to understand how the past thought about tomorrow, this book recognises architectural models as a vital and often overlooked material means of revealing crucial evidence of how Britain's future was planned. In challenging the prevailing emphasis of historical analysis on the tangible events and outcomes of past realities,[6] this study also embraces a growing cross-disciplinary interest in exploring the 'horizons of expectation'[7] that formed in any given period, and in recognising the value of understanding anticipatory practices,[8] seeks to bring to life the hopes and dreams of the past. This book, in encompassing visions of both the built and unbuilt environment therefore presents a history of the ideas behind yesterday's dreams of tomorrow, told through architectural models. Across six themed chapters, individual models serve to illustrate the possible futures they were made to represent while collectively charting a century of evolving ideas about how we might live, work, relax, and move. By entering the orderly miniature realm of Model Britain we are able to explore a fictional yet tangible reality where competing visions of yesterday's future reside side by side, allowing for an understanding of how the past imagined tomorrow and how the paths actually taken through the many different ideas put forward during the twentieth century were ultimately chosen.

## Miniature Dreams

Architectural models have long been recognised as a powerful medium through which grand and hopeful visions of the future can be expressed, but it was during the twentieth century that the model's position in this manner really came to prominence in Britain, in no small way due to the establishment of architectural modelmaking as a dedicated occupation under the auspices of John Thorp, the founder of Thorp Modelmakers, but also due to the scale of change to Britain's built environment that took place as the century progressed. While the nineteenth century had seen Britain transformed through massive population growth, rapid industrialisation and urbanisation, the development of the railways, and the scouring of the natural landscape for resources such as coal, the changes that occurred during the twentieth century were arguably just as profound. Technological advances, the consequences of two World Wars, a shift in ideology to favour state intervention in addressing social issues, a desire to meet the increasing aspirations of the working classes, and the ongoing necessity of dealing with the consequences of the unplanned nature of Britain's urban development during the previous century fuelled a relentless expansion and renewal of the built environment. Approximately eighty percent of England's housing stock was built between 1900 and 2000,[9] as were similar proportions of Britain's schools and hospitals. Half of the nation's road network was laid out, including over two thousand miles of motorways, all of its power stations and airports, and hundreds of shopping centres containing perhaps as much as twenty million square metres of retail space. Entire towns such as Milton Keynes, Crawley, and Cumbernauld were built to become home to over one million people, while massive shifts in how we lived and worked, combined with relentless technological innovation, additionally gave rise to new forms of buildings such as high rise office blocks, airports, and retail parks that characterise the manmade environment we experience today.

Fundamentally, architecture is an ideas business.[10] The job of an architect, and that of the other professions involved in shaping the built environment, is to imagine what could be. The ideas of architects, planners, and civil engineers, in outlining potential visions of tomorrow, are intrinsically hopeful, and the designers of Britain's buildings, towns, and infrastructure during the twentieth century invariably saw their interventions as positive. During the seductive process of shepherding an idea from concept to drawing to model, and – if fortune was on their side – to actual construction, it was a conviction in the positive benefits of an idea that fuelled its progression. In this manner everything they imagined was partially utopian,[11] projecting dreams of a better world into a future that was, in the context of their designs, firmly under their control.

Architectural models, made to explain and promote countless schemes from the most mundane housing estate or office building to vast speculative concepts for entire towns and cities, proved to be the perfect means through which these utopian ideas could be expressed, as being an abstraction of reality that becomes more perfect than can ever be achieved, utopia is in essence a model itself. In presenting an idealised state architectural models have therefore long been considered the ideal medium through which notions of utopia could be rendered comprehensible,[12] extending a sanitised realisation 'of what architecture promises, yet can never attain.'[13] Operating as worldbuilding tools,[14] the realities that architectural models create are shaped by the ideological assumptions behind the designs they are made to represent, and in their miniature existence stand as parallels, substitutes, or surrogates of full-sized futures, creating carefully choreographed fictional spaces that form gateways to different worlds.

The making of presentation models, used not as study or sketch aids to guide the development of an architectural design but as a means of communicating those designs to someone else, usually a client or the public, has, from the start of the twentieth century onwards, been the specialism of the professional modelmaker, trained in the interpretation and translation of an idea into scaled, three-dimensional form. Their role is to present the originator's ideas through the creation of a model that is attuned to the experiences, expectations, and cultural and ideological frameworks of its intended audience, and it takes the skill of the modelmaker to overcome the inherent distortions and compromises that such communication entails, as well as adding the creative refinements that make models such engaging spaces within which complex ideas can be housed (Figure 0.3). Acting as worldmaker as much as modelmaker, their task is to balance the model's dual existence as both artefact and representation, their creations projecting 'a reality of their own while also anticipating a reality beyond.'[15] Scale becomes an important tool, generating a distance from reality that results in a cognitive detachment that draws the viewer ever deeper into the fictional world the model creates.[16] In providing us with a density of information that is hyper-real, the process of miniaturisation grants a sense of spatial and conceptual authority that is difficult to obtain in the real world, with reality replaced by a fictitious and abstract state, 'timeless and separated from its surroundings,'[17] at a scale over which we can dominate.

Models are therefore powerful instruments that aid visionary thinking, and it was this ability that placed architectural models central to the expression of so many hopeful ideas about the future of Britain's built environment during the twentieth century. As purer, more utopian expressions of what was planned, those same models today offer a unique insight into the dreams, hopes, debates, and ideologies that were encoded into them before reality took hold. Whether models of projects that were built, or of alternatives that never saw the light of day, in all of them it is possible to examine the miniature dreams of past generations just as they were imagined, and to explore them is to embark on a journey to investigate yesterday's visions of the future in their unfiltered, idealised forms.

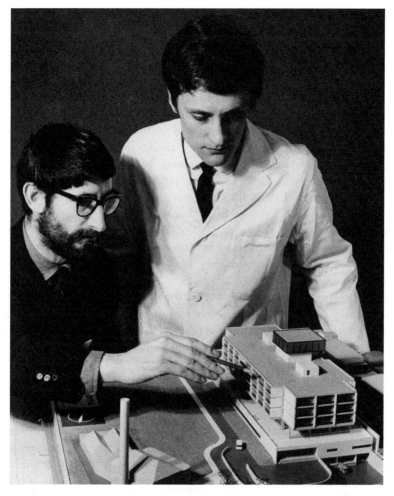

FIGURE 0.3    A modelmaker at Thorp noting final adjustments to an architectural model, c1965. Courtesy Thorp Archive, AUB.

### The Model as Evidence

By using architectural models as primary sources this book approaches its subject from a position whereby all proposals are considered at the point of public reveal when their futures were as yet undetermined, allowing for an appreciation of the dreams they hold within the contexts of the times in which they were formed. In doing so, this book discusses the different ideas relating to place, home, work, leisure, citizenship, and transport that lie behind them with the intention of illustrating the breadth of ideas that were put forward, whether ideologically or commercially driven, and how architectural models were used to communicate those dreams to the public. To aid this discussion, this book employs the conceptual notion of Model Britain as a metaphorical parallel to the real Britain where we are able to tour the multitude of past possible futures that architectural models represent. In drawing from this parallel history of Britain's built environment, this book champions models as important sources of evidence and recognises the unique insights they provide into the ideas, values, and aspirations that shaped the designs they were made to communicate. In doing so, this study consciously avoids repeating my previous work on the history of architectural modelmaking in Britain by respectfully positioning modelmakers in the background. The skills of the modelmaker and the materiality of architectural models nevertheless play an important role in what follows, however, with individual models considered as constructs, 'the result of a series of choices about what to show and how to show it.'[18] Analysing decisions relating to materials, scale, and composition reveals useful information about which messages particular models were trying to convey and which they might have been trying to hide. The richness of information a model contains, communicating through three-dimensional storytelling, is therefore invaluable, and having served as the mediator between an architect, planner, or engineer and their clients and the public, models also provide an insight into the processes of persuasion that were taking place at the time. Nick Dunn and Paul Cureton have noted that the 'purpose and power' of any representation of the future comes from the visualisation itself,[19] and so in 'reading' models, their lack of neutrality as a communication medium is acknowledged, with a consideration of the context of that communication being necessary to fully understand the messages they contain.

Architectural models themselves are ephemeral objects, generally being discarded after their job has been completed, and this is likely why they have been an underutilised source of historical evidence; to compile a history using models, you first have to find them, and this can quickly become a problematic exercise as collections of surviving models such as those belonging to the RIBA and the V&A are highly selective. It is for this reason that the archive of Thorp Modelmakers is of such value, with the collection containing over 30,000 photographs and documents that chart the company's long and illustrious history, and with Thorp having photographed a significant number of the 10,000 architectural models they made during the twentieth century, the records held within the Thorp Archive are uniquely comprehensive. A detailed account of the company and its significance can be found in my previous work,[20] but as the first, oldest, and, for most of its 140-year history, the largest firm of architectural modelmakers in Britain, Thorp made more models than anyone else. Thanks to the foresight of its founder John Thorp (Figure 0.4), his son Leslie, and the owners and directors of the company that followed them, the record of the company's work remains remarkably intact, including more than 16,000 photographs of the architectural models they made between 1899 and 1996. The completeness of the archive, now held by Arts University Bournemouth, is exceptional, and it was through my work leading the cataloguing of the collection that I began to realise its potential in terms of not just understanding the history of architectural modelmaking but also in revealing an entirely new perspective on the history of architectural design and the built environment.[21] Covering more than 3500 separate projects spanning the entirety of the twentieth century, the archive's photographic record reveals a remarkable progression through time as new ideas were being tested and explored in model form, some of which were ultimately built while others were not. The collection therefore provides a valuable opportunity to understand the development of Britain's homes, workplaces, leisure facilities, and transport infrastructure through the evidence provided by the models that Thorp made for hundreds of different architects, planners, property developers, and engineers.

FIGURE 0.4    John Thorp, right, with a team of modelmakers in the workshops at 98 Gray's Inn Road, 1930. Courtesy Thorp Archive, AUB.

Archival research is by no means immune from bias, selection, or the pitfalls of contemporary interpretation, however, as no historical source can offer unmediated access to what has gone before and even the most complete archive is only able to put forward a partial and selective representation of events. Archives do nevertheless provide an important means of accessing evidence from as close to the time being studied as possible,[22] and the insights they put forward can be highly valuable, as evidenced by David Dean's use of the RIBA's drawings collection for *The Thirties: Recalling the English Architectural Scene*,[23] and Alastair Forsyth's *Buildings for the Age*,[24] which draws from the photographic archive of the National Monuments Record, both of which use specific archival collections to contribute a greater understanding of the history of the twentieth century built environment. An obvious limitation of relying on a single archive such as Thorp's, however, is that despite their dominance, Thorp did not by any means make every architectural model made in Britain during the twentieth century, and so there are many models of notable projects that are today deemed central to the history of Britain's built environment that are not represented in the collection. This is more than compensated by the archive's breadth, however, and it is the archive's inclusion of the ordinary alongside what is now deemed iconic that gives it such value to this study as nowhere else can be found so complete an unfiltered record of the everyday commissions of architectural models over so long a period of time.

## Scope and Contents

The structure of this book has been organised thematically and within each of the six main chapters that follow different visions of the future of Britain's built environment are explored by drawing from the evidence provided by more than 120 architectural models made by Thorp during the twentieth century and contextualising the ideas behind them within the architectural, social, and economic circumstances of their times. Chapter 1, Place, considers architectural models that portrayed future visions of the structure and lay-out of Britain's towns and cities, while Chapter 2, Home, examines the ideas behind models that depicted proposals for both private and public housing. Chapter 3, Work, explores architectural models that reflected changing ideas about the future of the workplace, particularly offices and industrial buildings; Chapter 4, Leisure, considers models that evidence how architects responded to changing social and cultural aspirations in designing future shopping centres, holiday parks, and other leisure venues; Chapter 5, Citizenship, examines architectural models that chart shifting visions of the future of public buildings; and Chapter 6, Transport, explores models that outline how the future of Britain's transport infrastructure was imagined in response to rapid technological advances. These six themes were chosen as together they describe the functions of much of the artificial landscape of Britain while also allowing for an investigation of the major influences that shaped the built environment throughout the twentieth century. The individual models featured were selected from the many thousands recorded in the Thorp Archive to be representative of the collection as a whole in order to reflect the rise and fall in demand for models of particular types of buildings and structures as the century unfolded. The models described therefore act as windows into the ideas that shaped the designs they represent and so at times both the models and even the proposals themselves fade into the background, allowing the ideological changes of the twentieth century to be brought forward to explore the driving forces behind the dreams of the future that each model was made to convey. Although focused on Britain, the global context of many of the influences expressed is also considered where appropriate, and the conclusion highlights broader themes from across the chapters while also summarising the value of using architectural models as evidence in this way.

With each chapter dedicated to a single theme, this book, and the models it describes, can only ever provide snapshots of the different ideas outlined, offering fleeting glimpses of how they were developed and communicated as the twentieth century progressed. As an examination of the evidence that the architectural models made by a single company of modelmakers provide of how yesterday imagined tomorrow, this is not an in-depth study of any single period, movement, or building type, and its intention is to consider projects as they were first unveiled, regardless of whether they were realised or not, in order to bring to life some of the hopeful optimism that surrounded them at the time. The historical narrative that this book puts forward is therefore ultimately one of ideas, and it aims to encourage the further use of architectural models as a form of historical evidence by revealing how they captured just some of yesterday's dreams of a better tomorrow during a century of unrelenting change.

## Notes

1 Peter Downton, 'Temporality, Representation and Machinic Behaviours,' In *Homo Faber: Modelling Architecture*, eds. Peter Downton et al. (Sydney: Archadia Press, 2007), 46.
2 Karen Moon, *Modelling Messages* (New York: Monacelli Press, 2005), 104.

3 M. Topalovic, 'Models and Other Spaces,' *OASE* 84, 2011, 38.

4 David Edgerton, *The Rise and Fall of the British Nation* (London: Penguin, 2019), 174.

5 Edgerton, *The Rise and Fall of the British Nation*, 174.

6 David Engerman, 'Introduction: Histories of the Future and Futures of History,' *The American Historical Review* 117, no. 5, December 2012, 1402.

7 Reinhart Koselleck, *Futures Past: On the Semantics of Historical Time* (New York: Columbia University Press, 2004), 255.

8 Zoltan Boldizsar Simon and Marek Tamm, 'Historical Futures,' *History and Theory* 60, no. 1, March 2021, 3.

9 'English Housing Survey 2014 to 2015: Housing Stock Report,' Ministry of Housing, Communities & Local Government, 2015, https://www.gov.uk/government/statistics/english-housing-survey-2014-to-2015-headline-report.

10 Christopher Beanland, *Unbuilt* (London: Batsford, 2021), 10.

11 Nathaniel Coleman, *Utopias and Architecture* (London: Routledge, 2005), 17.

12 Alexander Schilling, *Architecture and Model Building* (Basel: Burkhauser, 2018), 122.

13 Christian Gerrewey, '"What are Rocks to Men and Mountains?" The Architectural Models of OMA/Rem Koolhaas,' *OASE* 84, 2011, 36.

14 Thea Brejzek and Lawrence Wallen, *The Model as Performance* (London: Bloomsbury, 2018), 11.

15 Brejzek and Wallen, *The Model as Performance*, 13.

16 Topalovic, *Models and Other Spaces*, 37.

17 Markku Lahti, 'The Magical World of Models,' In *Little Big Houses*, ed. Jari Jetsonen (Helsinki: Building Information Ltd, 2000), 163.

18 Moon, *Modelling Messages*, 12.

19 Nick Dunn and Paul Cureton, *Future Cities: A Visual Guide* (London: Bloomsbury, 2020), 5.

20 David Lund, *A History of Architectural Modelmaking in Britain: The Unseen Masters of Scale and Vision* (Abingdon: Routledge, 2022).

21 For more information on the Thorp Archive, visit aub.ac.uk/thorp-archive.

22 Laura Millar, *Archives: Principles and Practices* (London, Facet, 2017), 6.

23 David Dean, *The Thirties: Recalling the English Architectural Scene* (London: Trefoil books, 1983).

24 Alastair Forsyth, *Buildings for the Age: New Building Types 1900–1939* (London: HM Stationery Office, 1982).

# 1

# PLACE

Among the many thousands of architectural models that Thorp made during the twentieth century, the naming conventions applied to different types of models gave a clear indication of their purpose. Commissions were generally assigned the title of the road on which a project was being proposed, such as Eyre Street, Cromwell Road, or Hatton Gardens, for example, and these suggested a relatively confined development such as an office building, apartment complex, or housing estate. At the other end of the scale, however, were models that were simply recorded as Canterbury, Liverpool, or as one particularly impressive model made in 1952 for the planners William Chapman and Charles Riley was titled, Aberdeen (Figure 1.1). These were not models of individual buildings but rather planning and masterplan models of entire places, with the Aberdeen model outlining a wholescale reimagining of the city centre. Often made at smaller scales and encompassing large urban areas complete with miniature roads, railways, parks, and sometimes hundreds of carefully made buildings, these were intended to communicate broad and often ambitious visions of the future of Britain's cities, towns, and neighbourhoods.

The ideas that these models put forward were generated in response to the fundamental question of how and where we should live in the future, a question that preoccupied many architects and planners during the twentieth century,[1] and which to a certain extent underpins the entirety of this book as answering it by necessity also generated thoughts about how we might work, relax, and travel. It was also a question that resulted in the commissioning of an enormous number of architectural models and in using just some of those models as evidence of how the future of our towns and cities was imagined, this chapter and the next share many themes and ideas as the twin notions of place and home are deeply entwined. Place is the most appropriate concept to begin with, however, as before models of the specific buildings in which we spend so much of our lives are considered, it is first necessary to take a broader view to examine some of the different ideas about the overall structure and organisation of Britain's towns and cities that were explored and projected through planning and masterplan models.

The notion of place is a somewhat contested concept,[2] and while it is generally understood that a place might be where we live or work, we also recognise that it is not as

DOI: 10.4324/9781032715728-2

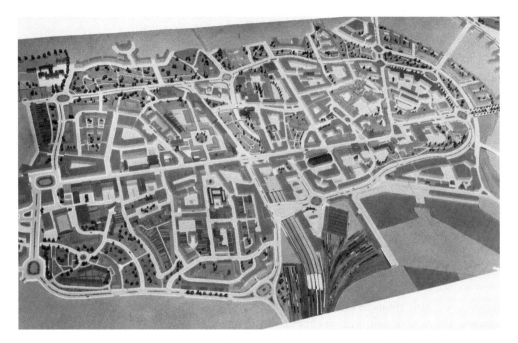

FIGURE 1.1    Model of a proposed rebuilding of Aberdeen. Planners: William Chapman and Charles Riley. Made by Thorp, 1952. Courtesy Thorp Archive, AUB.

small as our home or office, and that neither it is as large as a county or nation. Places are the middle ground, areas that exist on the scale of neighbourhoods, villages, towns, and cities; they are locations with a defined character and identity. During the twentieth century urban planning and architectural design offered the means by which a sense of place could be constructed and in doing so they positioned architectural models as the principal medium through which the future form of Britain's towns and cities was deliberated, with architects and planners able to plot the broad arrangement of buildings, roads, and public spaces without necessarily having to think about the details. Planning and masterplan models, when presented to the public, allowed for grand visions to be expressed on a more relatable, human scale, providing an instant overview of the principles guiding the layout of a new town, suburb, or area of urban renewal. The most well-documented models of this kind were those made to communicate the plans for the postwar New Towns but held within the records of Thorp's work are many photographs of less well-known schemes, the majority of which described possible futures that never came to pass.

On its most fundamental level, urban planning, as the process by which land use is determined,[3] is an 'art of arrangement,'[4] organising and structuring the relationships between different building types and zones of activity and function. Planning, therefore, encompasses not only the design of the physical infrastructure of a place, but its social and economic organisation as well. To indulge in the act of planning is to operate in the world of vision and ideals, dreaming not only of alternative physical structures but also alternative means of organising societies as a whole.[5] The notion of comprehensive planning that grew in prominence during the postwar era was predicated on the idea that everything needed to be planned, driven by an underlying modernist philosophy,[6] and following the Second World War an entire generation of modernist planners and architects eagerly began organising the land.[7] Modernists equated design with morality, firmly of the belief that they could quite literally build a better world,[8] and propelled by this conviction untested ideas were imposed on a public that had little say as to whether they consented to the experiments or not.

The desire, the urgency even, to address the questions of where and how we should live during the twentieth century was largely a response to the appalling conditions that had developed in many of Britain's larger towns and cities during the latter decades of the previous century. The rapid growth of the population of cities such as Birmingham, for example, which increased by a factor of ten between 1800 and 1900, had resulted in dire and squalid living conditions, and politicians and social reformers soon recognised that urban growth could no longer be left unchecked, although most early interventions centred on improving basic living conditions through legislation to control sanitation and access to daylight rather than considering the shape and form of the urban environment itself.[9] During the early decades of the twentieth century, however, a 'universally shared belief in the desirability of planning'[10] began to take hold that was largely inspired by the visionary ideas of Ebenezer Howard and whose idealistic and utopian dream of how our towns and cities could be better arranged can be seen echoing throughout this chapter.[11] From the Garden City movement to the New Towns, and to vast speculative concepts such as Motopia and Sea City, these were all visions of radical change that sought to bypass the limitations of short-term solutions that targeted the specific problems of individual towns and cities alone.[12]

Most of the models featured in this chapter are, therefore, unashamedly utopian in nature, attempting to capture individual visions of what the ideal form of Britain's future towns and cities should be like. The ideas behind them combined the exploration of both architectural and social solutions,[13] bringing together the hopefulness and order of an organised template for the built environment with enlightened concepts of social justice,[14] and architectural models proved to be a highly accessible means by which those ideas could be communicated to an often curious public, with architects and planners choosing to represent their concepts 'not in dry formulas but through three-dimensional models of their total approach.'[15] City models in particular, which acted as 'highly persuasive vehicles for socio-political concepts'[16] where the citizens of the model world behaved like pieces on a chessboard and obediently submitted to the philosophies of their creators, formed an illusion of compliance that reinforced a conviction that the real world would respond in the same manner, leading to accusations that architects and planners became lost in the models they fetishised.[17] The development of their visions of a better future nevertheless required the making of 'dedicated physical, mental, and emotional spaces for that imagining,'[18] and architectural models met this requirement superbly well, as their continued use in this regard today serves to demonstrate.

In the discussion of the models that follows, the evolution of how the broad future landscapes of our cities, towns, and neighbourhoods were projected over time can be seen, with each model offering an insight into a unique vision of future while also reflecting the shifting ideological positions that dominated twentieth century thinking. Across what is ultimately only a small selection of the many planning and masterplan models that Thorp made during the twentieth century, the rise and fall of top-down approaches to urban planning can be observed alongside changing attitudes towards conservation and the question of whose voices the different approaches to planning actually considered: those of architects, planners, and developers certainly, but what about those of ordinary people? The models of the projects described, whether realised or otherwise, therefore provide important glimpses into a century of hopeful visions of the future of Britain's towns and cities, and also the changing identities of the dreamers who were imagining them.

### Escape to the Country

In the opening decades of the twentieth century, if you needed an architectural model and did not want to make it yourself, you asked John Thorp. Holding an almost total monopoly as the owner of the sole firm of dedicated architectural modelmakers in Britain at the time, the highly detailed and sophisticated models that Thorp and his team of modelmakers produced ideally suited the ambitions of the new century, and it was to John Thorp that many architects and planners turned for help in expressing their bold ideas. Thorp's representation of natural landscapes in particular meant that the company's models were ideally placed to communicate the leading concept of the age relating to the future of Britain's towns and cities, the Garden City. So dominant was this idea that during the first three decades of the twentieth century, almost all of the planning or masterplan models that emerged from Thorp's workshop were in some way related to Ebenezer Howard's dream of building entirely new communities in the countryside. Thorp's 1913 model of Worthing Garden City was an early example and could at first glance be mistaken for an aerial photograph of an established English country village, complete with mature trees and neatly lawned gardens (Figure 1.2). This was, of course, an illusion, as at the time Worthing Garden City did not exist, nor would it ever as the idealistic vision the model portrayed was ultimately never built.

By the time the model was unveiled the Garden City movement was already fifteen years old. Ebenezer Howard's 1898 book *To-Morrow: A Peaceful Path to Real Reform*, retitled *Garden Cities of To-morrow* in 1902, had outlined a convincing and practical solution to the perceived problems of the inner cities that sought to combine the best elements of both town and country to create a new kind of settlement – town-country – from which 'will spring a new hope, a new life, a new civilisation.'[19] Industry and housing would be separated from one another by bands of trees and grass, zoning the land in a planned manner as opposed to the unregulated evolution of existing towns and cities. Howard also called for social change, proposing that the citizens of the Garden Cities would own the land they were built on in order to use the rental income to pay for the provision of community services, imagining a future in which the basic goodness of mankind would be harnessed in the creation of a more positive society.[20] Howard's ideas were quickly put into practice with the construction of Letchworth Garden City, designed by Raymond Unwin and Barry Parker, underway in 1904, with further projects soon following such as Hampstead Garden Suburb in 1907, Worthing in 1913, and Welwyn Garden City in 1920. By as early as 1914 over fifty Garden City-inspired projects had been announced and over 11,000 homes built.[21]

The Worthing model was likely made to help raise money for the first phase of the proposal by attracting investors. The vision championed by Howard and his disciples

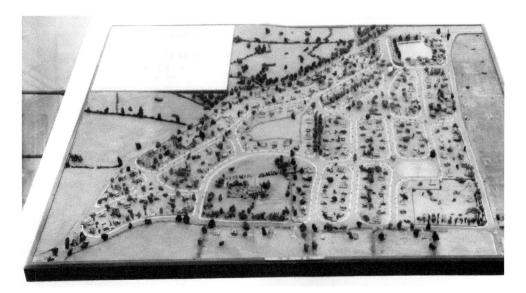

**FIGURE 1.2**  Model of Worthing Garden City. Client: Worthing First Garden City Ltd. Made by Thorp, 1913. Courtesy Thorp Archive, AUB.

relied on private promoters and private funds, there being no state coordinated approach to planning at the time. As had been the case for the development of Letchworth, a First Garden City limited company was established to realise the dream of a Garden City at Worthing, enthusiastically supported by the local town council. The chosen site was on land that had previously been part of the Offington Park estate, with the stately home of Offington Hall itself visible in the lower centre of the model. Detached houses can be seen situated on large plots of land with amenities including tennis courts, open public spaces, and a church adding to the impression of a well-planned community. Initial interest in the proposal was high, but with the outbreak of the First World War in the following year, building work was placed on hold. With Britain in a very different place both socially and economically following the armistice in 1918, revised plans in both 1920 and 1923 failed to secure the necessary funding. By the time the first handful of houses were built on the site in 1925, the momentum for a fully-fledged Garden City at Worthing had fallen away, with the Offington Park estate that occupies the land today a much less ambitious example of an upmarket interwar housing development.

Although the specific vision of a Garden City at Worthing was never realised, the model clearly evidences the enthusiasm for Howard's concept and the merging of town and country that was at its heart, and just a few months later John Thorp was commissioned to make a similar model to illustrate a proposal for a Garden Village at nearby Angmering-on-Sea in Sussex (Figure 1.3). Unlike Worthing, Angmering-on-Sea was actually built and with every road lined with carefully tended flowerbeds and spacious grounds surrounding each property, this was one of many models Thorp made at the time that sought to capture the dream of a new community that while inspired by the past was improved by the deliberate nature of its planning.

Garden Villages, Garden Suburbs, and Garden Estates were names applied to what were effectively watered-down versions of Ebenezer Howard's dream of the town-country

FIGURE 1.3   Model of Angmering-on-Sea Garden Village. Architect: unknown. Made by Thorp, 1913. Courtesy Thorp Archive, AUB.

Garden City, developed by some of Howard's followers to provide a smaller-scale solution that could be realised more easily than a full-blown Garden City such as Letchworth or Welwyn. The idea was to build the residential element of a Garden City on the outskirts of an existing town which would provide local employment as Howard had envisioned but without having to build entirely new industrial areas. Planned to contain around two hundred homes built to a high standard and with a generous allocation of green spaces, outdoor leisure facilities, and community centres to encourage a sense of family and belonging,[22] these were mostly smaller developments, but ones that still embraced the central tenet of holding the land in trust for the benefit of the community. Angmering-on-Sea was built according to these principles, although from the very start it was intended to be an exclusive estate, offering the benefits of town-country life only to those who could afford it. The model itself is quite revealing in terms of the quality of the environment that was planned for Angmering's inhabitants, adhering to the vision for the community that was advertised at the time as being where 'nature's free gifts coupled with man's progressive ideas, are helping to form an up-to-date resort on Utopian lines.' Depicted on Thorp's model was a provision of one tennis court for every four houses, a formal garden with a long pergola-covered walkway along the seafront, and a formal promenade with a beachside pavilion, while on the far left of the model just below one of the tennis clubs was a corner parade of shops and public house.

Both the Worthing and Angmering models were aimed at potential investors, putting forward idealised visions of Howard's utopian dreams of prosperous and socially minded communities, but after the First World War, local authorities and speculative builders alike began to add the Garden prefix to 'almost any housing scheme where a few original trees survived.'[23] The types of model that Thorp was asked to make changed accordingly, as rather than being directed at raising capital funds these were targeted at prospective homebuyers. Thorp's 1919 model of the proposed Kingsbury Garden Village in Neasden, commissioned by Metropolitan Railway Company Estates, captured both the change in model design and the shift to a wholly commercial vision of the future that was behind it (Figure 1.4). Outlining a broad estate of semi-detached houses laid out in much higher densities than in the earlier Garden City and Garden Village designs, Thorp's model gave little indication of where the proposed development sat in relation to its surroundings, deliberately omitting the massive railway depot that existed immediately to the south, a rather manipulative approach that reflected the new audience for the model and an early example of the selective editing and distortion that modelmakers were often encouraged to implement. The railway was the sole the reason for this estate being proposed, however, with the Metropolitan Railway having set up its own property development arm in order to utilise the excess land that had been purchased for the building of the railway as it reached outwards from central London, with Kingsbury one of the first major developments of what the railway quickly began to promote as 'Metro-Land.'[24] Home buyers

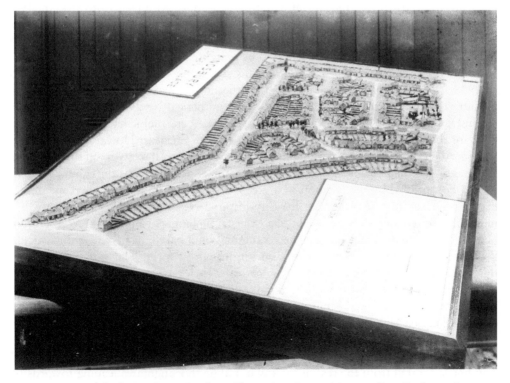

**FIGURE 1.4** Model of Kingsbury Garden Village. Developer: Metropolitan Railway Company Estates. Made by Thorp, 1919. Courtesy Thorp Archive, AUB.

could purchase standard houses off plan or commission an architect or builder to design one to their own specification,[25] and while the company's publicity referred to Kingsbury as a 'Model Garden Village,'[26] in reality this was nothing more than an ordinary housing estate, devoid of any of the social ambitions of the Garden City movement and an early sign of what was to come with the relentless expansion of suburbia along the routes of existing transport corridors (see Chapter 2). In selling prospective buyers the same dream of town-country promised by the Garden Cities, Metro-Land was in fact building over the very countryside that featured so heavily in the railway's stylish promotions, and the depiction of just a handful of trees on Thorp's model of Kingsbury stands in stark contrast to the lush greenery seen on the models of Worthing and Angmering-on-Sea.

Despite the commercialisation of the Garden City concept evidenced by models of suburban housing developments such as at the Kingsbury, Ebenezer Howard's vision nevertheless endured and by the time the Garden City Association, established by Howard in 1899, changed its name to the Town and Country Planning Association in 1940, the movement's ambitions had expanded. In calling for the building of a swathe of brand new Garden City inspired communities up and down the country in response to not only the existing problem of the inner cities but also the unfolding devastation of Britain's towns and cities that was taking place during the war, the dream of the Garden City was enshrined in the burgeoning discipline of town planning. It was in this manner that the principles of the Garden City formed the basis of the postwar rebuilding program and the creation of the New Towns. These generated an avalanche of architectural models but while the Garden City movement had provided Thorp with plenty of work, the New Town models were largely made by the in-house modelmaking workshops set up by the New Town Development Corporations, although Thorp did make what was likely one of the first models of the New Town vision to be presented to the public.

Following John Thorp's death in 1939, his son Leslie took over the company, and in 1943 Leslie Thorp was commissioned by the newly formed Ministry of Town and Country Planning to make a large model of a hypothetical New Town that was needed to illustrate the broad principles the planner Patrick Abercrombie had established as the basis for their design (Figure 1.5). As a disciple of both Ebenezer Howard and Raymond Unwin, Abercrombie had been brought in by the Ministry to start work on the rebuilding of London and the plans he outlined made the radical proposal that the capital's growth should be curtailed by the creation of a green belt to surround it and over one million people rehoused in a series of Garden City-inspired New Towns orbiting the city. The model illustrated an early attempt by the Ministry's planners to put form to Abercrombie's ideas, and in depicting an imagined community not based on anywhere in particular it needed to capture the New Town vision in its purest form. The difference between this and the Kingsbury model of a commercial development is clear, and not just in terms of the improvements in modelmaking techniques that took place during the twenty years between them. The Abercrombie model was a return to the idealistic utopianism of the earlier Garden City models, and it was here, visually at least, that Howard's vision was most clearly presented, with hundreds of individual miniature trees emphasising the merging of town and country at its heart. With an industrial area to the left of the railway line separated from the rest of the town, public thoroughfares leading towards the central shopping area, a mix of individual houses with gardens and large blocks of flats situated in landscaped grounds, and the entire town well-connected to a passing dual

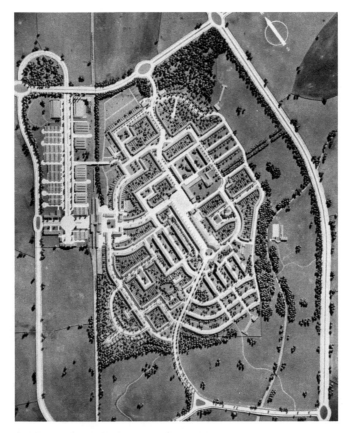

**FIGURE 1.5**  Model of a hypothetical New Town. Planner: Patrick Abercrombie. Made by Thorp, 1943. Courtesy Thorp Archive, AUB.

carriageway, this was a model of Ebenezer Howard's dream updated for the demands of the impending postwar era and an indication that the physical, if not the social, form of the Garden City had by then been fully adopted as the state-approved vision of the future of Britain's towns and cities. As the 'grandfather' of the many hundreds of models produced during the development of the New Towns, it was both Thorp's first and last contribution to the project, however, as the planning and masterplan models the company was commissioned to make in the decades that followed captured far more commercial ideas of what the future of the nation's towns and cities should be like.

## Urban Visions

While the postwar dream of the New Towns was being implemented, Thorp's attention was largely focused on making models of an altogether different set of futures that were directly targeted on what both the New Towns and Garden Cities had hoped to leave behind, the inner cities themselves. Between 1950 and 1965, Thorp's order book was almost overwhelmed by the demand for models of unflinchingly modernist urban redevelopment projects put forward by an eager generation of planners and architects who were set on creating a brave new world.[27] The wholescale adoption of the clean sweep approach of modernism after the Second World War was in part a reaction to the war itself, but also to the class divisions and perceived grandeur of prewar life.[28] Modernists viewed the future as one where creative people such as themselves would grasp modern materials and technologies and direct them in the pursuit of a brighter tomorrow,[29] accompanied by a Keynesian assumption that state intervention in the nation's economy would lead to growth.[30] By investing public money in regenerating and renewing Britain's urban environment, consumer demand would increase which would in turn boost the country's economic output, and so when considering the future of bomb-damaged city centres, thinking big was encouraged. This approach was not always one that the public responded to positively, however, and as the many dozens of planning and masterplan models made by Thorp during this period illustrate, the sheer scale and boldness of most of the redevelopment projects envisioned by the proponents of comprehensive planning approaches often struggled to navigate the opposing interests of personal versus public benefit and short-term versus long-term gain.[31]

Thorp's 1954 model of New Barbican is a prime example of the radical approaches to thinking about the future that characterised this period and provides an important insight into not just what might have been but also the limits of public support for such all-encompassing urban redevelopments at the time (Figure 1.6). Patrick Abercrombie's Greater London Plan that first proposed the New Towns had also highlighted that the district to the north of St. Paul's Cathedral would be best utilised if given over to commercial use. The area, known as Barbican, had been the centre of London's rag trade and its cloth-filled warehouses had been almost completely obliterated by incendiary bombs during the Second World War. Following Abercrombie's advice, in the early 1950s various proposals for commercial developments on the site were put forward while at the same time residents living in the surrounding areas began to campaign for much needed housing instead. In order to protect the original commercial vision of the district a pressure group called the New Barbican Committee was formed and in 1954 commissioned the architect Sergei Kadleigh of Kadleigh, Whitfield & Horsbrugh to design an alternative proposal for a mixed-use development.[32] Kadleigh's enormous scheme, unveiled to the public with Thorp's impressive concept model centre stage, was described at the time as a 'superhuman building for a superhuman city'[33] (Figure 1.7). Covering forty acres and raised on a plinth covering four floors of warehouse space and parking for several thousand cars, the tallest tower would have held thirty-four floors of offices and flats. This was bold thinking from an architect who just two years before had created a similar controversy with his design for High Paddington, an urban development that proposed stacking eight thousand people into a huge megastructure suspended over Paddington goods yard.

Thorp's model of New Barbican was highly abstract, using stacks of polished clear Perspex to give an impression of the overall masses of the proposed buildings and it was unlikely to have helped convince the public of the proposal's merit. While this is a common approach for representing design concepts at an early stage today, in the 1950s this abstract composition was highly unusual and would have made it rather difficult to interpret. What the model did make clear was that Kadleigh's plan would utterly dominate the skyline and having strayed too far from the original brief it was dismissed out of hand. Threatened by the proposal nevertheless, the London County Council quickly produced

**FIGURE 1.6**  Model of New Barbican. Architect: Sergei Kadleigh. Made by Thorp, 1954. Courtesy Thorp Archive, AUB.

**FIGURE 1.7**  The unveiling of the New Barbican model at a press conference in London, 1954. Courtesy Thorp Archive, AUB.

**FIGURE 1.8**  Model of Motopia. Planner: Geoffrey Jellicoe. Made by Thorp, 1959. Courtesy Thorp Archive, AUB.

a model of its own plans in response,[34] and two years later Chamberlin, Powell & Bon's upmarket residential proposal was approved in a rejection of Abercrombie's commercial vision for the area in favour of one that more closely matched the views of local people instead.

As dramatic as it was, Kadleigh's plan for a high density urban future squeezed into the existing cityscape was far from the most radical proposal that Thorp was asked to make in miniature during the 1950s, and just a few years later the landscape architect and town planner Geoffrey Jellicoe suggested an even more startling vision, proposing an extraordinary combination of hard Corbusian modernism and more relaxed Howardian town-country utopianism in the form of Motopia, the enormous model of which Thorp's modelmakers spent six months constructing (Figure 1.8). Having designed the original masterplan for the Hemel Hempstead New Town in 1947,[35] Motopia was one of several projects Jellicoe worked on as part of the Pilkington Glass Age Development Committee, all of which positioned megastructures as the future solutions to the issues facing Britain's urban environment. Following the Garden City and New Town tradition of bypassing the problems of existing towns and cities to the extreme, Motopia was a proposal for an entirely new city with an initial population of 60,000 people to be built outside London on open farmland near Staines.[36]

Jellicoe's assertion about the future of cities was that existing ones offered very little hope of improvement, wondering if we were 'in perpetuity condemned to the presence of noise, dirt, smell, and a permanent sense of danger, or whether there is an ideal environment that would give us the best of all worlds,'[37] echoing Ebenezer Howard's town-country vision once more. Motopia was his solution, an example of top-down planning at its most forceful, and Jellicoe drew from an unusual mix of the Georgian streets of London and Bath, Le Corbusier's La Ville Radieuse, and the Garden City movement to propose something quite astonishing, a city in a single building, suspended on pillars above a continuous public park, with its road network elevated to run along the rooftops. This was a vision of Howard's town-country projected through the prism of mass car ownership, 'an extreme display of the determination to bring order and control to the motorised city.'[38] Jellicoe was insistent that the future should embrace the 'separation of mechanical and biological man,'[39] noting that cars were threatening to take over our lives. The resolution of the conflict between the pull of urban living, technology, and modernity on the one hand, and that of the human desire to embrace the natural world on the other, Jellicoe believed, was to bring people back down to nature and force traffic into the air. Main roads would traverse the roof of the entire structure, with ramps down to mews streets underneath where parking for the apartments below would be easily accessed. Garden flats with wide balconies would look down on an unbroken natural landscape with the idea being that once you had driven home everything else you might need would be within a pleasant walk through carefully tended parkland.

The model of Motopia was oddly diagrammatic despite its apparent level of detail as while the landscaping was fully realised and tiny vehicles can be seen using the integrated rooftop road system, the megastructure itself was rendered fairly stark and uniform, quite different to Jellicoe's description of the facades being divided into sections that would be designed by different architects. The illustrations of Motopia that Jellicoe commissioned revealed more of his inspiration of a London Square filled with individual town houses surrounding a private garden, and the sense of character Jellicoe wanted for the city is strangely missing from the model itself. In his 1961 book about the proposal, Jellicoe described Motopia as if it had already been built, commenting on how easy and convenient life in the city was and how happy people were with their balcony gardens,[40] embodying the modernist assumption that everyone else would share the same enthusiasm for his personal dream of how we should live. The model, with its projection of a tidy and obedient world, reinforces this view and it is therefore not surprising that so many projects of this scale and ambition used architectural models as their main means of expression. In the model world people enjoy the new community that has been created for them, everything works, and everyone is happy.

The contrasting visions of the future of Britain's towns and cities that were put forward during the postwar era in models of projects such as of Motopia and New Barbican demonstrate the twin tools that were available to planners when dealing with the problems of urban sprawl and war damage – redevelop what was there or move it somewhere else.[41] The issues facing planners in the 1950s and 1960s were principally identified as being problems of land use, therefore you could solve them and bring about social change by building things rather than using policies or legislation.[42] In most cases urban regeneration was directed by the public sector, particularly local councils, but the private sector was increasingly becoming involved by the middle of the 1960s as they had the funds to build what councils desired. Commercially driven regeneration projects were focused on maximising land use in order to derive the most profit available, entirely understandable from a business perspective, but as many of the models Thorp made during this period evidenced, such a focus on short-term return on investment was rarely compatible with the wider needs of society.

The masterplan model of Russell Diplock's unbuilt 1965 design for St. James' Square in Edinburgh stands as a particularly startling example of this approach, where architects and property developers conspired to take the modernist vision of clearing out and starting again from scratch and overlay it with commercial zeal (Figure 1.9). For anyone familiar with Edinburgh's city centre it takes a moment before the location it depicted becomes clear, so radical were the changes proposed. The city had identified St. James' Square for redevelopment in 1964 with indicative plans unveiled for a new inner ring road, the demolition of tenement blocks, and the building of new government offices and a shopping centre. This was to be a commercial development with the city corporation inviting developers to pitch their own proposals. The architect Basil Spence became involved as a consultant, initially working for the Taylor Woodrow team until they were eliminated from the competition, after which he switched to the developer Hammerson and their architects Russell Diplock Associates. Spence had wanted to preserve the original street layout as had been requested by the city corporation but Diplock's proposal showed an astonishing disregard for the city's heritage, driving a motorway through the centre and building an ultra-modern replacement for the nineteenth century Catholic

**FIGURE 1.9**  Model of the unbuilt St. James' Square development. Architect: Russell Diplock. Made by Thorp, 1965. Courtesy Thorp Archive, AUB.

**FIGURE 1.10**   The new road network and cathedral featured in the St. James' Square model. Courtesy Thorp Archive, AUB.

cathedral (Figure 1.10). This overtly commercial vision nevertheless adhered to the prevailing view within planning circles that the radical rebuilding of Britain's cities was necessary in order to accommodate the projected growth of urban traffic,[43] with local councils often all too eager to destroy their own communities' heritage in the name of progress.[44]

Not all visions of the future of Britain's towns and cities were quite so disregarding of what already existed, however, and the boldness of the St. James' Square proposal, in being driven by commercial considerations, is neatly contrasted by an altogether calmer model Thorp made in 1963 to illustrate Geoffrey Jellicoe's plan for the redevelopment of the City of Gloucester (Figure 1.11). Instigated by the city council, a much more sensitive approach is evidenced, although the model stands as an uncomfortable reminder of how even the most idealistic of proposals can be so poorly put into practice. The Gloucester model had a singular task to perform – to outline Jellicoe's plan for the city as it would be in twenty years' time, offering a very specific vision of the future as it would be in 1982. Built almost entirely from timber rather than the plastics common in most postwar models, the model very effectively used the contrast between light and dark woods to signify areas identified for redevelopment and those that were to be protected. The simple elegance of the model also reflected a more considerate approach to preserving the city's heritage than was on display in the model of St. James' Square and the language of using natural materials in a model is still used today to denote a sympathetic development in keeping with its existing surroundings. As such the model was comfortably abstract, making it clear that while Jellicoe had determined where redevelopment should take place, he was not specifying the actual forms that those developments should take. This

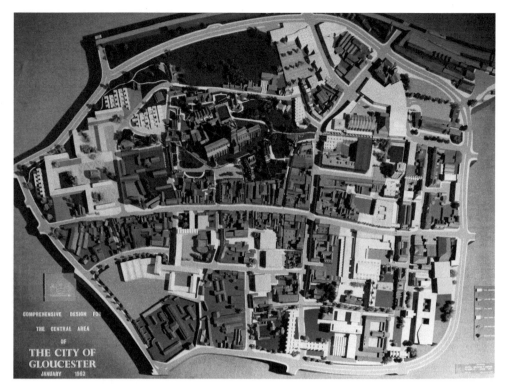

COMPREHENSIVE   DESIGN   FOI
THE   CENTRAL   AREA
OF
THE CITY OF
GLOUCESTER
JANUARY   1962

**FIGURE 1.11**   Model of the proposed redevelopment of Gloucester City Centre. Planner: Geoffrey Jellicoe. Made by Thorp, 1963. Courtesy Thorp Archive, AUB.

was a physical model of a conceptual one – a series of principles for the future development of the city to adhere to.

The terms of reference given by the city council at the start of the project included the preparation of a 1:500 scale diagrammatic model and Jellicoe made good use of the model to illustrate his aim of embracing the city's heritage while simultaneously unlocking poorly used space for redevelopment. Increasing the density of the city centre and linking the cathedral more obviously to the commercial district were prime considerations and a new one-way traffic system was proposed to allow the city centre itself to be pedestrianised.[45] As the model illustrates (Figure 1.12), any new developments would be low rise so not to detract from the cathedral, but Jellicoe, as his Motopia concept had demonstrated, was not afraid of progress. In the introduction to his report, Jellicoe noted that 'the recognition and acceptance of the principles of comprehensive development are vital to the plan.'[46] By identifying and purchasing valuable space that was not being used efficiently, particularly private houses with front gardens near the city centre, the city could then sell this land on for commercial development to benefit the community as a whole.

The model of Jellicoe's plan makes an interesting comparison to the city as it exists today and stands as a reminder that the concept of comprehensive planning, even this sensitive in approach, rarely worked as intended, as anyone familiar with Gloucester's actual history following 1962 will appreciate. Although used as the basis for the 1966–1974 redevelopment of the city centre, what was ultimately built was far more radical

**FIGURE 1.12**    Close-up of the Gloucester model showing the cathedral and proposed new shopping centre. Courtesy Thorp Archive, AUB.

and less sensitive to the city's heritage than Jellicoe had envisaged, and Thorp's model of the original proposal provides clear evidence that such grand visions of the future rarely come to fruition in the manner projected by their miniature counterparts. During the postwar era, urban redevelopment of the kind imagined by the models of Gloucester, St. James' Square, Motopia, and New Barbican had nevertheless become the 'planner's panacea,'[47] and despite a growing focus on the neighbourhood unit, the provision of public spaces, and the desire to develop genuine communities,[48] there was something irresistible about the notion of radical change, no doubt exacerbated by the intrinsic appeal of the models themselves. By the late 1960s, architects and planners were being accused of getting lost in such models, and in taking the top-down ideology of comprehensive redevelopment to its extremes, set about proposing highly speculative solutions to the question of place that were far more suited to the fantasy world of models than the real world they wished to change.

## Impossible Dreams

As will be seen across many of the chapters that follow, the late 1960s and early 1970s was a period characterised by a fascination with radical and outlandish proposals of all kinds, and in terms of planning models Thorp's order book during this time was dominated by a series of models of wildly impractical schemes. Thorp, by then under

**FIGURE 1.13**   Model of the proposed River City development in Liverpool. Architect: Richard Seifert and Partners. Made by Thorp, 1966. Courtesy Thorp Archive, AUB.

the ownership of Ray Pfaendler after Leslie Thorp's death, remained the leading firm of architectural modelmakers in Britain despite growing competition, and it was during this period that the company became known as the go to company for spectacularly large and impressive models to illustrate the very boldest speculative ideas. The designers behind these projects were usually well aware that these models would be as tangible as their proposals would ever become, using them instead as a means of making ideological statements about how they saw the future of Britain's urban environment. By this time a new and influential voice had also entered the stage alongside the architect and the town planner, the property developer, whose power had emerged after the end of building controls in the mid-1950s. The king of these developers was Harry Hyams, who in 1966 commissioned Thorp to make a model to illustrate his proposal for River City in Liverpool (Figure 1.13). Having made his fortune building speculative office developments such as Centre Point and Gateway House, Hyams looked for commercial opportunities to take underutilised land and turn a profit from it. While this was perhaps removed from the mostly egalitarian aims of the planners and architects so far featured in this chapter, the role of private investment in regenerating the inner cities had become increasingly important during the postwar era, and with River City Hyams demonstrated that property developers could think on a scale just as large as socially conscious utopian dreamers such as Howard, Abercrombie, and Jellicoe.

In proposing an idea beyond what was presently achievable, River City acted as a signal of intent. The 'utopian impossibility'[49] of proposals such as this were characteristic of large-scale modernist redevelopment plans, dealing with broad-brush concepts without needing to attend to the detail, although by the time the project was unveiled the public's view of earlier postwar developments had already soured, with few having delivered the improvements they had promised.[50] The model of River City, complete with neatly positioned cars and people, presented a convincing impression of the overall dream and yet

**FIGURE 1.14**  Model of the proposed River City development in Liverpool. Architect: Richard Seifert and Partners. Made by Thorp, 1966. Courtesy Thorp Archive, AUB.

was conveniently able to avoid any discussion of its obvious impracticalities. Designed by Richard Seifert, River City was a vision of commercially led urban regeneration of dramatic proportions. By the 1960s Liverpool's fortunes were in rapid decline with its waterfront docks largely abandoned, and the approach taken by Hyams and Seifert was similar to that proposed by Russell Diplock in Edinburgh, simply sweep the decay aside and replace it with prosperity. As the model of the proposal made by Thorp in 1967 shows, the entire waterfront was to be razed to the ground and an entirely new mixed development of offices, homes, and shops built in its place (Figure 1.14). The tallest tower was to have been forty-two storeys high and the whole site intended to provide a new urban community for fifty thousand people.[51]

Hyams' plan garnered much attention but no serious support and was scaled down in 1970 and repromoted as Aquarius City, but even this project was too ambitious to secure

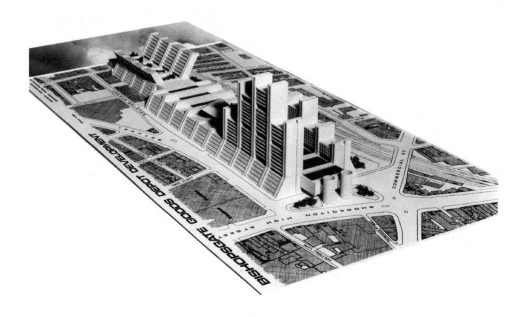

**FIGURE 1.15** Model of the proposed Bishopsgate Goods Station redevelopment. Architect: Batir Associates. Made by Thorp, 1972. Courtesy Thorp Archive, AUB.

the necessary funding. What it did generate, however, was a great deal of publicity for Hyams and reignite the debate about how derelict urban areas such as Liverpool's waterfront should be regenerated. This discussion was still ongoing when an equally speculative proposal was unveiled in 1972 for the redevelopment of Bishopsgate Goods Station in London. The scheme, put forward by Batir Associates and likely designed by Rodney Gordon, was perhaps less radical than River City but still demonstrated the big thinking approach of modernist utopianism, applying the megastructure concept to a large derelict site on the edge of the City of London (Figure 1.15). With the model of the proposed development made by Thorp presented simply on an oversized map, it is at first difficult to gauge the sheer size of Gordon's design, but this was a bold proposal for a location that even today remains partly undeveloped. The goods station at Bishopsgate had been severely damaged by fire in 1964 and left abandoned, and when offered for sale in the early 1970s the site attracted the attention of land hungry property developers. Various ideas were put forward of what to do with the large and well-connected plot of land, but surprisingly little information has survived about any of them, Batir's proposal included.

Studying the largely balsa wood model more closely the scale of this particular vision of London's future becomes clear. The plan was for a single building that would occupy three entire blocks and rise thirty storeys over its surroundings, by far the largest single development that had been seriously proposed for the city at the time. The elevated nature of the design suggests that it was intended that the railway yard would remain underneath, or possibly be replaced by an underground parking area. Roads appear to pass through the building with a large entranceway leading off Commercial Street, but other than the overall form of the design it is hard to discern much detail. Indeed, it is not even certain that Rodney Gordon was the actual architect behind the proposal, although there are similarities with his earlier work at the Owen Luder Partnership where he was responsible for the brutalist Tricorn Centre in Portsmouth, and Gordon was certainly working at Batir at the time. It is hard to imagine that such a bold proposal received a warm response, and as with Hyams' and Seifert's proposal for River City in Liverpool, the Bishopsgate concept was perhaps a few decades too early, as while today part of the site has been filled by Shoreditch High Street station, the remainder of the still derelict goods station is earmarked for a £900 million mixed-use development centred around a cluster of forty-storey office towers that is not too dissimilar from what Batir had proposed in 1972.

Thorp's reputation for making technically complex models of speculative schemes was largely fuelled by the company's impressive models for the Pilkington Glass Age Development Committee, several of which appear in this book, including the Motopia model described above. Chaired by Geoffrey Jellicoe, Ove Arup, and Edward Mills, in 1968 the Committee commissioned Thorp to build what proved to be one of the most challenging models the company ever made, that of Sea City (Figure 1.16). Designed by Hal Moggridge, John Martin, and Ken Anthony, Sea City was an ambitious proposal for a self-sustaining city of thirty thousand people to be built in the North Sea. Their vision was a radical take on the question of where and how people should live, moving far beyond the idea of Garden Cities, New Towns, and urban regeneration, and in predicting future shortages of food, oil, gas, and land, Sea City was envisaged as a floating island that would be independently powered by water turbines and built to serve various sea-based industries such as fishing and mining.[52]

Thorp's model was unveiled at a press conference in London by Tony Benn, then Minister of Technology, but the model had been designed to act as more than just a visual explanation of what was being proposed and had already been through extensive wind tunnel testing to prove the engineering principles of its forward-thinking design. As the model shows, Sea City's concrete outer sea wall would enclose an internal lagoon, with ten thousand people living in glass-fronted houses stacked over sixteen terraced levels within the wall itself and twenty thousand more living on floating islands below (Figure 1.17). The sea wall was to be nearly two hundred feet high and it was specifically designed to deflect the strong sea winds up and over the lagoon, the waters of which would be heated so that rising air currents would help carry the air above the city to create a calmer climate below.[53] The wind tunnel tests successfully demonstrated this in principle, and the model was also colour coded to highlight the different facilities that would be included for its citizens. Schools, churches, parks, football pitches, and even a marine zoo would be provided, while a marine college was planned to help train people for employment at fish farming plants or in the dredging of sand from the seafloor. Transport to and from the city was to be handled by hovercraft and helicopter, and the entire structure would be a mile long and three-quarters of a mile wide.[54]

Sea City, while being a relatively detailed proposal that caught the public's imagination, was entirely speculative in nature and had little hope of ever being realised. Its designers and the Glass Age Development Committee knew that, but they still saw value in presenting such an audacious dream. Building Sea City might have been out of their reach, but perhaps the idea would inspire more modest attempts to solve the problems

FIGURE 1.16    Model of Sea City. Client: Pilkington Glass Age Development Committee. Made
by Thorp, 1968. Courtesy Thorp Archive, AUB.

they had identified. With photographs of the model featuring heavily in newspapers and
magazines over the following year, their vision was widely shared and even made an
appearance on the children's television program Blue Peter where it likely sparked the
interest of many young future architects. When featured in a 1972 book on future urban
structures,[55] the Sea City model was merely one of many, with almost every single project
represented by a grand and impressive architectural model of a utopian megastructure of
one kind or another. This was, by the early 1970s, the way in which such ideas were presented,[56] leading to criticisms that models such as Sea City were encouraging architects
and planners to spend more time indulging in fantasy than improving the reality around
them.[57] Arthur Drexler in his critique of modernism wrote that the 'model generated its
own truth,'[58] noting how the artificial and perfect world of the model was inherently
seductive, with reality being reduced to being a superfluous copy of the models that
preceded it.[59] With the dominance of modernist thinking and the era of grand utopian

**FIGURE 1.17** Close-up of the Sea City model. Courtesy Thorp Archive, AUB.

visions of place that accompanied it reaching its end, however, the demand for models that so successfully turned fantasies into tempting miniature realities fell away, with Sea City standing as the most ambitious speculative masterplan model Thorp ever made, and also – in terms of British projects – one of the last.

## A More Human Tomorrow

By the start of the 1970s, the nature of the planning and masterplan models that Thorp was commissioned to make had undergone a significant change. Gone were the modernist, top-down comprehensive planning interventions of the postwar era, and in response to the rise of the conservation movement and a downturn in Britain's economic fortunes, the proposals being put forward were on an altogether more human scale that better reflected the ambitions of individual communities.[60] This was largely a consequence of the shift towards private funding for the building of new communities and the regeneration of existing ones, driven by the commercial logic that as people were more likely to buy what they actually wanted, it was financially prudent to offer it to them, as the next chapter will explore further. The commercial pressures of private development often proved to be stronger than any socially focused ideology, however, and while the idea of large-scale 'grand plans' for the future of Britain's towns and cities had fallen out of

**FIGURE 1.18**    Model of New Ash Green. Developer: Span/Bovis Homes. Made by Thorp, 1971. Courtesy Thorp Archive, AUB.

favour, the voices of ordinary people still struggled to be heard when it came to determining what the overall shape and structure of their urban environments should be, an issue that was visible in many of the planning models of the time.

In 1971, Bovis Homes commissioned a model to illustrate their plans to expand the recently built village of New Ash Green in Kent, having purchased it from the original developer, Span (Figure 1.18). Thorp's colourful model conveyed the full extent of the increase in size being proposed, with areas already completed or under construction identified as those with street plans inserted under the orange Perspex. What the model did not make clear, and likely deliberately so, was that Bovis' new plans for the village involved an almost total rejection of Span's original vision of building a carefully planned community that was designed around the noble ambition of actively improving society.[61]

New Ash Green, originally designed for Span by the architect Eric Lyons, had been intended to show that private developers and architects working together could improve the quality of new housing in Britain.[62] Envisioned as a template for a new kind of community, New Ash Green was planned as a large village of 5,000 people and positioned as an alternative to both local authority housing developments and expensive private estates.[63] Lyons was adamant that modernist architects had failed to pay sufficient attention to the importance of landscaping,[64] particularly in the New Towns which he felt were uniformly suburban and bare,[65] and for New Ash Green, Lyons designed clusters of small neighbourhoods of around one hundred homes that were arranged facing landscaped paths rather than roads, following the American Radburn approach originated by Clarence Stein and Henry Wright during the 1920s.[66] Neighbourhoods were separated from each other by generous wedges of communal green spaces, all arranged around a pedestrianised village centre. Each neighbourhood was given its own residents' association to coordinate the management and maintenance of the cluster, giving people a level of control over their community that echoed Ebenezer Howard's ideas of common ownership and local accountability, although Lyons was careful to downplay the similarities.[67] Nevertheless, this was clearly a vision of the Garden City applied to the baby boom generation. Crucially, Lyons determined that while the village should be designed with the car in mind, it should not take prominence, grouping parking spaces together to encourage chance neighbourly encounters as people walked along the woody paths to their homes.

With the first residents moving in during 1968, just three years later Span had run into financial difficulties and it was at this point that Bovis took over. While proposing to follow the broad physical layout of Lyon's masterplan, the new Bovis neighbourhoods were to be built at a much higher density than the existing ones and without the emphasis on communal space and landscaping that had been central to the original concept.[68] Bovis also tried unsuccessfully to abolish the resident's associations, and while the village subsequently grew to become a highly desirable place to live, Span and Lyon's utopian dream was never fully realised in its intended form, with a more conventional profit-driven vision of the future in place that was not quite what its early residents had signed up for. Thorp's model, by indicating the size of the expansion that was planned without communicating how it was to be carried out, demonstrated how fragile the new humanist dreams of the community were when held against the commercial ambitions of developers.

By the 1980s the power of the private developer had become absolute and the dreaming of the future of Britain's towns and cities had effectively been privatised, with commercial interests replacing ideology in terms of deciding how and where people should live. Architectural models of whole towns and villages disappeared almost completely from Thorp's order book and were replaced instead by an almost endless run of models of privately led urban redevelopment projects, particularly within London's Docklands. The 1986 model of Richard Seifert and Partners' proposal for Glengall Cross was just one of many that showcased the dramatic regeneration of the Isle of Dogs that was by then underway, and which exemplified the human scale yet blandly corporate visions of the future that developers craved (Figure 1.19). Designed for the property company LET, Glengall Cross was conceived as a mixed development of housing, shops, and offices that would link the new Crossharbour Station on the Docklands Light Railway with the western side of Millwall Dock. This was a purely commercial development, an example of market forces taking the lead with top-down planning reduced to an absolute minimum, and taking its inspiration from the Baltimore Harbour and Quincy Market regeneration

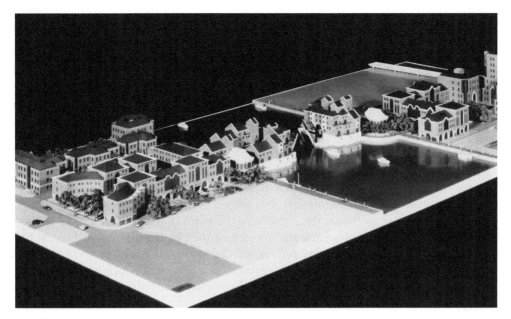

**FIGURE 1.19**  Model of Glengall Cross. Architect: Richard Seifert and Partners. Made by Thorp, 1986. Courtesy Thorp Archive, AUB.

projects in the United States, public space became private space. As the model neatly captured, this previously derelict location was reimagined as a bustling thoroughfare complete with happy shoppers, private boats moving through the water, and a frequent DLR service that has just departed the station (Figure 1.20). This was a welcoming vision of a low-rise, high-profit property-led regeneration project in the heart of an abandoned industrial wasteland.

Many of Thorp's models from the 1980s reflected the same urban regeneration policies that were focused on using legislation to unlock private investment.[69] The idea was to free market forces to intervene where governments had previously led the way by providing incentives for private developers to build on an enormous scale through the relaxation of planning restrictions and tax burdens in designated Enterprise Zones. London's Docklands was by far the largest of these and through the creation of the London Docklands Development Corporation to promote opportunities in the area, it became a highly attractive location for developers to invest.[70] Challenging the enduring separation of housing, leisure, and industry into different zones that had been central to Ebenezer Howard's Garden Cities, the intention for developments such as Glengall Cross was to encourage mixing of work and leisure in an attempt to return a sense of life and activity into the evenings that had been lost in many urban centres. Dockside and riverside locations became prime targets for redevelopment across the country after the success of London's Docklands, and while overtly commercial in origin, the bringing together of work, housing, and leisure in one location did at least adhere to the human-scale approach to planning that had emerged during the 1970s and which had been evident in the original design of New Ash Green. As such, the vision laid out by the model of Glengall Cross was in sharp contrast to the centralised comprehensive planning concepts seen

FIGURE 1.20    Model of Glengall Cross. Architect: Richard Seifert and Partners. Made by Thorp, 1986. Courtesy Thorp Archive, AUB.

in earlier models, with the development rising from an almost total absence of planning regulations with profit motive alone left to instigate change, only some of which benefited the individuals who would work and live there, while all of them benefited the developer.

Just one year after the Glengall model was made, Thorp produced another model of an urban regeneration project that pitched a similarly commercial development in a far more sensitive area that generated a significant debate around whether the voices of those being impacted by the overall planning and redevelopment of Britain's towns and cities finally deserved to be heard more loudly. The model was made for the 1987 competition for a scheme to replace William Holford's Paternoster Square in the City of London, the design of which was completed in 1956 although the development was not fully opened until 1967. Built on land surrounding Paternoster Row, an area immediately north of St. Paul's Cathedral that had been almost totally destroyed during the Second World War, Holford's modernist design had made use of raised pedestrian walkways rather than the existing street plan in an attempt to improve the flow of road traffic, and the stark block-like forms of its buildings stood in harsh contrast to the classical architecture of St. Paul's. At the time, Holford's masterplan had been lauded as 'a splendid example of the English planning tradition,'[71] but it quickly became seen to have been a monumental mistake that was totally out of keeping with its surroundings.

For the 1987 competition to replace Holford's scheme, eight architectural practices including those of Arup Associates, Norman Foster, Richard Rogers, James Stirling, and

**FIGURE 1.21**   Model of an unbuilt proposal for Paternoster Square. Architect: RHWL. Made by Thorp, 1987. Courtesy Thorp Archive, AUB.

RHWL, well known for their work on the Crucible and Old Vic theatres, were invited to submit new designs to the developer.[72] RHWL's design, as with all the competing entries, was defiantly modern, and as the model of their proposal made by Thorp illustrates (Figure 1.21), was not a dramatic departure from Holford's original scheme. Featuring monolithic office towers, theirs was nevertheless a bold proposal, but very tellingly the model did all that it could to say otherwise. Made entirely from timber, it is quite hard to determine which buildings were being proposed and which ones were already there, giving the impression that the whole development would blend into its surroundings. This was likely due to the fact that models of all eight entries in the competition were to be presented to a very harsh critic of modern architecture and planning, Prince Charles.[73] Arup and Richard Rogers were jointly named as the competition winners, but when Charles was asked to vet the schemes, he promptly rejected Rogers' design. Rogers then resigned in protest when it became clear that Prince Charles intended to block any development that would repeat what he saw were the same mistakes as the one being demolished.[74] From this point on the Paternoster Square competition became a tug of war between opposing viewpoints – not just of which style of architecture the development should adopt, but whose visions of the future were more important, those put forward by architects and planners or those held by the public?

Charles was adamant that his objections to modern architecture and urban planning, and specifically to the proposals that had been put forward for Paternoster Square, were not just his alone and that he was speaking for the public at large.[75] By backing an alternative proposal by the neoclassical architect John Simpson in a speech in December that year, during which he eviscerated all the official competition entries and the state of the architectural profession in general, Charles ignited a fierce battle for public opinion.[76] Maxwell Hutchinson, the then President of the RIBA, wrote an entire book accusing the Prince of Wales of undemocratic interference,[77] which was precisely the charge that Charles had laid at the architectural profession by claiming that architects were ignoring the 'deep-rooted feelings of ordinary people.'[78] What people actually wanted, he suggested, were cities that operated on a more intimate, friendly, and civilised scale,[79] pointing his finger equally at private developers, architects, and planners, and he even highlighted one of Thorp's own models of a Pilkington Glass Age Development Committee project as an example of everything that was wrong with how the future of the built environment was being planned. All of the official entries in the Paternoster competition, including RHWL's, aimed to make bold interventions rather than blend into their surroundings, and with such an intense debate raging the competition stalled as architects such as Quinlan Terry and Leon Krier put their support behind both Charles' call for more respectful architecture and planning and Simpson's alternative plan for the site.[80] It took until 1996 before a classically-inspired proposal by William Whitfield was finally accepted and which was completed in 2003, the design of which adopted a much more human scale approach to its layout and form.

As the final model in this chapter, Thorp's depiction of RHWL's 1987 proposal, in attempting to hide its boldness, says much about the shifting balance of opinion during the late twentieth century as to whether architects, planners, and developers should give people what they wanted or what they thought the people needed. Throughout the twentieth century, the visions of social reformers, government ministries, speculative developers, town planners, and architects were all seen and heard, whether through models or completed projects on the ground. The views of ordinary people remained curiously overlooked, however, and while the controversy that erupted over the Paternoster Square competition acutely highlighted their absence, it took the intervention of someone who occupied a position that was far from ordinary to do so. Without the top-down approach to planning that dominated the postwar era, the private, commercially-driven visions of the future that replaced them in the latter decades of the twentieth century still firmly placed the dreaming of the overall structure and organisation of Britain's towns and cities in the hands of a few, but as the models featured in the next chapter demonstrate, when it came to the actual buildings in which people lived – their homes – the dreams and aspirations of ordinary people proved to be much harder to ignore.

## Notes

1 David Jeremiah, *Architecture and Design for the Family in Britain, 1900–1970* (Manchester: Manchester University Press, 2000), 3.
2 Tim Cresswell, *Place: An Introduction* (Oxford: Blackwell, 2015), 34.
3 Barry Cullingworth and Vincent Nadin, *Town and Country Planning in the UK*, 15th Edition (Abingdon, Routledge, 2006), 2.
4 John Gloag, *The Englishman's Castle* (London: Eyre & Spottiswoode, 1945), 11.
5 Peter Hall, *Cities of Tomorrow* (Oxford: Blackwell, 2002), 3.
6 Justus Dahinden, *Urban Structures for the Future* (London: Pall Mall Press, 1972), 7.
7 David Kynaston, *Austerity Britain* (London: Bloomsbury, 2008), 158.
8 Juliet Gardiner, *The Thirties: An Intimate History* (London: Harper Collins, 2011), 327.
9 Andrew Tallon, *Urban Regeneration in the UK*, 2nd Edition (Abingdon: Routledge, 2013), 9.

10 Gavin Stamp, *Interwar: British Architecture 1919–1939* (London: Profile, 2024), 32.

11 Hall, *Cities of Tomorrow*, 2.

12 Robert Fishman, *Bourgeois Utopias: The Rise and Fall of Suburbia* (London: Basic Books, 1982), x.

13 Fishman, *Utopias*, 6.

14 Fishman, *Utopias*, 3.

15 Fishman, *Utopias*, x.

16 Thea Brejzek and Lawrence Wallen, *The Model as Performance* (London: Bloomsbury, 2018), 92.

17 Arthur Drexler, 'Engineers Architecture: Truth and its Consequences' In *The Architecture of the Ecole des Beaux-Arts*, ed. Arthur Drexler (London: Secker and Warburg, 1977), 15.

18 Madeline Ashby, 'Prediction Fiction,' *RSA* Journal 1, 2023, 15.

19 Ebernezer Howard, *Garden Cities of Tomorrow* (London: Faber and Faber, 1945), 48.

20 Frederick Osborn and Arnold Whittick, *The New Towns: The Answer to Megalopolis* (London: Leonard Hill, 1969), 56.

21 Mark Swenarton, *Homes for Heroes* (London: Heinemann, 1981), 23.

22 Fishman, *Utopias*, 14.

23 Gloag, *Englishman's Castle*, 156.

24 Sheila Taylor and Oliver Green, *The Moving Metropolis* (London: Lawrence King, 2001), 17.

25 Christian Wolmar, *The Subterranean Railway* (London: Atlantic, 2005), 239.

26 Metropolitan Railway, *Metro-Land: British Empire Exhibition Number* (Metropolitan Railway, 1924), 82.

27 Hall, *Cities of Tomorrow*, 237.

28 Andrew Marr, *The Making of Modern Britain* (London: Macmillan, 2010), 244.

29 Gardnier, *The Thirties*, 327.

30 Tallon, *Urban Regeneration*, 11.

31 Cullingworth and Nadin, *Town and Country Planning*, 5–7.

32 John Grindrod, *Concreteopia* (Brecon: Old Street, 2013), 406.

33 Wilfred Burns, *British Shopping Centres* (London: Leonard Hill, 1959), 97.

34 Lionel Esher, *A Broken Wave: The Rebuilding of England 1940–1980* (London: Allen Lane, 1981), 116.

35 Christopher Beanland, *Unbuilt* (London: Batsford, 2021), 101.

36 Geoffrey Jellicoe, *Motopia* (London: Studio Books, 1961), 143.

37 Jellicoe, *Motopia*, 8.

38 Jeremiah, *Architecture and Design for the Family*, 175.

39 Jellicoe, *Motopia*, 12.

40 Jellicoe, *Motopia*, 15.

41 Tallon, *Urban Regeneration*, 31.

42 Tallon, *Urban Regeneration*, 30.

43 Otto Saumarez Smith, *Boom Cities* (Oxford: Oxford University Press, 2020), 17.

44 James Stourton, *Heritage* (London: Head of Zeus, 2022), 25.

45 Geoffrey Jellicoe, *A Comprehensive Plan for the Central Area of the City of Gloucester* (London: Jellicoe, Ballantyne and Coleridge, 1961), 1.

46 Jellicoe, *A Comprehensive Plan for the Central Area of the City of Gloucester*, 4.

47 Miles Glendenning and Stefan Muthesius, *Tower Block: Modern Public Housing in England, Scotland, Wales, and Northern Ireland* (London: Yale University Press, 1993), 119.

48 Glendenning and Muthesius, *Tower Block*, 97.

49 Nathaniel Coleman, *Utopias and Architecture* (London: Routledge, 2005), 72.

50 Joseph Rykwert, *The Seduction of Place* (Oxford: OUP, 2000), 4.

51 Joseph Sharples, *Liverpool* (London: Yale University Press, 2004), 106.

52 *Sea City*, directed by H.G. Casparius (Pilkington Glass Age Development Committee, 1968).

53 *Sea City*.

54 *Sea City*.

55 Dahinden, *Urban Structures*.

56 Fishman, *Utopias*, x.

57 J. Esche, 'Architecture in Miniature,' In *Idea and Model*, eds. Marg Von Gerkan and Partner (Berlin: Ernst and Son, 1994), 23.

58 Drexler, *Engineers Architecture*, 15.

59 Drexler, *Engineers Architecture*, 15.
60 Catherine Croft. 'David Rock: Architecture is the Land of Green Ginder, or Form Follows Culture,' In *The Seventies*, eds. Elain Harwood and Alan Powers (London: The Twentieth Century Society, 2012), 67.
61 Grindrod, *Concretopia*, 285.
62 Elain Harwood, 'Building for Span and the Public Sector,' In *Eric Lyons and Span*, ed. Barbara Simms (London: RIBA, 2006), 54.
63 Grindrod, *Concretopia*, 278–279.
64 Barbara Simms, 'Community and Common Space,' In *Eric Lyons and Span*, ed. Barbara Simms (London: RIBA, 2006), 97.
65 Jan Woudstra, 'Landscape First and Last,' In *Eric Lyons and Span*, ed. Barbara Simms (London: RIBA, 2006), 38.
66 Alan Powers, *Britain: Modern Architectures in History* (London: Reaktion, 2006), 30–31.
67 Patrick Ellard, 'New Ash Green: Span's Latter 20th Century Village in Kent,' In *Eric Lyons and Span*, ed. Barbara Simms (London: RIBA, 2006), 79.
68 Ellard, 'New Ash Green,' 91.
69 Tallon, *Urban Regeneration*, 4.
70 Alastair Goobey, *Bricks and Mortals* (London: Century Business, 1992), 23.
71 Frederick Gibberd, *Town Design* (London: The Architectural Press, 1962), 162–163.
72 Maxwell Hutchinson, *The Prince of Wales: Right or Wrong? An Architect Replies* (London: Faber and Faber, 1989), 28–29.
73 Hutchinson, *The Prince of Wales*, 29.
74 HRH The Prince of Wales, *A Vision of Britain: A Personal View on Architecture* (London: Doubleday, 1989), 69.
75 HRH The Prince of Wales, *A Vision of Britain*, 72.
76 Andreas Papadakis, *Paternoster Square and the New Classical Tradition* (London: Academy Editions, 1992).
77 Hutchinson, *Prince of Wales*.
78 HRH Prince of Wales, *A Vision of Britain*, 12.
79 HRH Prince of Wales, *A Vision of Britain*.
80 Papadakis, *Paternoster Square*.

# 2

# HOME

In anticipation of its Ideal Home Exhibition returning after an enforced absence during the Second World War, in 1944 the Daily Mail newspaper published the *Daily Mail Book of Post-War Homes*. Its editor, Mrs M. Pleydell-Bouverie had one particularly strong piece of advice for her readers when considering a new home in the forthcoming era of peace: 'Study the models. They may be the models of your future home.'[1] Architectural models have long been associated with domestic space, with the first known reference to their use in Britain being a record of a model of the proposed rebuilding of Longleat House that was made in 1567.[2] During the seventeenth century it was not uncommon for older architectural models to be turned into dolls houses, and the charm and sense of intimacy exuded by models of the buildings we call home has lost none of its appeal in the centuries since. Pleydell-Bouverie's advice for future home buyers to pay close attention to models of what was being proposed demonstrated the continued value of architectural models in communicating notions relating to domesticity during the twentieth century, as with the concept of home ultimately describing an imaginary space[3] that encompasses 'emotional, spiritual and moral values' as well as the practical provision of shelter,[4] it was therefore well-suited to being expressed through the miniature world of architectural models. In heeding Pleydell-Bouverie's advice today, a great deal can therefore be learned by studying yesterday's models of the future of home to understand how those visions changed over time.

Following the previous chapter in which planning models were used to explore how the question of where and how we should live was considered at the structural scale of Britain's towns and cities, this chapter examines architectural models as evidence of the changing approaches to the design of our homes. In doing so, it continues to address an emerging theme from the previous chapter, the question of voice, as through the middle decades of the twentieth century planners, architects, and politicians set about a wholescale rethinking of the domestic landscape that imposed ideologically driven views of how people should live and in what kinds of buildings with little regard to the opinions of those who would be asked to live in them. This is not to say that the homes that were built were unwelcome, but the selection of models discussed in this chapter nevertheless

DOI: 10.4324/9781032715728-3

evidences the conflict between the top-down imposition of new ways of living and the humbler but no less important aspirations of ordinary people. As was also the case in the previous chapter, the twentieth century's deliberation of the nature of the homes we occupied largely stemmed from the overhanging problems of the previous one hundred years. The same concerns that drove a desire to consider the broader planning of Britain's towns and cities also fuelled a re-evaluation of the design of the specific buildings we live in. Investigations by concerned reformers into the living conditions of the working classes during the late nineteenth century had highlighted deeply troubling statistics such as that forty percent of families in Edinburgh in the 1880s were occupying single rooms[5] and that even by 1900 a third of Birmingham's population was still living in back-to-back houses with no inside plumbing. Charitable trusts sprang up in an attempt to alleviate the worst of these conditions but the problems were just too enormous to tackle without government co-ordination. By the turn of the century, the London County Council, which had begun to rehouse slum dwellers during the 1890s, had also started to construct new, additional housing space which broadly followed the principles of the Garden City movement.[6] The 1918 Tudor Walters Report on the provision of public housing further embedded the Garden City's housing ideas by recommending a preference for low-density estates to be built in short terraces or semi-detached pairs with wide frontages in order to maximise the available daylight.[7] With local councils made responsible for meeting the housing needs of their populations in 1919, the importance of housing as a means of social reconstruction came to the fore[8] while at the same time the dream of home ownership became the ultimate status symbol for the growing middle classes.[9]

The notion of home also became a deeply political one during the early twentieth century. With suffrage extended in 1918 to women over the age of twenty-one who either owned property or were married to men that did, in the early twentieth century homeownership became inextricably linked to political enfranchisement.[10] During the postwar rebuilding of Britain's war-damaged towns and cities the provision of social housing then became a national political mission with building controls placing the state firmly in charge of meeting the country's housing needs. Fuelled by the combined ideological conviction of modernism and the formation of the welfare state, home building shifted into a high-density, high-rise overdrive.[11] The state-sponsored application of modernist ideas lacked an interest in the needs of the individual, however, and often failed to appreciate the public's deeply engrained instinct for privacy,[12] with the diverging approaches of both public and private housing provision during the second half of the century clearly seen in the models of future visions of the nation's housing that Thorp made, as is the eventual triumph of the latter over the former under the political agenda of the Thatcher government of the 1980s.

Most of the models discussed in this chapter were made as sales tools, designed to entice prospective buyers of privately built homes or to convince a community of the merits of building new social housing. As early as 1924 an article in *The Building News* recommended the use of architectural models for advertising purposes,[13] while in 1937 the modelmaker Edward Hobbs wrote that 'whatever one may feel about house models in estate agents and builders' offices, the acid test is, does the model attract clients and help to make sales?'[14] The answer to Hobbs' question was a resounding yes, and the sight of models of proposed housing estates, tower blocks, and gated apartment complexes became all too familiar during the second half of the twentieth century. Models such as these comprised a significant proportion of the commissions Thorp received during its long history, recording so much of value in terms of understanding the different ideas that were put forward about what our future homes should be like. From the political preferences for private or state-provided housing, debates around the merits of high or low-density communities, the virtues of flats versus houses, of low rise versus high rise, of communal spaces versus privacy, and to the longevity of the simple aspiration of home ownership, the models that follow provide an insight into the changing dreams of the future put forward as the century unfolded.

What the models featured in this chapter ultimately make clear, is that the dreams of those designing tomorrow's homes were not always aligned with the dreams of those inhabiting them. As the aspirations of ordinary people captured in the *Daily Mail Book of Post-War Homes* demonstrated in 1944, what families, and particularly women in those families, wanted was the simple dream of privacy in the form of a house with a garden and the modern provisions of a fitted kitchen and a plumbed bathroom. Pleydell-Bouverie positioned her book as a chance for 'women to tell authority what they want,'[15] noting that men had always considered the design of the domestic space to be a man's job.[16] As such, the book's survey of what women wanted from their postwar homes neatly summarises the themes that are evident in the models discussed in this chapter, as no matter how hard architects tried to project different visions of the future from the one expressed above, people largely wanted what they had already imagined. The brief appearance of high-rise, high-density housing in the middle of the century evidences this difference of views, with the architectural models that follow demonstrating that the history of housing in Britain during the twentieth century ended as it began, with the dream of low-density, pitched roof semi-detached houses with gardens defining the image of the ideal home for much of the population.

### Dreams of Aspiration

The advice given in the 1944 *Daily Mail Book of Post-War Homes* to study architectural models before buying a new house was a reminder of just how central models had been to the Daily Mail's Ideal Home Exhibition ever since its founding in 1908. By the time of the fifth exhibition in 1912, John Thorp had produced so many models of houses for display there that he printed a promotional advert highlighting his work (Figure 2.1). Depicting six models of large, architecturally notable houses with an impression of substantial gardens, these, as with all the models displayed at the Ideal Home Exhibition, were deeply aspirational in nature. Models such as these provided a lucrative stream of income for John Thorp before the First World War, who advised potential clients on the benefits of realising their new home in model form before committing to the architect's plans, noting that for a villa or private house the cost of a model should be no more than half a percent of the actual building, which amounted to around five guineas at the time.[17] Thorp's models were aimed at wealthy families planning their dream homes and in projecting visions of an idealised future there was no better marrying of medium and message than found in the models he exhibited at the Ideal Home Exhibition.

The models of private houses that Thorp was commissioned to make during the early decades of the twentieth century, whether for the Ideal Home Exhibition or otherwise (Figure 2.2), reflected the growing aspirations of home ownership and the desire for domestic luxuries that emerged as the expanding middle classes sought to embrace

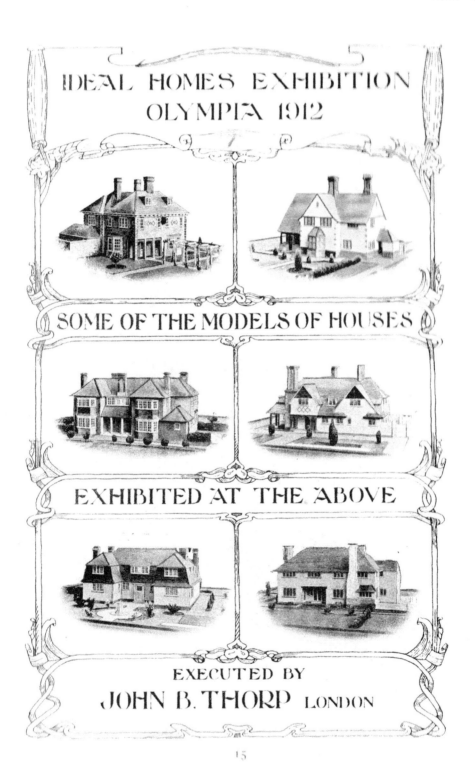

IDEAL HOMES EXHIBITION
OLYMPIA 1912

SOME OF THE MODELS OF HOUSES

EXHIBITED AT THE ABOVE

EXECUTED BY
JOHN B. THORP LONDON

15

**FIGURE 2.1** Illustration promoting John Thorp's display of models at the 1912 Ideal Home Exhibition. Courtesy Thorp Archive, AUB.

**FIGURE 2.2**  Model of a private house. Architect: Unknown. Made by John Thorp, c1920. Courtesy Thorp Archive, AUB.

modernity and the social, cultural, and material changes that it involved.[18] Before the First World War housing was a fairly stagnant sector of Britain's economy,[19] and while the number of people living in urban areas had expanded from nine million in 1851 to over twenty eight million in 1911,[20] the overwhelming proportion of the population, some ninety percent, were renting their homes.[21] The quality of much of Britain's housing stock, particularly for the working classes, was in a desperately poor state, but with the development of the early Garden Cities (as outlined in the previous chapter), the idea that things could get better, that it was possible, and indeed acceptable, to aspire to better living conditions, began to take hold. For the public, the Ideal Home Exhibition was the place where the small but valuable dream of home ownership could be indulged.

The Ideal Home Exhibition was in essence a giant model itself. Filled with full-size mock-ups of entire houses, room settings, and gardens, in addition to many scale models such as those provided by Thorp, it was an opportunity to experience the future of the home made real and was perhaps the most widely accessed portal into the imaginary world of Model Britain that ever existed. Created by the Daily Mail newspaper, the intention was to break open the closed housebuilding market and encourage competition as a means of boosting the paper's advertising revenue. When purchasing a house of the type illustrated by Thorp's models, the architect tended to recommend the fittings and decorations from suppliers who were giving them commission on the sales, and in recognising this the Daily Mail saw an opportunity to 'undermine the influence of the architect and remove his stranglehold from the home buying industry,'[22] by holding an exhibition where the public could see all the different options available to them. This would then encourage the manufacturers of wallpapers, paints, sinks, and bathrooms to switch their advertising from the trade press directed at architects and builders to national newspapers in order to reach home owners themselves. Enormously successful, in the first year twenty thousand people visited the exhibition, with attendance growing to half a million by 1926 and 1.3 million in 1957.[23] Both architects and the building trade embraced the exhibition with enthusiasm, with over four hundred entries into the architects competition for best new house at the inaugural 1908 exhibition, many of which were accompanied by architectural models.[24] From 1918 onwards, the full-scale House of the Future mock-up became the focus of the entire exhibition, each year anticipating the latest trends in architectural and interior design. Models of houses designed by architects and individual housebuilding companies were produced in their hundreds and through both full size and miniature visions of future ideal homes, women were explicitly targeted as the leading consumers of modernity and encouraged to dream about what tomorrow's domestic world might be like. Here were expressed the aspirations of ordinary people from the working and middle classes: of light and airy homes, a garden, and most of all, the latest labour-saving devices and home conveniences.[25]

Following the end of the First World War the British public's dreaming of a better way of living intensified[26] and for many families the possibility of moving into a home with even just inside bathrooms became an enormously attractive proposition.[27] As electric lighting and devices such as vacuum cleaners became increasingly common in wealthier houses, a rethinking of the layout and composition of the British home took place, and with the inclusion of central heating and running hot water becoming desirable selling points for new homes, in 1924 John Thorp was commissioned by the National Radiator Company to make a cut-through model of their 'Ideal Cookanheat'[28] heating system to illustrate how it could be retrofitted into existing homes. The model showed a stove and boiler in the kitchen range recess, four radiators, a cold water cistern in the roof, hot and cold water circulation pipes, and that most modern of conveniences, a heated towel rail in the upstairs bathroom (Figure 2.3).

The National Radiator Company, founded in the United States in 1902, had quickly opened a factory in Hull to supply the British market with boilers and home heating equipment and by the 1920s was operating out of showrooms in London, Brighton, and Birmingham. Having redesigned their range to be more suitable for British homes, Thorp's model was likely made for display in their flagship London store, promoting their system at a time when the desire for such simple amenities as running hot water and central heating had been exacerbated by the decline in the number of households employing servants after the First World War. With fewer domestic servants around the need for labour-saving devices in the home increased and the model of the heating system would have acted as a convincing sales tool to persuade interested homeowners of the benefits such a system would bring in reducing the time spent on chores.

Such simple yet important dreams of the future of Britain's homes were not just restricted to the working and lower-middle classes during the interwar years, with the wealthier segments of society also embracing the aspiration for better and more efficient living, and in 1930 Thorp was asked to make a large model of Clifton Court, a mansion

FIGURE 2.3 Sectional model of the 'Ideal Cookanheat' system. Client: National Radiator Company. Made by John Thorp, 1924. Courtesy Thorp Archive, AUB.

block under construction in Maida Vale in London (Figure 2.4). Occupying an entire city block, the proposal for Clifton Court was a vision of convenient but luxurious living close to the centre of the city that was put forward near the end of a trend for wealthy families living in the countryside to buy urban boltholes that were used for just a few months of the year. Such developments were highly exclusive and residences in Clifton Court came with maids' quarters, fitted kitchens, and spacious plumbed bathrooms as standard. Thorp's model of Clifton Court was made to illustrate the first phase of the development and is missing the matching mock Tudor extensions on either side and the strangely contrasting rear block built to face Northwick Terrace that was completed with a neo-classical façade of yellow brick, stuccoed entrances, and a flat roof. Likely for display in an estate agent's office to showcase the proposal to potential buyers, the model's fine detailing and inclusion of several luxury motor cars helped to communicate the dream of high-quality city living.

Clifton Court's adoption of the mock Tudor or Tudorbethan style of architecture reflected the popularity of the Tudor and Elizabethan periods at the time and which had become viewed as being central to the creation of British national identity.[29] The strength of this association served to aid the design of domestic buildings to stubbornly resist the clean lines of modern architecture that had begun to dominate the architectural profession and the stark functionalism modernism offered did not fully capture the interest of the British public until after the Second World War. With private housebuilders rarely

FIGURE 2.4    Model of Clifton Court. Architect: Unknown. Made by John Thorp, 1930. Courtesy Thorp Archive, AUB.

offering anything but mock Tudor or neo-Georgian style properties, few modernist housing designs appear in Thorp's catalogue of work until the 1950s.

The convergence of the appeal of such stylistic nods to the past, the aspiration of home ownership, and the desire for improved standards of living during the early decades of the twentieth century is perhaps best encapsulated by a model of a hypothetical housing estate that Thorp was commissioned to make in the late 1920s for display in either an estate agents' window or the offices of one of the growing number of speculative house builders (Figure 2.5). Depicting at least nine pitched-roof detached houses with either brick, rendered, or half-timbered exteriors, a gated park to the front and an impression of further housing and open countryside to the rear, for many people this was the ultimate dream of home to be pursuing, that of suburbia. The vision presented by Thorp's model was of a future that had already begun to spread across vast swathes of the land (as demonstrated by the model of Kingsbury Garden Village in the previous chapter), bringing the domestic aspiration of home ownership within reach for millions of people, and through the development of the suburbs during the interwar years the balance between those renting their homes and those owning them began to change.[30]

Following the First World War class boundaries had become more porous and huge numbers of skilled manual and professional workers and their families sought to improve their social status by moving to speculatively-built suburban homes.[31] The majority of these homes were not as grand as those portrayed in Thorp's model of the hypothetical development, but with low interest rates and the growing availability of mortgages offered by building societies, the purchase of detached or semi-detached suburban homes became the proudly cherished fruits of social progression.[32] As Thorp's model shows, the influence of the Garden City movement persisted in the suburbs, albeit superficially, utilising its preferred arts and crafts cottage style of architecture on a much larger scale.

FIGURE 2.5   Model of a hypothetical suburban housing development. Developer: Unknown.
Made by Thorp, c1929. Courtesy Thorp Archive, AUB.

Behind the visual similarities, the suburban dream was almost the opposite of Ebenezer
Howard's vision of the Garden City, however, and the growth of suburbia was criticised
at the time for creating a space that rather than combining the benefits of town and
country as Howard had proposed, instead lacked the advantages of either.[33] For the eager
home buyer of the interwar years, the privacy and standard of living the suburbs offered
were nevertheless irresistible and Thorp's model was made to quite literally sell this
dream. Largely built by speculative house builders such as Ideal Homes, Wates, Taylor
Woodrow, and Wimpey, enormous numbers of new homes were built each year with
Ideal Homes completing ten thousand in 1930 alone.[34] Having followed existing services
such as water, gas, electricity, and, as pioneered by the Metropolitan Railway, the expansion of the railways, the 'octopus' of suburbia quickly spread its tentacles.[35] Fierce competition saw a lowering of prices that further fuelled demand, with over four million new
homes built in Britain between the two World Wars, and by the end of the 1930s a third
of Britain's housing stock was less than twenty years old due to the scale of building that
had taken place.[36] Consequently, the dream of a home-owning future in more spacious,
better appointed houses compared to the Victorian and Edwardian terraces of the inner
towns and cities became an aspiration shared by millions. The suburban vision of the
future of home captured in Thorp's hypothetical model was selling not just a new space
but a new set of values and a very different way of living that offered young families everything they could hope for.[37] This was a dream of modernity rather than of modernism,

looking as much to the past as it was to the future,[38] and clearly visible in Thorp's models is the combination of overt symbols of progress such as motor cars and central heating with the invented tradition of the mock Tudor semi.[39] Architects at the time may well have derided such ordinary dreams,[40] but the speculative house builders who turned those dreams into reality were all too aware that when it came to thinking about the future of their homes, people were not rational, but emotional.[41]

## A Question of Space

Among the many architectural models Thorp made prior to the Second World War, there is one type of housing that is notable by its absence, the transformative social housing projects instigated by local authorities during the interwar years that provided much-loved, high-quality homes for countless families over many decades. The bulk of Thorp's home-related commissions during this period were for private houses, the simple reason being that private house builders needed to sell their designs while local authorities did not, meaning their need for expensive models was much diminished. Where Thorp did make a handful of models of social and charitable housing, however, an important comparison can be made between the differing approaches taken to private and public housing that highlights one of the key debates that dominated future visions of public housing from the 1920s right through to the 1970s, the issue of density.

Dating to around 1920, Thorp's model listed in the company's archive as 'Houses for Chorleywood' is a bit of a mystery, with almost no surviving information relating to the scheme it was made to illustrate (Figure 2.6). Given the timing of the model and the presence of a prominent memorial statue, it is likely that this was a proposal for memorial homes, one of many such plans put forward by charitable foundations in Britain following the First World War. These particular homes were never built and neither was the memorial itself, Chorleywood instead erecting a memorial hall in 1921, but as an early form of social housing the design of the proposed buildings themselves is important to note. Each block contains four reasonably large terraced houses with passageways between the inner terraces to provide access to the rear, and while there was to be a small public park around the war memorial, the houses themselves do not have private gardens. Compared to another model of an unbuilt proposal for private housing in Flackwell Heath dating to the early 1930s, the differences in approach become clear (Figure 2.7). Planned for the corner of Links Road and Links Way in what was then a small and relatively undeveloped village, the scheme presented in Thorp's model suggests a strong Garden Village influence (as shown in the models of Worthing Garden City and Angmering-on Sea in Chapter 1), with detached houses set in spacious gardens and a tennis court complete with pavilion providing a recreational centre for this proposed new addition to the village community. Flackwell Heath offered a future vision designed to appeal to the aspirational dreams of the middle classes, while Chorleywood put forward a more charitable vision of providing much-needed homes for those in need. Crucially, one was low density while the other was high density, characterising a clear dividing line between socio-economic groups.

Density was a core issue that shaped the design of all forms of public housing right from the very beginning of the twentieth century. While memorial homes, like the almshouses that preceded them, had specific missions to achieve, social housing in the form

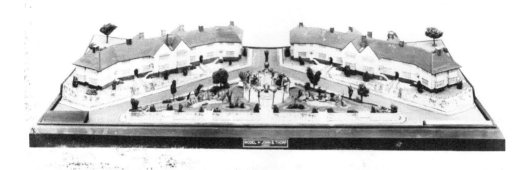

FIGURE 2.6   Model of an unbuilt proposal for memorial homes in Chorleywood. Architect: Unknown. Made by John Thorp, c1920. Courtesy Thorp Archive, AUB.

FIGURE 2.7   Model of an unbuilt proposal for housing in Flackwell Heath. Developer: Unknown. Made by John Thorp, c1931. Courtesy Thorp Archive, AUB.

of council estates was more broadly aimed at families who couldn't afford the speculative private housing that was springing up in Britain's suburbs. As such a conflict arose whereby the desire of local councils to implement the ideas of the Garden City movement and to provide healthy and affordable homes for the masses clashed with the economic realities of needing to reduce costs by using as little land as was necessary.[42] The template put forward by the Garden City movement offered a highly appealing low-density alternative to inner city slums but space pressures and the high costs involved limited their appeal as a realistic solution for providing publicly funded mass housing for the working classes.[43] Proposals for private estates such as shown in Thorp's Flackwell Heath model were highly attractive, but with local authorities initially confining their building programmes to existing urban sites with costly land values, higher densities were ultimately required.[44] Following the First World War, the twin drivers of slum clearance and the 'Homes for Heroes' initiative to build high-quality houses for those returning from the battlefield served to raise the provision of publicly-funded homes up the political agenda,[45] and by the start of the 1920s the Tudor Walters report on housing conditions and the 1919 Housing Act had established both the imperative for local authorities to provide social housing and the suggested high density template for them to follow. In starting to build on the open countryside, council-funded cottage estates of plainly decorated semi-detached houses with gardens in tree-lined cul-de-sacs became a common sight, with over seven hundred thousand such homes built between the two wars.[46] With local authorities having become major housing suppliers for the first time, council estates served as 'vehicles of modernisation and social mobility,'[47] providing an opportunity for lower earning working class families to realise many of the same aspirations of home-owning suburbanites and extending a profoundly welcome increase in living standards for millions of people.

After the Second World War, the demand for social housing grew even further, and between 1945 and the mid-1960s, Thorp, now led by John's son Lesile, saw a wholesale change in the types of housing models the company was commissioned to make. Whereas before the war Thorp's client base had been almost entirely private house builders, the imposition of building controls until 1954 saw their order book dominated instead by local authorities, with postwar dreams of the future of the home deeply connected to the emerging ambitions of the welfare state. In 1947, Leslie Thorp was asked to make a model that not only began a long trend of commissions for social housing projects but also demonstrated just how urgent the need to build more homes had become, as while density remained a vital concern it was suddenly no longer as important as the speed with which new homes could be built. Thorp's model of a pair of Cornish Unit prefabricated houses was made to be presented to Princess Elizabeth in commemoration of the gifting of two such houses by the Duchy of Cornwall to the Princess on the occasion of her marriage (Figure 2.8). Constructed in the small village of Bray Shop in Cornwall, the Princess Villas were opened by Elizabeth herself in 1949, with the Duchy having donated the land to the local council and the Princess' gift used to pay for two of the six houses the council was building to provide much-needed accommodation for displaced families from war-damaged towns and cities such as nearby Plymouth. The Type 1 Cornish Unit prefabs built at Bray Shop were designed by the architect Arthur Edgar Beresford for the Central Cornwall Concrete & Artificial Stone Company, which had developed a means of making prefabricated concrete panels from sand waste extracted from their China clay pits.[48] More than forty thousand Cornish Unit homes were built for local authorities in less than ten years, one of several types of prefab that provided a much needed stop-gap solution to Britain's housing crisis in the late 1940s.

With over three million houses destroyed and half a million severely damaged during the Second World War, it was estimated that nearly 800,000 houses were urgently needed,

**FIGURE 2.8**    Model of a pair of Cornish Unit homes to be gifted to Princess Elizabeth. Architect: Arthur Beresford. Made by Leslie Thorp, 1947. Courtesy Thorp Archive, AUB.

which was considerably more than it was possible to build using established construction methods.[49] In response the 1944 Housing Act authorised £150 million of government funding to build temporary homes.[50] Over the next five years 156,000 were constructed, largely out of prefabricated concrete and steel components in order to halve the cost and dramatically speed up the time it took to build a new home.[51] Taylor Woodrow's Arcon prefab was the most numerous of the types built, with over 43,000 constructed, with 30,000 of the Uni-Seco type and thousands more of more than a dozen other manufacturers' homes providing high-quality temporary accommodation. While the designs themselves were approved by the central government, it was left to local councils to determine where to put them, either as infills to replace bombed-out houses or in whole new estates.[52] The Cornish Units depicted in Thorp's model, while prefabricated, were not designed as temporary structures, however, it having been quickly realised by the government that the prefabrication approach could also be applied to the building of permanent dwellings.[53] The dream of future housing that the Cornish Units made real closely followed the interwar aspirations of privacy, a garden, and the provision of good quality kitchens and bathrooms. In being quick and cheap to construct, this dream was brought to more people more rapidly than might have been otherwise possible, and the six Cornish Units built at Bray Shop are still serving as social housing today, albeit having been heavily modernised.

By the end of the 1940s, alongside the switch from private house builders to local authorities as the main clients commissioning housing models from Thorp, an almost

**FIGURE 2.9**  Model of an early proposal for the Cleve Hall estate. Architects: Camberwell Borough Council Architects' Department. Made by Thorp, 1950. Courtesy Thorp Archive, AUB.

total change of the types of housing themselves had also taken place, with models of flats replacing those of houses and evidencing a new and persistent vision of the future of where and how we should live that dominated the next twenty years. For the most part, both private and social housing during the interwar years had adhered to the widely shared expectation that a home equated to a house and a garden, and regardless of whether they were constructed as spacious, low-density detached or semi-detached pairs, or in high-density terraces, the overall vision remained the same. Following the Second World War, the paths available to owner-occupiers and social tenants to pursue that dream began to diverge, and one of the earliest surviving records in Thorp's archive of a model that captured the alternative route for social housing is that of a 1950 model of a proposed housing estate at Cleve Hall in Camberwell (Figure 2.9). Illustrating an early design put forward by the Borough Architects' Department, with six-storey blocks of flats positioned in green open spaces surrounded by trees and communal tennis courts, this was a much bolder vision than the three-storey pitched roof designs that were actually constructed on the site between 1952 and 1956. As the model indicates, density remained a crucial issue when imagining the future of state-provided housing, and compared to Thorp's hypothetical model of suburbia shown earlier in this chapter, the ideology shaping the design of postwar public housing can be clearly seen. In the suburban model individualism and a high value assigned to privacy is visible in the fenced and gated gardens and the variety of styles applied to the design of each detached house. In the Cleve Hall model, there is no clear demarcation of ownership, no fences to separate privately held land, and an overriding sense of uniformity rather than individuality. Even the way such estates were described says much about the differences in their underlying visions: public housing versus private homes.

Between 1946 and 1951, some 800,000 council homes were built,[54] and fuelled by visions of density, modernity, and higher living standards,[55] the construction of flats rather than houses became the norm. Flats had formed a small part of social housing plans in London since the 1890s, but by the 1930s a perceived failure of the council-built Garden Estates to meet the housing needs of the capital's poorest families had stimulated a desire among both architects and planners for radical solutions that rejected traditional forms of housing in favour of high density flats.[56] By the time Thorp's model of Cleve Hall was made the enthusiasm for flats rather than houses had spread to most urban local authorities in Britain, with flats and maisonettes accounting for more than half of all council building undertaken between 1945 and 1964.[57] The original plan for Cleve Hall, as the model illustrates, was heavily influenced by Scandinavian modernism, with the point block approach of situating vertically stacked homes within attractive green spaces for their occupants to enjoy offering a more humanist alternative to the formalist ideas of Le Corbusier's slab wall high density housing that was dominating architectural thinking at the time. The Lawn in Harlow became the first development of this type to be completed in Britain in 1951, while the London County Council's influential Roehampton Estate adopted both approaches, including eleven-storey point blocks of flats in a park-like landscape on a much larger scale than had originally been planned for Cleve Hall.

The thinking behind the proposal for Cleve Hall, and countless other high-rise estates that followed, was driven by a combination of the aesthetic preference of postwar modernist architects and the need to achieve higher densities with limited land to build on, but also the changing makeup of the families they were designed to house.[58] Between 1921 and 1961, Britain's population increased by eight million people but the number of separate households almost doubled from eight to fifteen million.[59] Individual households were therefore getting smaller, with an average of 3.1 people in each house in 1961 compared to 4.6 in 1901.[60] These changes stimulated the adoption of mixed developments that sought to combine both high- and low-density housing within a single estate. A close examination of Thorp's model of Cleve Hall reveals that a small number of two-storey houses or maisonettes had indeed been included, attempting to cater for the increasingly varied future requirements of Britain's postwar families. The modernist dream of high rise, high density living for the masses was formed in deliberate opposition to that which had shaped suburbia in meeting the domestic aspirations of the public during the interwar years, however.[61] Suburbia, including both private and council-built housing, while immensely popular with its residents, was quietly loathed by many postwar architects and planners, primarily because they deemed the suburbs to be completely out of control due to their lack of centralised planning.[62] Decrying 'infinite horizons of semi-detached pairs...lost in acres of asphalt,'[63] architects and planners of the 1950s had little influence over what was being built there, but they did have control over the new generation of social housing projects that were then underway and through this control sought to prove that their own radical solutions were far more effective in addressing the nation's housing needs. The high density visions of the future of Britain's homes that they projected, while having logically argued their necessity amongst themselves, rarely served to spark the imagination of the public they were being built for, however.[64] While all new homes were gratefully welcomed, a survey conducted in 1943 revealed that only five per-cent of people would actively choose to live in a flat given a choice, while the following year, Pleydell-Bouverie's survey for the *Daily Mail Book of Post War Homes* emphatically claimed that with ninety percent of the population preferring homes over flats, 'Britons [were] still at heart, homelovers,' arguing that 'True family life is impossible without privacy and independence.'[65]

Despite this clear view from the public, even into the 1960s the architectural models of social housing projects that Thorp was commissioned to make continued to reflect architects' wholesale embracing of the flat, with even more emphatically high-rise visions

**FIGURE 2.10**  Model of St. James's Grove. Architect: Clifford Culpin and Partners. Made by Thorp, 1969. Courtesy Thorp Archive, AUB.

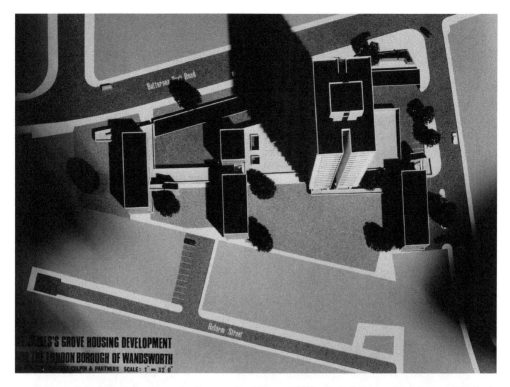

**FIGURE 2.11** Model of St. James's Grove. Architect: Clifford Culpin and Partners. Made by Thorp, 1969. Courtesy Thorp Archive, AUB.

of the future being expressed, and in 1965 Thorp commissioned the architectural photographer Henk Snoek to record, in dramatic imagery, their model of a twenty-one-storey block of council flats designed by Clifford Culpin and Partners for Wandsworth Borough Council (Figure 2.10). Approved for construction in 1969, the 114 homes at the St. James's Grove development were contained in five buildings with the site dominated by the sixty-seven metre tall Castlemaine Tower. Sixty houses were demolished to build the estate, with the new development almost doubling the density of homes on the same plot of land. The low angle of Snoek's photograph of the model demonstrates the sheer size of the main tower, particularly when compared to the height of the surrounding trees and the vehicles parked on the street. With the prevalence of such tower blocks today, it is perhaps difficult to imagine the response from local people when this model was unveiled, and how utterly exciting and modern it must have seemed compared to the Victorian terraces that the development was proposing to replace. As a wider photograph of the model shows (Figure 2.11), this comparison was made deliberately more challenging by the model omitting any of the surrounding buildings. In only showing road outlines there was no clear indication of just how dominant St. James's Grove was going to be, although the shadow being cast by the tower might have given cause for concern to anyone living on Battersea Park Road.

Residential tower blocks of this kind had been springing up all over Britain during the 1960s, with projections made at the time that in the future up to thirty percent of the population would be living in high-rise flats.[66] Incentivised through a storey-height subsidy from 1956 onwards that encouraged local authorities to build ever taller housing blocks, and constructed using prefabrication methods that had been developed during the building of the postwar prefabs such as the Cornish Units, high-rise council housing such as this was quick and relatively cheap to build.[67] In 1960 alone, approvals for the construction of high-rise flats reached fifteen thousand, increasing to a peak of twenty thousand in 1968[68] and providing a total of over 400,000 much needed high-quality new homes. St. James's Grove was planned towards the end of this trend, however, and by the time of the Ronan Point disaster in 1968, architectural opinion had finally caught up with public opinion in turning back to more low-rise forms of housing. While Thorp's model beautifully captures the dream of high-rise high density living, it was nevertheless a dream that only circulated within the provision of social housing, with few private high-rise housing blocks built until the latter decades of the century as the home-buying public still aspired to the dream of a house with the garden. [69] The high-rise vision of future social housing expressed in the many models of similar developments proposed during the 1960s was ultimately moving down a very different path to that of private housing, but with the state building fifty-one percent of all housing built in England between 1945 and 1969, sixty-four percent in Northern Ireland, and eighty-five percent in Scotland,[70] this was a dream that spread regardless of whether ordinary people shared it or not.

### Visions of Privacy

Just two years after Thorp was commissioned to make the model of St. James's Grove, a model of an altogether different vision of a high-density future housing scheme by the same architectural practice, now renamed The Culpin Group, was again photographed by Henk Snoek. As a low rise development, Thorp's model of Blackwell Street in Brixton was built at twice the scale of the St. James's Grove model, and while allowing for more detail, the two models were executed in a similar style (Figure 2.12). Comparing the low rise buildings on the St. James's Grove model to the Blackwell Street model, the fact that these two developments were designed by the same company becomes obvious, but the height and arrangement of the buildings indicate a radical difference between them. At only five storeys tall and designed around enclosed and more private shared green spaces, Blackwell Street offered a vision of social housing that was on a much more human scale. Today known as the Church Manor Estate, the development was built during the late 1960s with the old Blackwell Street itself and the surrounding Victorian terraces demolished to create three hundred new flats built facing Vassall Road on Church of England land for Lambeth Council.

By the late 1960s the public's general dislike of high-rise council flats had been matched by a critical reappraisal of their success[71] and architects began to favour low rise but still high-density schemes that were not too dissimilar to the principles that had guided Victorian housing developments.[72] Modernism had started to lose its unwavering confidence and with architects and planners having prioritised their adherence to ideology over the community values of the people they were trying to house,[73] it was finally recognised that high-rise council flats, while appreciated by their occupants, were not what people ideally wanted. Perhaps as a sign of class snobbery, flats of any kind had always been seen as

**FIGURE 2.12**  Model of the Blackwell Street development. Architect: The Culpin Group. Made by Thorp, 1971. Courtesy Thorp Archive, AUB.

an 'un-British' form of housing by much of the public,[74] no doubt due to their European heritage, and by the 1970s the design of social housing had switched back to the horizontal from the vertical once more, as the long run of flats in Thorp's model illustrates. The vision portrayed by the model was guided by a desire to provide as much privacy as was possible in a high-density estate, with carefully shielded balconies and terraces, stepped-back facades, and more intimate communal gardens. In contrast to the differences noted earlier between Thorp's model of suburban housing and that of Cleve Hall, in the model of Blackwell Street it is once again possible to distinguish individual homes, with the uniformity and anonymity present at both Cleve Hall and St. James's grove somewhat diminished. This was still a vision of state-provided homes, however, and with the number of public sector rentals increasing from eighteen to thirty percent of Britain's total housing stock between 1950 and 1972, and private rentals falling from forty four percent to thirteen,[75] it was a vision that had many years of life left in it. Council homes of all types were being built at a rate of over 150,000 per year by the time Blackwell Street was proposed, but what changed during this period was the type of homes being built, with the number of new high-rise flats being approved plummeting from 20,000 in 1968 to just thirty seven by 1978.[76] In part this was a consequence of not only architects and planners listening to public opinion, but following the 1967 Housing Subsidies Act the height subsidy that had encouraged tall residential buildings had been removed, ending the incentive for councils to build ever taller blocks of flats.[77]

Through the late 1960s and early 1970s, Thorp began to receive an increasing number of orders for models of privately-built housing developments once more, and with developers having largely steered clear of flats altogether in adhering to the home-buying public's preference for semi-detached and terraced houses alongside lower priced maisonettes, the record of the models Thorp made quickly shifted, with fewer models of flats, more of private housing estates, and a greater sense of individuality and privacy in the designs of the buildings they were made to represent. By the middle of the 1970s, the growth of the private rental market had begun to reflect a wider dissatisfaction with the results of a generation of state-provided housing,[78] with the modernist visions behind them deemed by many commentators at the time to have failed to meet the needs and aspirations of ordinary people.[79] A 1975 model of a proposed mixed development of private housing designed by Arthur Mull Associates for a site on the corner of Broadway and Princes Gate in Peterborough demonstrated this change of attitude particularly well (Figure 2.13). With a combination of flats and townhouses arranged around a shared central courtyard, this was a low rise proposal with a pitched roof, familiar brick construction, and plenty of parking for residents, all composed on a human scale. The ideas driving architectural design during the 1970s were largely centred on notions of community, communication, and the environment,[80] and while Mull's scheme was never built, the influence of these ideas can be clearly seen in Thorp's model. Having abandoned high-rise housing approaches, architects were keen to experiment with ways of increasing the density of low rise developments, exploring different arrangements to avoid

FIGURE 2.13   Model of an unbuilt proposal for Broadway in Peterborough. Architect: Arthur Mull Associates. Made by Thorp, 1975. Courtesy Thorp Archive, AUB.

**FIGURE 2.14** Model of Chapel Lane. Developer: Sunley Homes. Made by Thorp, 1976. Courtesy Thorp Archive, AUB.

properties overlooking one another, and by reducing, or, as in the case of the Peterborough scheme, eliminating front gardens entirely.[81] Speculative house builders had always paid more attention to the dreams of ordinary people, as was the commercially sensible thing to do, and they understood, as the architectural historian John Gloag memorably wrote in 1945, that the 'liking of privacy is as widespread in England as the love of liberty.'[82] For all the experimentation with different forms of state-funded housing during the twentieth century, for the British public their vision of the future of home stubbornly refused to change – a simple house with a garden. With the building of new social housing much reduced by the start of the 1970s, models of speculatively built housing estates by developers such as Barratt Homes, Wimpey, Bovis, and Bellway Homes instead began to dominate Thorp's order book from the mid-1970s onwards, fuelled even further during the 1980s by the Thatcher government's embracing of the dream of home ownership as the ultimate marker of aspiration and social mobility.

Thorp's 1976 model of the Chapel Lane housing development made for Sunley Homes was typical of countless such models made to be displayed in estate agents' offices and marketing suites across Britain during the late twentieth century, and which poured out of Thorp's workshops in quite staggering numbers (Figure 2.14). Adhering to Pleydell-Bouverie's 1944 advice to 'study the models' when considering a new home, developers were well aware of the convincing power of an architectural model to help a potential buyer place a deposit on what was usually little more than either an empty field or a chaotic building site at the time. The style adopted for these models was one of clear yet restrained detail, enabling aspiring homeowners to imagine themselves walking along the street or turning onto their driveway in their car. With little information in Thorp's archive as to where in Britain Chapel Lane even was, a search of all roads with that name suggests that Sunley's specific proposal for this site was never built, but the broader vision portrayed by the model was realised time and time again across the country, the private developer's housing estate becoming one of the defining elements of the built environment in late twentieth century Britain.

At the end of the 1970s a third of Britain's housing stock was still owned by local authorities, so significant had the push for council housing been during the post-war era, however private ownership of homes had nevertheless also been increasing since the Second World War, rising from twenty-six percent in 1945 to sixty-seven percent in 1983.[83] Following the relaxation of building controls in 1954, the surviving prewar regional house builders and their new postwar competitors began to balloon in size, with companies such as Bellway, Barratt, and Wimpey leading the market.[84] By 1980 Barratt Homes was building over ten thousand new homes a year, with over three hundred completed estates across Britain.[85] Following the continued postwar demographic trend of fewer multigenerational families and longer life expectancies, it was predicted that more separate but smaller family homes would be needed, which developers such as Barratt and Sunley duly provided.[86] The houses proposed in the Chapel Lane model are a little more unusual in being three-storey townhouses, but the influence of the Radburn approach that was applied to the design of New Ash Green (as outlined in Chapter 1) can be seen, and the preservation of a large number of mature trees and the provision of shared green spaces demonstrates a more considered approach to conservation than was prevalent in the state-funded social housing projects of the 1950s and 1960s featured earlier in this chapter.

The vision of home that models of projects such as Chapel Lane put forward was one of home ownership, privacy, and safety – the latter having become a core weapon in the attack on postwar social housing that emerged during the late 1970s and early 1980s. Connections were drawn between the design of high density council estates and the high incidence of crime and anti-social behaviour within them, and whether this was true or not, high level walkways, secluded corners and underpasses, and the prevalence of shared spaces were all castigated as design flaws that created the conditions where crimes were more likely to be committed.[87] Architects at the time responded that people and not buildings were responsible for crime,[88] but regardless of which view was correct, it provided a useful excuse to justify a reduction in public spaces in new housing developments, with a return to private, fenced, and non-overlooked gardens and well-lit, overlooked streets and pathways. By the early 1990s, the increasing importance being given to safety and privacy concerns in the design of new housing developments also served to give rise to a new vision of private homes that for the first time wholly embraced high density living in flats, or rather in apartments as they were referred to in order to distinguish them from the postwar council blocks.

Two models made by Thorp in 1993 were typical of the designs of such developments at the time, presenting a very different feel to earlier models of flats such as Cleve Hall and Blackwell Street. The first, of a Berkeley Homes apartment block, Oakleigh Park (Figure 2.15), included underground parking, secure entrances, and the ubiquitous Juliet balcony, all of which supported an impression of a secure and highly private development. The second, made for an unknown developer, not only incorporated all of the above, but with a generous central courtyard garden and pastiche architectural features presented a direct call back to early twentieth century mansion blocks such as Clifton Court (Figure 2.16). The return to brick construction, pitched roofs, and traditional

FIGURE 2.15    Model of Oakleigh Park. Developer: Berkeley Homes. Made by Thorp, 1993. Courtesy Thorp Archive, AUB.

FIGURE 2.16    Model of an unidentified apartment building. Made by Thorp, 1993. Courtesy Thorp Archive, AUB.

**FIGURE 2.17**    Model of Priory Wharf. Architect: Briarcroft. Made by Thorp, 1990. Courtesy Thorp Archive, AUB.

details was a clear sign that these private complexes were a world apart from the social housing blocks of a few decades before. Modernism was banished and in applying the architectural language of the traditionally built house to high density living, flats, in their modern guise as apartments, become an increasingly popular form of private housing for the first time. Developers were keen to benefit from the greater profits available from high-density schemes while the extension of mortgages and the lower prices of one- or two-bedroom apartments compared to a house made them appealing choices for many homebuyers. Visions of home ownership, safety and security, and high density living were combined, and with the role of the state in providing homes massively curtailed following the privatisation of council housing through the Right to Buy scheme of the 1980s, the private developer became the key realiser of the nation's dreams of what the future of Britain's home should be like.[89] Driven by the commercial logic of providing people with what they wanted, private developers embraced both the low-density housing estate and high density 'luxury' apartments in unison, as the final model in this chapter, Thorp's 1990 model of Briarcroft's design of Priory Wharf in Birkenhead, clearly demonstrates (Figure 2.17).

Proposed as the start of an urban regeneration project on the site of a disused railway yard and infilled dockyard on the banks of the Mersey, Priory Wharf was built in 1992 and contained a mix of both large, terraced townhouses and apartments generously arranged around a shared green space with views overlooking the estuary. The model, with its depiction of couples strolling along the waterfront, presented an image of urban tranquillity but also a curious merging of earlier dreams of the privacy of a house, the landscaped communality of postwar social housing such as was envisaged for Cleve Hall, and the inward-facing luxury and security of the mansion block. In this privatised vision of the future of the home the simple domestic aspirations of ownership, higher quality living standards, and privacy can be seen to have triumphed over the state provision of mass housing, and Thorp's order book ended the twentieth century just as it began, dominated by models of private houses and luxury flats, demonstrating that for all the alternatives put forward during the twentieth century, the futures people wanted in terms of their ideal homes remained remarkably constant throughout.

## Notes

1 M. Pleydell-Bouverie, *The Daily Mail Book of Post-War Homes* (London: Associated Newspapers, 1944), 119.
2 Mark Girouard, *Robert Smythson and the Architecture of the Elizabethan Era* (Chicago: University of Michigan Press, 1966), 57.
3 Alison Blunt and Robyn Dowling, *Home* (Abingdon: Routledge, 2006), 2.
4 Deborah Ryan, *Ideal Homes 1918–1939: Domestic Design and Suburban Modernism* (Manchester: Manchester University Press, 2018), 19.
5 Sam Wetherell, *Foundations: How the Built Environment made Twentieth-century Britain* (Princeton: Princeton University Press, 2023), 79.
6 Susan Beattie, *A Revolution in Housing* (London: The Architectural Press, 1980), 85.
7 Ryan, *Ideal Homes*, 37.
8 Mark Swenarton, *Homes for Heroes* (London: Heinemann, 1981), 136.
9 Helen Barrett and John Phillips, *Suburban Style* (London: MacDonald Orbis, 1987), 14.
10 Ryan, *Ideal Homes*, 29.
11 Miles Glendenning and Stefan Muthesius, *Tower Block: Modern Public Housing in England, Scotland, Wales, and Northern Ireland* (London: Yale University Press, 1993), 2.
12 Paul Oliver, Ian Davis, and Ian Bentley, *Dunroamin: The Suburban Semi and its Enemies* (London: Barrie and Jenkins, 1981), 136.
13 'The Fascination of Models,' *The Building News*, March 28, 1924, specially reprinted copy of the original article made by John Thorp, Thorp Modelmaking Archive.
14 Edward Hobbs, *House Modelling for Builders and Estate Agents* (London: The Architectural Press, 1937), vii.
15 Pleydell-Bouverie, *The Daily Mail Book of Post-War Homes*, 12.
16 Pleydell-Bouverie, *The Daily Mail Book of Post-War Homes*, 15.
17 John Thorp, *Models of Buildings, Estates, Works, etc. For Exhibitions or Law Cases* (London: John. B. Thorp, 1913), 27.
18 Ryan, *Ideal Homes*, 57.
19 Martin Pugh, *We Danced All Night* (London: Vintage, 2009), 58.
20 John Burnett, *A Social History of Housing 1815–1985* (London: Methuen, 1986), 141.
21 Fred Wellings, *British Housebuilders: History & Analysis* (Oxford: Blackwell, 2006), 35.
22 Deborah Sugg Ryan, *The Ideal Home Through the 20th Century* (London: Hazar, 1997), 11.
23 Ryan, *The Ideal Home Through the 20th Century*, 7.
24 Ryan, *The Ideal Home Through the 20th Century*, 23.
25 Ryan, *The Ideal Home Through the 20th Century*, 34.
26 Andrew Marr, *The Making of Modern Britain* (London: Macmillan, 2010), 201.
27 Peter Hall, *Cities of Tomorrow* (Oxford: Blackwell, 2002), 79.
28 Edward Hobbs, *Pictorial House Modelling* (London: Crosby, Lockward and Son, 1926), 109.
29 Ryan, *Ideal Homes*, 137.
30 Hall, *Cities of Tomorrow*, 77.
31 Ryan, *Ideal Homes*, 18.
32 Burnett, *A Social History of Housing*, 252.
33 Burnett, *A Social History of Housing*, 256.
34 Wellings, *British Housebuilders*, 42.

35 Clough Williams-Ellis cited by Alan Powers. 'Models for Suburban Living,' In *Eric Lyons and Span*, ed. Barbara Simms (London: RIBA Publishing, 2006), 24.
36 Peter Scott, *The Making of the Modern British Home* (Oxford: Oxford University Press, 2013), 233.
37 Roger Silverstone. 'Introduction,' In *Visions of Suburbia*, ed. Roger Silverstone (Abbingdon: Routledge, 1997), 3.
38 Ryan, *Ideal Homes*, 19.
39 Ryan, *Ideal Homes*, 19.
40 Hall, *Cities of Tomorrow*, 80.
41 Burnett, *A Social History of Housing*, 256.
42 Swenarton *Homes for Heroes*, 36.
43 John Boughton, *Municipal Dreams: The Rise and Fall of Council Housing* (London: Verso, 2019), 30.
44 Swenarton, *Homes for Heroes*, 34.
45 Neal Shasore, *Designs on Democracy* (Oxford: Oxford University Press, 2022), 297.
46 Swenarton, *Homes for Heroes*, 1.
47 Wetherell, *Foundations*, 116.
48 Elizabeth Blanchet and Sonia Zhuravlyova, *Prefabs: A Social and Architectural History* (Swindon: Historic England, 2018), 56.
49 Andrew Marr, *A History of Modern Britain* (London: Macmillan, 2007), 73.
50 John Grindrod, *Concretopia* (Brecon: Old Street, 2013), 22.
51 Blanchet and Zhuravlyova, *Prefabs*, 30.
52 Blanchet and Zhuravlyova, *Prefabs*, 32.
53 Blanchet and Zhuravlyova, *Prefabs*, 25.
54 Boughton, *Municipal Dreams*, 105.
55 Glendenning and Muthesius, *Tower Block*, 1.
56 Alan Powers, *Britain: Modern Architectures* (London: Reaktion, 2007), 65.
57 Burnett, *A Social History of Housing*, 301.
58 Boughton, *Municipal Dreams*, 115.
59 Burnett, *A Social History of Housing*, 279.
60 Burnett, *A Social History of Housing*, 279.
61 Oliver et al., *Dunroamin*, 24.
62 Oliver et al., *Dunroamin*, 18.
63 Albert William Cleve Barr, *Public Authority Housing* (London: Batsford, 1958), 60.
64 Powers, *Britain*, 66.
65 Pleydell-Bouverie, *The Daily Mail Book of Post-War Homes*, 19.
66 Glendenning and Muthesius, *Tower Block*, 61.
67 Owen Hopkins, *Lost Futures* (London: RCA, 2017), 31.
68 Powers, *Britain*, 134.
69 Wetherell, *Foundations*, 77.
70 Glendenning and Muthesius, *Tower Block*, 2.
71 Burnett, *A Social History of Housing*, 302.
72 Burnett, *A Social History of Housing*, 311.
73 Oliver et al., *Dunroamin*, 24.
74 Glendenning and Muthesius, *Tower Block*, 24.
75 David Crawford, *A Decade of British Housing 1963–1973* (London: The Architectural Press, 1975), 19.
76 Grindrod, *Concretopia*, 339.
77 Glendenning and Muthesius, *Tower Block*, 32.
78 Elain Harwood and Alan Powers, 'From Downturn to Diversity, Revisiting the 1970s,' In *The Seventies*, eds. Elain Harwood and Alan Powers (London: The Twentieth Century Society, 2012), 11.
79 Geraint Franklin and Elain Harwood, *Post-modern Buildings in Britain* (London: Batsford, 2017), 24.
80 Catherine Croft, 'David Rock: Architecture is the Land of Green Ginder, or Form Follows Culture,' In *The Seventies*, eds. Elain Harwood and Alan Powers (London: The Twentieth Century Society, 2012), 65.

81 Crawford, *A Decade of British Housing*, 16.
82 John Gloag, *The Englishman's Castle* (London: Eyre & Spottiswoode, 1945), 9.
83 Burnett, *A Social History of Housing*, 282.
84 Wellings, *British Housebuilders*, 66.
85 Wellings, *British Housebuilders*, 86.
86 Burnett, *A Social History of Housing*, 279.
87 Wetherell, *Foundations*, 14; Hopkins, *Lost Futures*, 18.
88 Jonah Lowenfeld, 'Estate Regeneration in Practice: The Mozart Estate, Westminster, 1985–2004,' In *Housing the Twentieth Century Nation*, eds. Elain Harwood and Alan Powers (London: The Twentieth Century Society, 2008), 166.
89 Boughton, *Municipal Dreams*, 5.

# 3

# WORK

The British Empire Exhibition, held in Wembley between April and November 1924, and again from May until October the following year, was the largest exhibition ever staged in Britain. Intended to show how Britain was still a major player on the world stage following the First World War, twenty-seven million people visited the two hundred acre site to explore the vast Palaces of Industry and Engineering and the many pavilions that represented the fifty-eight territories of the Empire. The aim of the exhibition was to outline the potential of exploiting the collective raw materials of the Empire to fuel Britain's economy, albeit with little consideration of how this would negatively impact the inhabitants of its overseas possessions, such were the attitudes of the time. The focus of the exhibition was centred on industry and trade, and its pavilions positively over-flowed with models. Alongside countless engineering models of locomotives, ships, and machines were hundreds of architectural, landscape, and planning models that were built to outline different visions of Britain's future industrial facilities. The dedicated Hall of Models within the transport section of the Palace of Industry featured more than one hundred such models alone, including Thorp's impressive depiction of Hull Docks (Figure 3.1), while an even larger model of Liverpool Docks made by an unknown model-maker attracted constant crowds who were enticed by its moving ships.[1]

Models such as these were common sights at exhibitions throughout the twentieth century where the world of work and new developments in industry and commerce could be proudly displayed through miniature representations of the future buildings, structures, and landscapes that would house the activities that would fuel Britain's economic growth. Thorp inevitably made an enormous number of these models, as well as many others that were for client and planning approval rather than public display, and this chapter examines twenty two of these models in order to consider some of the different ideas that shaped how future offices, factories, and other industrial workplaces were imagined during a century in which rapid social, economic, and technological change necessitated the creation of entirely new building types. This chapter therefore contains a notable shift in emphasis compared to the previous two chapters in that whereas the ideas that shaped the future visions of place and home that were captured by the architectural

DOI: 10.4324/9781032715728-4

FIGURE 3.1    Model of Hull Docks made for display at the British Empire Exhibition. Made by
John Thorp, 1924. Courtesy Thorp Archive, AUB.

models of the time were largely generated by architects and planners themselves, in the
case of the design of Britain's workplaces architects were more often reacting to external changes beyond their control, although the models featured nevertheless evidence a
range of striking and innovative solutions put forward to meet the evolving needs of their
clients. This chapter also deliberately limits its exploration of models of the built environment of work to offices and industrial buildings as these were perhaps the most recognis-
able types of workplaces during the twentieth century. Models of future civic buildings,
schools, hospitals, shops, and transport facilities that also served as places of work are
addressed later in this book, leaving this chapter to explore architectural models that evidence the broad changes to the design of Britain's offices, factories, ports, power stations,
and other industrial buildings that took place in response to the development of entirely
new industries and technologies.

After the home, the workplace is one of the most familiar elements of the built environment as it is in work that we spend more of our waking hours than anywhere else.
Where we worked, doing what tasks, and in which types of buildings changed dramatically during the twentieth century as the rise and fall of different industries and the
invention of new technologies and processes instigated massive social and economic
change. Factories, once seen as symbols of both human achievement and human suffering,[2] changed out of all recognition through automation, while offices grew from simple
spaces in which the activities of a business were directed and into expressive statements

of corporate identity. Through much of the twentieth century neither attracted much attention from ambitious architects, however, with industrial buildings in particular having been seen as unappealing commissions due to their functional constraints.[3] Industrial architecture, as Frederick Gibberd observed, nevertheless required the skills of engineers, architects, and landscape designers in order for it to succeed,[4] and in many of the models described in this chapter the merging of all three disciplines can be seen.

The overall history of the imagining of Britain's future offices and industrial workplaces during the twentieth century that Thorp's models evidence can be encapsulated by a single notion: change. Very little in the world of work remained constant and the models that Thorp was commissioned to make reflected this, with countless new proposals for offices, factories, warehouses, and entirely new structures such as oil rigs and nuclear power stations emerging from the company's workshop. Britain began the new century uniquely rich among nations, benefiting from its position as the birthplace of the industrial revolution and as the keeper of a global empire.[5] A Victorian attitude towards work endured for some time, with most men spending the bulk of their time 'from late childhood to their deathbeds' working either in a factory, workshop, or on the land,[6] and through the first few decades of the twentieth century more and more people found their work heading indoors as the role of agriculture declined and the factory, and later the office, grew in importance.[7] Change began to accelerate further following the First World War, during which the state had been drawn into an unprecedented intervention in the workplace with over three million industrial workers taken into government employment.[8] After the Second World War this state intervention expanded once more with the application of the nationalised wartime economy to meet the aims of post-war reconstruction.[9] Industry in the form of heavy manufacturing began to be replaced by the production of consumer goods, while new service industries such as distribution and warehousing demanded brand new types of building.[10] A trend of consolidation saw the growth of ever larger companies that dominated their respective markets, while technological advances in the second half of the century saw the productivity of an hour of labour increase by a factor of four.[11] As the type of work in which people were employed changed, so too did the environments in which they were based, with the proportion of workers employed in service industries increasing from forty-three percent to seventy-nine percent of the workforce between 1900 and 1990[12] while those working on the land fell from twenty-two percent to two percent over the same period.[13]

In response to all of these changes, architects and engineers were constantly tasked with developing new visions of how these dramatic shifts in work could be accommodated through the creation of factories, offices, and other workplaces that in many cases had no prior examples to draw from. What should a nuclear power station look like? Or a container port? How could modern architecture be used to convey messages of corporate identity? And what exactly was a business park and where should it be located? The visions that developed in response to these questions were captured in the architectural models of the time, with perhaps as many as 6000 of the 10,000 architectural models made by Thorp during the twentieth century being of workplaces such as factories and offices. Some of these models were used for public display in exhibitions such as the 1924 model of Hull Docks, while others were made to explain the functions and operation of a proposed building to stakeholders, and following American practice, by the 1950s the use of models had become an integral part of the planning of industrial sites, both in terms of their external design and internal layouts.[14] Taken together as a body of evidence, what these models collectively reveal is just how rapidly the nature of work, and the buildings in which that work was carried out, evolved. As will be seen, the forms of both the factory and the office ultimately began to converge as the makeup of Britain's industrial output moved from heavy industry to manufacturing and ultimately to the provision of services, and the distinctions between what were previously separate locations for industrial and office-based work began to blur. The workplace, in providing the surroundings in which the nation's economic activities could take place, served to shape much of Britain's built environment during the twentieth century and the architectural models that follow document just how dramatically the visions of its future changed.

### New Work for a New Century

During the first decades of the twentieth century, the models of factories and offices that John Thorp was commissioned to make were incredibly varied, their diversity reflecting a growing uncertainty about what the future of the workplace was to be. The nature of work itself was already quickly evolving as while established industries such as coal mining continued to employ over one million people, this was contrasted by a long-term shift from agriculture to manufacturing and the emergence of new industries fuelled by technological developments such as the wireless and the telephone.[15] In determining what the most suitable workplaces for the new century should be like, architects had to carefully balance the traditions of the past with the ambiguous demands of the future. Two of Thorp's earliest twentieth century models, one of the Brilliant Sign Company's proposed Paragon Works made in 1907, and one of a new headquarters for James Carter & Company made in 1910, demonstrated the breadth of approaches that were taken in crafting visions of how future industrial buildings should be designed.

The model of the Brilliant Sign Company's Paragon Works outlined a proposal for a two-storey building to house the firm's new workshops, depicting the extensive glazing along one wall that would provide generous natural lighting, hoists to haul goods up to the first floor, and an unpaved yard with both horse-drawn carts and early motor vehicles ready to ship the company's wares (Figure 3.2). By 1907, the Brilliant Sign Company was on its way to becoming the world's largest sign maker and the model was intended to show how their new three-acre manufacturing site in Shepherd's Bush would be organised. The overall arrangement was functional and followed an established pattern that was commonplace at the time, with the lack of visible power cables suggesting that the company had no need as yet to be connected to the growing electricity network. As such, the proposal for Paragon Works encapsulated a vision that cautiously straddled two eras, a projection of a Victorian factory template lightly modified to suit the modernity of the twentieth century. This was to be a medium-sized specialist workshop located on a new site on the edge of a built-up area, producing a new product but using traditional hand skills and manufacturing techniques. It was also largely hidden from public view, the buildings set back from the road behind a high front wall, a private business in a private location. For many companies at the time this was the ideal vision of the future, practical and familiar, yet comfortably removed from the squalid conditions of the thousands of small-scale workshops in Britain's towns and cities where so many businesses such as

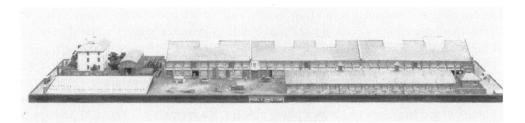

FIGURE 3.2 Model of Paragon Works. Client: The Brilliant Sign Company. Made by John Thorp, 1907. Courtesy Thorp Archive, AUB.

FIGURE 3.3 Model of James Carter & Company's Raynes Park headquarters. Architect: unknown. Made by John Thorp, 1910. Courtesy Thorp Archive, AUB.

this were operating from, often in buildings that followed the same design principles as factories from two centuries before.[16]

While Paragon Works was a subtle progression from what had come before, just three years later a completely different vision of an industrial building was put forward that took a far more confident leap into the modernity of the new century. In John Thorp's model of the new headquarters of James Carter & Company, Britain's leading supplier of seeds, gone were the realistic depictions of worn bricks, dirty rooftops, and horses and carts that were visible in the Paragon Works model, replaced by an almost sculptural, idealised representation of the pristine architecture alone, with the building shown surrounded by tidy lawns on a raised and substantial baseboard (Figure 3.3). Comparing the two models the distance between them seems far greater than just three years, the later model seemingly belonging to a different age, both in terms of the model's aesthetics and the design of the building it was made to represent. James Carter & Company had been based for many years in Holborn, not far from Thorp's workshop, and the model they commissioned Thorp to make was of their proposed new headquarters in Raynes Park, a nineteen-acre site that was to include glasshouses, seed beds, warehouses, and testing grounds. The building depicted was a combination of offices, warehouses, and laboratories, all contained behind an ornate and rather triumphant facade. This was clearly more than just a practical industrial building, instead acting as a proud statement of the company's identity.

The care with which the new building was conceived by its unknown architect suggests that it was intended to make a bold impression, an early example of what later became a common approach during the interwar years for companies to face their factories with grand frontages to act as a physical form of advertising.[17] This was perhaps the key difference between the visions laid out for James Carter & Company and the Brilliant Sign Company works, with the former being purely practical and hidden from public view while the latter was deliberately intended to be seen. The growth of light industries during the early twentieth century enabled a greater number of buildings such as the James Carter headquarters to adopt a less functional appearance, often humanising the environment around them with careful landscaping,[18] which in the case of a seed supplier was highly appropriate and the company become noted for its colourful flower displays. The imposing architecture, which was more readily associated with public buildings (see Chapter 5), was a clear sign of things to come, designed to convey a sense of efficiency and cleanliness, influenced by North American factory exteriors and offering a direct contrast to the utilitarian image of Victorian brick-built mills and factories.[19]

Following the First World War, this more ostentatious approach to the design of industrial buildings expanded, with buildings such as Owen Williams' modernist factory for Boots in Nottingham, influenced by Peter Behrens's AEG turbine hall, setting new standards for the architectural quality of factories and warehouses during a period in which pride in Britain's industrial success rose to a new peak. Such the pace of change, however, that the conversion and adaptation of existing buildings was often the only way to keep up with the challenge of accommodating entirely new industries and novel modes of commerce. Many of the industrial models Thorp made during the interwar years reflected this and in 1928 the company was commissioned to make a model of what was then the busiest exhibition centre in Britain, the British Industries Fair complex, which had opened in 1920 in a converted aircraft hangar at Castle Bromwich aerodrome (Figure 3.4). Trade exhibitions had become an important part of Britain's commercial activities, and as with the 1924 British Empire Exhibition, were also a symbolic means of expressing industrial pride. As the Castle Bromwich site continually expanded, so too a greater sense of grandeur was included in its design, with Thorp's model commissioned to show how the proposed new entrance and outdoor exhibition space would be incorporated into the existing site. Held each spring and billed as the greatest trade fair in the world, the British Industries Fair had a global reputation and was evidence of the dramatic shift away from the nation's reliance on heavy industries and towards the production of consumer goods that was by then well underway.[20] Thorp's roofless model clearly shows the scale of the indoor space, able to hold more than one thousand exhibitors displaying their latest goods, and it is likely that the model was prepared for George V's visit to the Fair that year, an opportunity to show the King-Emperor himself how Britain's Imperial economy was modernising.

The need to convert existing buildings to meet the changing demands of industry was perhaps best evidenced the following year by Thorp's 1929 model of the MG car factory in Abingdon (Figure 3.5). Depicting how MG intended to convert an unused tannery into a state-of-the-art car factory, the model itself was a return to the style of the 1908 Paragon Works model, animated with realistic planting and twin parades of trucks and

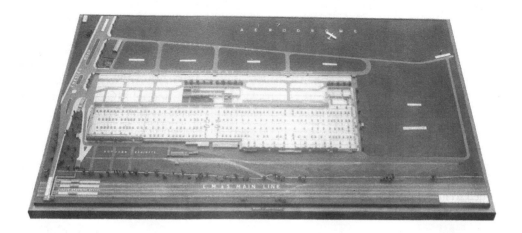

**FIGURE 3.4** Model of the British Industries Fair, Castle Bromwich. Architect: unknown. Made by John Thorp, 1928. Courtesy Thorp Archive, AUB.

**FIGURE 3.5** Model of the MG Car Factory in Abingdon. Architect: unknown. Made by John Thorp, 1929. Courtesy Thorp Archive, AUB.

cars emerging from the main factory doors. This was likely to reflect the increased output that the plant's modern production line would produce, with twin elevated assembly lines running through the building and completed vehicles trundling off the end to be driven directly to the company's test track before being delivered to waiting customers. The challenge for the plant's designers was how to incorporate the latest production methods into the infrastructure of the existing building and while the model showed that the factory was to follow a relatively traditional approach to its external design, inside, a revolution in manufacturing was planned.

The reuse of existing buildings was common for the early motor industry, with the first car plants in Britain having been built on a decidedly ad hoc basis as and when demand required, such as Daimler opening in a disused mill in 1896 and Austin in an abandoned print works in 1905.[21] By the time of Thorp's model of the proposed MG factory in Abingdon, however, Britain was in the process of overtaking France as the largest car manufacturer in Europe as the economic benefits of mass production began to take hold.[22] Ford had opened its first British car plant at Trafford Park in 1911 and the company's approach of using interchangeable parts and a continuous production line had transformed how the industry could operate. It was Ford's innovative production methods that the MG plant needed to incorporate and Abingdon was planned to be a totally modern factory, powered by electricity and organised around the principles of professionalism and organisation.[23] Emulating Ford's success, MG invested heavily in improving the working conditions at their new Abingdon plant, and as the model shows, staff tennis courts were planned alongside a social club, a football pitch, and a canteen, all reflecting a greater need for such facilities to attract workers to these new and rapidly expanding industries.[24] At the rear of the model the two storey office building can be seen, Thorp's model capturing what was then considered to be the ideal arrangement for a car factory with a double-floor administration block and an expansive single-storey production facility.[25]

Industrial buildings were not the only kind of workplace that Thorp was commissioned to make models of during the interwar years, as while the factory was undergoing a period of rapid change, so too was the office building, with new ideas about how future offices should be designed emerging in response to a dramatic growth of non-manual work. In the first half of the twentieth century the proportion of workers employed in non-manual sectors such as administration and finance increased from twenty percent to thirty percent, while the number of clerical staff trebled.[26] At the same time, the consolidation of smaller businesses into national and even global conglomerates led to a need for larger office buildings than had previously been the norm, with London's streets comprehensively redeveloped to house the corporate headquarters of industrial giants such as Unilever, Shell, BP, and ICI.[27] All of these projects called for architectural models, and by the 1920s John Thorp's order book was beginning to be dominated by commissions for large and architecturally challenging models of office buildings. The demand for office space in London had skyrocketed following the First World War and with high prices within the square mile making areas to the west of the City increasingly attractive, a speculative office boom began to spread through the West End and the Embankment that served to significantly reshape much of the capital.[28] Central to this was the London County Council's 'New London' redevelopment of Aldwych and The Strand which was envisaged as a repositioning of London as a grand imperial city at the heart of the British Empire.[29] Bush House, designed by the American architect Harvey W. Corbett, was one of many speculative office buildings constructed as part of the project. Funded by the American industrialist Irving Bush with the intention of creating a major new trading centre to encourage international commerce, construction took place over several phases and by 1925 the central section had been completed. Thorp produced several models of the design as it developed, including a large-scale model of the main entrance that was a

**FIGURE 3.6**   Model of the main entrance to Bush House. Architect: Harvey W. Corbett. Made by John Thorp, c1923. Courtesy Thorp Archive, AUB.

stunning depiction of what was already the most expensive office building in the world (Figure 3.6). Planned to be the best serviced office building in the city,[30] Bush House extended a bold vision of international trade in luxurious surroundings. As an expression of London's modernity and global importance, Corbett's design for the main entrance included statues representing Britain and the United States holding a torch of progress over an altar to symbolise the friendship between the two nations,[31] a rather challenging detail that Thorp's modelmakers nevertheless recreated perfectly in miniature.

**FIGURE 3.7**   Model of Industry House. Architect: Frank Baines. Made by John Thorp, c1926. Courtesy Thorp Archive, AUB.

The growth in office space in London during the interwar years meant that Bush House was soon eclipsed by larger and equally impressive office buildings, and just two years later an even grander model emerged from Thorp's workshop of Frank Baines' design of the proposed Industry House at Millbank (Figure 3.7). Planned to house the headquarters of the newly merged Imperial Chemical Industries, Baines' design pushed the sense of corporate grandeur to new levels, with more than seven hundred rooms contained within a granite and Portland stone facade. Occupying a site on the embankment of the Thames that had been razed after a devastating flood in 1928,[32] Industry House and its mirror image companion Thames House framed the approach to Lambeth Bridge, acting as dominating expressions of London's commercial success. Reaching the maximum building height allowed by the London County Council, with their main cornices at eighty feet above street level, Industry House and Thames House were the largest office buildings in Europe at the time, and Baines' bold reimagining of Millbank served as a template for further development during the 1930s, with even the financial crash of 1929 doing little to slow long-term demand. With an increase in the number of office clerks from 478,000 in 1911 to 1.2 million in 1931,[33] the need for large office buildings such as both Industry House and Bush House was on a singularly upward trajectory, providing a steady stream of commissions for Thorp through to the start of the Second World War. For both offices and industrial buildings, however, the adaptations to accommodate the major shifts in the makeup of Britain's workforce that took place during the first half of the century were relatively minor in comparison to the revolutions that would follow in response to the profound technological and social changes of the postwar era. For the office in particular, new careers, new technologies, and new architectural ideas were set to inspire an explosion of different visions of the future, for which countless models were duly required.

### The Office of the Future

In 1956, Thorp was commissioned to produce a model of a new office development planned for Gracechurch Street in London (Figure 3.8). The building was to house the Midland Bank's overseas division and comparing this model to Thorp's prewar models of offices such as Industry House, a radical shift in appearance can be seen. Many of the speculative offices built in London during the interwar years had either been badly damaged or destroyed during the Second World War, with an estimated loss of twenty million square metres of office space,[34] and the resulting need to replace these buildings, as well as to accommodate a further expansion of the nation's economic activities, resulted in a ferocious office boom following the removal of building controls in 1954.[35]

**FIGURE 3.8**    Model of Midland Bank's Overseas Branch. Architect: unknown. Made by Thorp, 1956. Courtesy Thorp Archive, AUB.

It was during this postwar boom that the unwavering certainty of modernism was adopted as the architectural language through which countless visions of future office buildings were expressed, as evidenced by the clean lines and modern construction materials depicted in Thorp's model. Architects were keen to explore what the future of the office might be in the bright new postwar world, and with its prominent stairwell, wide expanses of glazing, flat roof, and imposing yet defiantly modernist entranceway, the unknown architect of the Midland Bank's overseas branch offered an elegant solution that suited the aesthetics of the New Elizabethan Age. Modernist buildings such as this were also much cheaper to build compared to those designed in a classical style, which no doubt did much to boost their popularity among profit-conscious postwar office developers.[36] The return to commercial building in London after the relaxation of building controls meant there had been a seventeen year gap since the last of the major interwar office buildings had been completed and in the intervening years new ideas about both office design and architecture in general had taken hold.[37] Many new operational concepts relating to office design were imported from the United States[38] and the Midland Bank building, with its strong statement of corporate identity, was an early example of this, although despite first appearances its overall form was still rather similar to the heavy masses of interwar office buildings such as Bush House. The building's stripping back of ornament and its clean lines clearly signal this as adhering to the vision of a 'gleaming, functional future' that modernism embraced,[39] but internally the design was not quite as forward thinking, with offices for individual staff still being provided, demonstrating an adherence to a traditional desire for clearly defined organisational hierarchies; the number of windows in your office remaining an important signifier of your seniority in the workplace.[40]

From the late 1950s through to the end of the 1960s, Thorp's workshop was brimming with intricate models of proposed new office buildings and by the end of that period, many of them displayed three major influences that were by then shaping how architects were imagining the future of the office to be: a shift to open plan layouts, a striving for ever taller buildings, and the dominance of the commercial property developer. Those influences were intimately linked as building high with flexible floorplans enabled developers to maximise their profits. Thorp's 1968 model of the unbuilt proposal for the Phoenix development on Cambridge Circus in London, designed by Steane, Shipman and Associates, captured the merging of all these influences in dramatic style (Figure 3.9). Made at a cost of £900 (some £13,000 today), the model showed the striking twenty-three storey main tower that faced onto the corner of Charing Cross Road and Shaftsbury Avenue, an eleven-storey side tower, and two five-storey podium buildings arranged around a generous public space with the intention of opening up views of the church of St. Giles in the Field (just out of view to the right of the photograph). This was a proposal for redeveloping an enormous site in the heart of London's west end that involved demolishing an entire range of buildings on Charing Cross Road and utilising an open-air car park behind that had been temporarily installed on the site of Second World War bomb damage. The imposing nature of the proposal was typical of the time, intended to join the enormous number of high-rise office blocks that were constructed across the capital during the 1960s, and given that commercial developers were not known for radical experimentation when it came to the specification of speculative office proposals,[41] the generous provision of public space was a particularly unusual feature of the design.

FIGURE 3.9   Model of an unbuilt proposal for the Phoenix development, Cambridge Circus. Architect: Steane, Shipman and Associates. Made by Thorp, 1968. Courtesy Thorp Archive, AUB.

The Phoenix development also characterised the shift towards open-plan office design that took hold during the 1960s, embracing new thinking about how offices should be organised that had already been adopted in both Germany and the United States and which when introduced by British architects brought about a transformation of how the nation's office buildings were designed.[42] The open-plan office layout quickly became standard within speculative developments, particularly those designed by the architect Richard Seifert, who throughout much of the 1960s worked in partnership with the property developer Harry Hyams (as seen in Chapter 1). Designing with no specific occupiers in mind, office buildings for rent benefited from the flexibility that open floor-plans provided, with lifts and services clustered in a central core. Most of Seifert's buildings followed this template, and with his offices just a few doors down from Thorp's workshop on Gray's Inn Road, Seifert was a frequent commissioner of the company's models, including a notable representation of an early proposal for the Kings Reach development on London's South Bank made in 1971 (Figure 3.10). Made solely from timber to outline the forms of the proposed buildings without any suggestion of the actual materials they would be made from, Thorp's model was carefully designed to conceal much of what Seifert had proposed as this particular iteration of the design had generated considerable controversy. The model included, in shape only, what was to have been a very tall glass-clad tower at the southwest corner of the plot and a riverside building with barrel roof detailing facing the Thames. It was these buildings that caused the

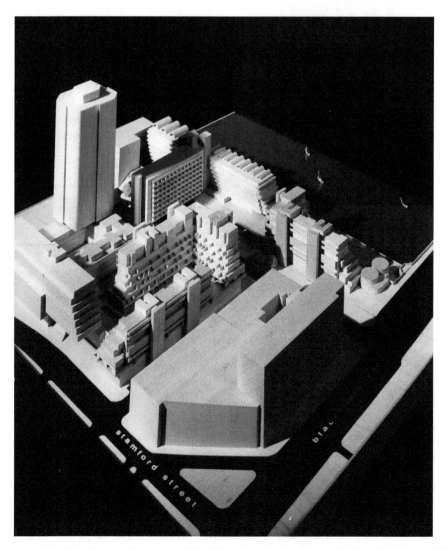

**FIGURE 3.10** Model of an early proposal for Kings Reach. Architect: Richard Seifert and Partners. Made by Thorp, 1971. Courtesy Thorp Archive, AUB.

most concern when the plans were first unveiled, with the Royal Fine Arts Commission demanding a reduction in height so as not to dominate the riverfront. With the project later reworked by Reginald Jenkins, one of Seifert's senior architects, the development as eventually completed in 1978 was far less imposing. As with the Phoenix proposal for Cambridge Circus, speculative office developments rarely considered the effect on their surroundings, seeking to extract maximum profit from their sites, although in this case Seifert had perhaps gone further than was palatable for such a prominent location.

Just a few months before completing the Kings Reach model, Thorp had made another model that resulted directly from a concern that the seemingly unending desire for both speculative and corporate office buildings in London had begun to create a much more fundamental problem than aesthetics, in having centralised both investment and employment in the capital at a time when a more equitable spread of economic opportunity was badly needed across the country. Thorp's 1970 model of Kodak House in Hemel Hempstead, designed by T.P. Bennett (Figure 3.11), was one of many the company made during this period of statement office buildings for regional employers outside London. These models, and the projects they represented, emerged as a result of the creation by the government of the Location of Offices Bureau in 1963, which was tasked with decentralising office employment away from the capital.[43] Developers wanting to build offices in London had to apply to the Bureau for strictly controlled permits which served to make building in other parts of the country more attractive. The result was an expansion of offices in other towns

**FIGURE 3.11** Model of Kodak House. Architect: T.P. Bennett. Made by Thorp, 1970. Courtesy Thorp Archive, AUB.

and cities, although inevitably more building was concentrated in the home counties, with fourteen million square feet of office space built in Middlesex between 1959 and 1970, six million in Croydon, and two million each in both Liverpool and Manchester over the same period. This was in comparison to an astonishing fifty-four million square feet of office space built in London between 1948 and 1961, however.[44]

The model of Kodak House has a particularly American feel about it and the building itself was unusually large for such a relatively small town, putting forward a vision of corporate power that was heavily influenced by the American slab-and-podium office block exemplified by Gordon Bunshaft's Lever House in New York and which was itself influenced by the ultra-modernist prewar ideas of Le Corbusier and Mies van der Rohe. First adopted in Britain with the design of Basil Spence's Thorn House in 1959 and Gollins, Melvin and Ward's Castrol House in 1960,[45] the sleek steel and glass approach of the International Style of modernism that characterised those earlier buildings had fallen out of fashion by the time of T.P. Bennett's design for Kodak House, however, and while following the same basic form, the building was clad with a dynamic concrete facade that took more of its inspiration from Gio Ponti's Pirelli Tower in Milan. This made the construction of Thorp's model particularly complicated, necessitating the use of bespoke injection-moulded parts to represent the building's distinct external profiles. Studying the model today reveals how prevalent the influence of American corporate office design had become by this period, with the podium structure containing not just offices but a restaurant, a staff cinema, and a gymnasium. As the European headquarters of Eastman Kodak and a major employer in the Hertfordshire town, such facilities were considered necessary in order to attract and retain staff in what was becoming an increasingly competitive marketplace, particularly outside of London.[46]

The design of Kodak House also needed to accommodate the increasing importance of information technology in office design as by the 1970s computers and automation had become central to how offices of the future were being planned. Postwar offices effectively took the form of 'paper factories,'[47] serving as spaces that were devoted to the collection and processing of paper-based information, but by the late 1960s much of how this processing was being carried out had begun to change. Office buildings such as Kodak House and the unbuilt proposal for the Phoenix development were normally designed to incorporate a single air-conditioned computer room in which much of an organisation's automated tasks would be carried out, but through the 1970s the move towards the distribution of computers to individual departments began to make such internal layouts out of date after less than a decade.[48] By the start of the 1980s, the introduction of the personal computer enabled a further change, with the computer fully liberated from its fortress-like room and onto individuals' desks,[49] which had major implications for the design of new offices.

Technology was not the only influence shaping 1980s visions of the future of the office, with major political and economic changes instigating a rethinking of both where offices should be located and how they should be designed. The desire to encourage the building of offices away from central London collapsed entirely after the 1986 'Big Bang' financial deregulation. This was intended to reposition the capital as a global financial centre and it sparked a wholesale rebuilding of office space that saw half of the City of London's offices rebuilt in just eight years,[50] a move that inevitably provided a welcome stream of model commissions for Thorp. The undeniable gravity of London in attracting

**FIGURE 3.12**  Model of an early proposal for the redevelopment of King William Street, London.
Architect: GMW. Made by Thorp, 1980. Courtesy Thorp Archive, AUB.

large-scale office developments had already begun to reassert itself before the Big Bang,
however, and in 1980 Thorp was commissioned to make the first of what would be a
long run of models depicting ambitious proposals for new projects in both the City and
the rapidly expanding Docklands development area. The model itself was rather unusual
in that it was able to depict two different proposals for the redevelopment of the lower
end of King William Street (Figure 3.12). Designed for Land Securities by the architectural practice GMW (formerly Gollins, Melvin and Ward), the full vision was of a pair of
octagonal office buildings connected by a two-storey bridge containing additional office

space that would span the main road. Both buildings would also contain basement levels that would provide access from Lower Thames Street. The model in this configuration presented a bold and no doubt controversial proposal that would have effectively blocked the view of London Bridge from the north, and it is perhaps unsurprising then that the entire right-hand building and the connecting bridge could be removed from the model to show an alternate proposal of just redeveloping the plot of thirty-three King William Street alone. It was this pared-back version that was approved for construction and which opened in 1983 as one of the first new blocks of the 1980s City property boom. Clad with polished granite and bronze-tinted glazing, the single building as built lacked the radical nature of the full proposal, however, with the unbuilt high-tech structural elements of the two-storey bridge serving to reflect the technological revolution that was taking place inside all offices at the time. The dominance of information technology in the form of computers, modems, faxes, and automated telephone systems meant that the future of office design was no longer projected as 'an accumulation of desks, arranged in rows and adding up to anonymous administrators,'[51] but was now perceived as 'networks linked by data transmission rather than lifts and corridors.'[52] As a result, it was perhaps symbolic that the physical bridge between the two buildings proposed for King William Street was never built, with connections increasingly being made through communications equipment alone.

Technology was to continue to shape future visions of office buildings throughout the final two decades of the century, as will be seen later in this chapter, and by the time of GMW's proposal for King William Street, how those visions were imagined was evolving as rapidly as they could be realised, with 1950s offices considered out of date by the 1970s, and 1960s offices deemed obsolete by the 1980s. This pace of change was nevertheless mild in comparison to the radical transformation of Britain's industrial sites over the same period, however, with the advent of entirely new industries requiring countless architectural models to communicate innovative ideas about what those future workplaces might be like.

### Industries for Tomorrow

Following the Second World War Britain was still a highly industrialised nation, but as the postwar economy went through a period of intense modernisation, the shifting makeup of its industrial output presented architects, planners, and engineers with the challenge of imagining how those industries should be housed, in what types of structures, and where. Manufacturing jobs in Britain reached their peak in 1951 but at the same time employment in sectors such as heavy engineering and textiles were undergoing a rapid decline.[53] In their place, new industries such as chemical and plastics production, food processing, electrical engineering, and telecommunications began to gain importance alongside the financial and service industries, but by the 1960s the effects of foreign competition in manufacturing had begun to shrink Britain's share of the global export market by as much as a third.[54] Amid a perceived industrial decline there was nevertheless an optimism that Britain would lead the world by embracing new and seemingly revolutionary industries such as nuclear power and automated production, with much discussion given over to where these new industries should be located.[55] Throughout the postwar era, Thorp's order book therefore witnessed an increased demand for large and expensive models commissioned not just on a practical level to explain where these new industries would be placed and what they would look like, but also on a symbolic level to convey visions of modernity, progress, and industrial pride. Many of these models were photographed in dramatic style by the leading architectural photographer of the time, Henk Snoek, who applied his strong sense of drama and high-contrast imagery to capture the often brutalist nature of the designs in their idealised, miniature forms.

Snoek's photography and both the practical and symbolic purposes of Thorp's models of postwar industrial architecture converged most spectacularly with a series of models Thorp made in 1965 of the proposed Dungeness B nuclear power station in Kent (Figure 3.13). The sensitivity of where to place the new industries of the postwar era was particularly important when it came to the building of Britain's nuclear power stations as these needed to be in remote areas close to sources of water and which due to their size would inevitably dominate the landscapes around them. These were structures that needed to be not just functional but architecturally appealing, and for Dungeness the architect Howard Lobb was brought in to oversee the design, having already worked on the Hunterston nuclear power station in 1960. Lobb had served as the co-ordinating architect of the Festival of Britain and was therefore an ideal choice to help express this grand vision of the Britain's future, one of a number of architects who had begun to turn

**FIGURE 3.13**   Model of the proposed Dungeness B nuclear power station. Architect: Howard Lobb. Made by Thorp, 1965. Courtesy Thorp Archive, AUB.

towards industrial architecture following the Second World War, no doubt drawn by the prestigious nature of many of the projects that were then underway.[56] Lobb's design for Dungeness B, with its modern lines of concrete and glass, made a bold statement that this was the future of how Britain would be powered,[57] and extended a vision of how science, technology, and engineering would open up new frontiers and reverse Britain's decline on the global stage.[58] As an entirely new building type, there were no precedents to draw from, and without the giant cooling towers or chimneys of coal-fired power stations, the design of Britain's nuclear power stations embraced a monumental brutalism that while very different in form to Giles Gilbert Scott's architecturally refined Battersea and Bankside power stations in London, were nevertheless created with the same 'scale and majesty' in mind,[59] as Thorp's models showed.

Two years later an even more dramatic vision of the future of industry was unveiled in a series of models made for the British Transport Docks Board to illustrate a proposed extension to Southampton Docks (Figures 3.14 and 3.15). Thorp's models, with their sleek, diagrammatic use of black Perspex and minimal detailing, demonstrated how planners and engineers were responding to the enormous changes instigated by the introduction of containerised freight. The concept, known as intermodal transport, proposed an unlocking of global trade through the adoption of standardised containers that would be able to be moved by sea, road, and rail without needing to be unpacked at each transition, reducing the number of man-hours required to unload a typical ship from 11,000 to less than 900.[60] In order to achieve this level of efficiency meant the complete renewal of the infrastructure involved, with new ships, lorries, wagons, births, and dockside cranes required. Mechanised handling at ports would enable twenty-four-hour operation, with new ways of working needed not just at ports, but across entire distribution and supply chains. The pace of change was astonishingly fast, with the standard sizes of containers having only been agreed in 1966 and yet just one year later Thorp's models were outlining the complete overhaul of Southampton's docks in response. Land reclamation at the site began just a few months later, and while

FIGURE 3.14   Model of a proposed extension to Southampton Docks. Client: British Transport Docks Board. Made by Thorp, 1967. Courtesy Thorp Archive, AUB.

**FIGURE 3.15**  Model of proposed facilities to be included in an extension to Southampton Docks. Client: British Transport Docks Board. Made by Thorp, 1967. Courtesy Thorp Archive, AUB.

the extension to the port was not built entirely as the model proposed (wider channels were needed for larger than anticipated ships), the vision that the models put forward, of a modernised, automated container port was one that would sweep away the traditional labour-heavy dockyard in less than a decade, with more than one hundred thousand jobs lost across the country as a result.[61]

Sensitivities around the scale of industrial change during the 1960s and the increasing use of rural and coastal locations resulted in a steady stream of models such as these, commissioned to not just explain what was planned but also placate as many environmental and aesthetic concerns as possible. In many cases the sheer size of what was being proposed necessitated very large models, and in 1969 another maritime model was produced to outline the new masterplan for the Isle of Grain oil refinery in Kent (Figure 3.16). As with the change to Britain's ports, oil refineries were another example of how the nation had come to be a net importer as its global economic standing gradually declined. The Isle of Grain refinery had opened in 1961 to process crude oil shipped from the Middle East to be used in Britain's growing petrochemicals industry, and having rapidly expanded, Thorp's model was made to show the site at its projected maximum when it would be capable of processing eleven million tonnes of crude oil each year. Depicting

FIGURE 3.16   Model of the Isle of Grain oil refinery. Client: BP. Made by Thorp, 1969. Courtesy Thorp Archive, AUB.

oil tankers docked at almost every jetty, the model put forward a deliberately ordered and tidy representation of the refinery, which was to contain more than one hundred storage tanks, twenty-two miles of roads, extensive railway sidings, and a central administration building, all on reclaimed land at the mouth of the River Medway. Outlining a vast industrial complex as sensitively as possible, the model accurately captured what was ultimately built, although the entire project was quickly deemed unnecessary as just three months later the first discovery of crude oil in the North Sea released Britain from its dependence on the Middle East and created a significant demand for models of an entirely different type of structure.

**FIGURE 3.17**  Model of the Sea Quest oil rig. Client: BP. Made by Thorp, 1969. Courtesy Thorp Archive, AUB.

The discovery of the North Sea oil fields proved to be a very lucrative development for Thorp for more than a decade as it involved the design and operation of what was for Britain an entirely new feat of engineering, the oil platform. Dozens of models were called for to outline not only what they would look like but also to explain to both the public and the riggers who would man them how they would function. Right from the very start Thorp's models were widely used in the press to illustrate what was happening and when BP's Sea Quest drilling rig located the first commercially viable oil field in 1969, it had already been immortalised in model form, photographs of which accompanied many newspaper articles in the weeks that followed (Figure 3.17).

Sea Quest, built in Belfast by the shipbuilders Harland and Wolff in 1966, was one of fifty rigs searching for oil in the North Sea in 1969.[62] Developed from drilling technology used in the Gulf of Mexico in the mid-1950s, Sea Quest was a mobile rig that could be towed to different locations, its triangular platform containing all the engineering and crew facilities needed for what could be an extremely arduous task. For engineers, when it came to designing permanent drilling platforms and the infrastructure necessary to bring the oil ashore, the specific requirements of working entirely isolated in the middle of the sea proved to be enormously challenging, with the largest platforms costing up to £10 million to build.[63] The vision put forward by the Sea Quest model was as much one of economics as it was of engineering given the potential independence and fuel security

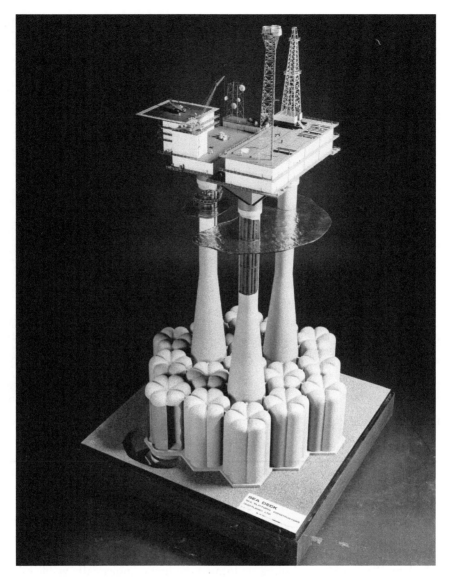

**FIGURE 3.18**   Model of the Brent Delta oil platform. Client: Sea Platform Constructors (Scotland) Ltd. Made by Thorp, 1974. Courtesy Thorp Archive, AUB.

that the discovery of oil beneath the North Sea would offer Britain, and by the 1970s models of the permanent oil platforms had become a regular line of work for Thorp (Figure 3.18), with each model symbolising an era of progress in which technology and economics appeared to have 'forced open the future'[64] through engineering projects that 'rivalled in scale some of the greatest schemes of the nineteenth or twentieth centuries.'[65]

With Thorp's models of Britain's postwar industrial future including offshore oil platforms, coastal refineries and ports, and rurally isolated nuclear power stations, the changing nature of where many of the nation's industries were to be located was clear to see. With the dominance of the midlands and the north of England declining as the economy of London and the southeast grew,[66] previously unindustrialised landscapes underwent rapid transformations to accommodate these new facilities, often after intense local debate. This shifting geography of work during the second half of the twentieth century in Britain was to accelerate further with the growth of the service economy from the 1980s onwards, as the growth of light industry and the service economy fuelled a merging of both location and form, and the types of building that Thorp was tasked with making in miniature shifted once more.

## Moving Out of Town

By the final decades of the twentieth century the British economy had been profoundly changed. Rather than processing raw materials and exporting manufactured goods to the rest of the world, goods were instead being imported, warehoused, and retailed through complex global supply chains.[67] The growth of financial services following the 1986 'Big Bang' deregulation and the dominance of consumer culture (see Chapter 4) further cemented a shift away from heavy industry with much of Britain's economic growth coming from services instead. As the need for specialised industrial buildings in specific locations lessened as a result, the late twentieth century saw a convergence of building types as the forms of work carried out within them slowly homogenised.[68] The boundaries between an office building and an industrial building increasingly began to blur, with a new type of urban space developing that was 'seized upon by industrialists, urban planners, politicians, and technocrats to form the foundations of a new economy and a new society.'[69] Known by a variety of names such as the business park, science park, and industrial estate, this was where work had begun its move out of town.

From the 1980s onwards a significant proportion of the architectural models that Thorp made reflected this trend with commercial property developers commissioning countless models of proposed business parks and industrial estates, most of which were built, an indication of the ease with which such proposals passed through the planning system. The industrial estate was by no means a new concept by this point, with the first estate, Trafford Park in Manchester, having opened in the 1890s, although out-of-town development had to wait for mass car ownership before it could really come into its own.[70] One of the earliest models of this kind that Thorp made was a 1970 model of the then proposed International Trading Estate in Hayes which demonstrated the interdependence of the industrial estate and Britain's road network particularly well (Figure 3.19). With ample parking and a turning circle for lorries, the site was close to both the M4 motorway and Heathrow Airport, location and access being the key selling points that encouraged businesses to flock to such new developments.[71] Parking, in particular, was central to the out-of-town dream and by the 1960s it was projected that perhaps as many as one parking space for every three employees might be needed in the future,[72] a significant underestimation of what was to come. The Hayes estate, with its relatively generous car park, was actually built, although not quite as tidily as the model suggested, providing over 800,000 square feet of modern light industrial and warehousing space on the site of an old jam factory. The model itself, with its simple diagrammatic baseboard and light timber buildings, emphasised the cleanliness of the site and by extension the cleanliness of the work that would be carried out within. This was a representation of the 'grand dream of organising industry,'[73] whereby the chaos of the nineteenth-century factory

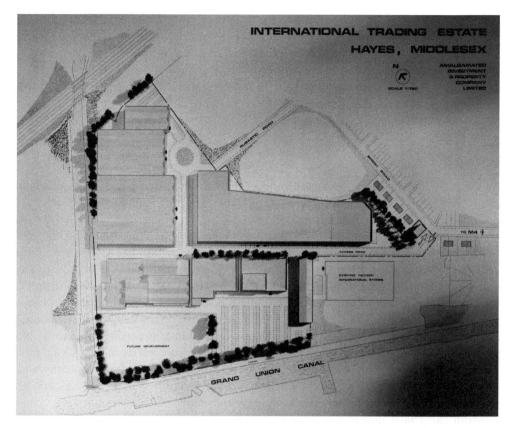

**FIGURE 3.19** Model of the proposed Hayes International Trading Estate. Developer: Amalgamated Investment & Property Company Limited. Made by Thorp, 1970. Courtesy Thorp Archive, AUB.

could be 'tamed, socialised, and beautified,'[74] ready for a post-industrial society where research and innovation would take the lead.[75]

The planner rather than the architect was the main figure involved in the expansion of the industrial estate, imagining flexible sites for general use rather than building for companies with specific needs,[76] and as political and economic tools, out-of-town locations promised to open up 'new and more radical futures,'[77] that embraced a flexible, landscaped, and sanitised vision of work. This was an attractive dream that appealed not only to industry, however, with office buildings following as well. Thorp's 1978 model of Clifford Culpin's unbuilt proposal for a new headquarters for the British Airports Authority (BAA) was an early example of this trend. Capturing the rush to occupy out-of-town office sites that would accelerate during the 1980s, the model presented a vision of a corporate headquarters seemingly embedded in the natural landscape (Figure 3.20). In place of the industrial estate here was an example of the office park, drawing from the imagery of the traditional English country house surrounded by parkland and which had been pioneered for office use by SOM's design for the Heinz headquarters in Hayes Park in 1965.[78] With its landscaped balconies, prominent roof lines, and extensive use of brick, the proposal was similar to not only Culpin's recently completed design for Wolverhampton Civic

**FIGURE 3.20**    Model of an unbuilt proposal for a new BAA headquarters. Architect: Clifford Culpin. Made by Thorp, 1978. Courtesy Thorp Archive, AUB.

Centre but also Arup Associates' designs for both Gateway House in Basingstoke and Gun Wharf in Chatham, all of which had been inspired by American and European roof garden concepts of the 1930s and the glazed winter garden and atrium concepts of 1960s American corporate architecture that were intended to create a healthier and more human type of office building.[79]

The BAA proposal put forward a radical alternative to the high-rise central London offices described earlier in this chapter and by exploring new ideas about both office work and office design the out-of-town corporate headquarters concept forced city centres to compete in order to retain jobs.[80] Fuelled by deindustrialisation, out-of-town locations became highly desirable for many businesses with a mass-migration of employment out of cities taking place, London losing half its manufacturing jobs between 1960 and 1980, for example.[81] For office-based work, the property crash of 1974 and the lack of new development until the start of the 1980s had also created an intense shortage of office space within the capital,[82] and given an increasing desire for more human scale developments with better road connections, and the impact of new technologies having generated an additional demand for non-manual occupations, there was a distinct lack of the types of properties businesses were looking for.[83]

Thorp's model of the unrealised BAA proposal was a hint of what was to come as by the mid-1980s the vision of the out-of-town corporate headquarters had expanded into

FIGURE 3.21    Model of an unbuilt proposal for Kings Ride Business Park. Developer: Slough
Estates. Made by Thorp, 1986. Courtesy Thorp Archive, AUB.

that of the business park, and the similarities between the 1978 BAA model and a later
1986 model for Kings Ride business park in Ascot are evident (Figure 3.21). This model,
again of an unbuilt proposal, was made for Slough Estates, the owner of one of the oldest industrial estates in Britain, and the very fact that this new development was planned
to be a business park rather than an industrial estate reflected how much the future of
work had changed since the original Slough Estate had been built in the 1930s. The architects of the project remain unknown but the same template that was followed for the
BAA proposal can be seen with generous landscaping and plenty of parking surrounding
American-inspired ranch-style buildings with low rise brick facades, pitched roofs, and
central atriums to provide natural lighting.

Business parks such as this were intended to open up the 'prestige and amenities' of
the out-of-town headquarters to a wider range of companies,[84] and it was here that the
distinction between office and industry became almost imperceptible. Despite their architectural similarities to the buildings on the left of the model, the larger right-hand buildings include loading bays, indicating that these were for light industry rather than office
work, an early example of the warehouse sheds of the service economy, landscaped for
show.[85] The business park concept had originally developed in the United States during
the 1960s. Bell Labs in New Jersey, with buildings designed by Eero Saarinen and landscaping by Hideo Sasaki, combined both architecture and planting to act as expressions
of corporate power,[86] while Stanford University's industrial park had initiated the 'campus' approach whereby universities invested in the construction of innovation quarters

**FIGURE 3.22**    Model of an early proposal for Delta Business Park. Developer: Taylor Woodrow. Made by Thorp, 1983. Courtesy Thorp Archive, AUB.

that were designed to mimic the feel of college campuses.[87] In Britain, Trinity College in
Cambridge was the first to import this approach in 1973 with the provision of a new science park aimed squarely at pharmaceutical and technology companies that were keen to
make use of the university's research expertise.[88] By the 1980s the notion of the high-tech
business park had firmly taken root on Britain with the planning and construction of
larger and more generalised sites than had been the case in the United States.[89]

Proposals such as Kings Ride were markers of a new post-industrial workplace, with
more than four hundred similar developments having opened in Britain by 1990.[90] The
largest developments such as at Stockley Park or Aztec West incorporated hotels and
conference facilities in addition to office, research, and light industry sites, while outdoor
spaces and pavement cafes brought a European feel to many.[91] The dominance of the
slab shaped office tower in Britain's towns and cities was being directly challenged by
the low rise nature of the business park and the placement of distribution and warehousing facilities next to corporate offices was starting to become the norm. Thorp's model
of Oxford Architects' masterplan for Delta Business Park in Swindon, made in 1983
for Taylor Woodrow (Figure 3.22), clearly demonstrates this merging of both form and
location, with corporate landscaping assisting the homogenisation of the workplace to
meet the demands of the increasingly globalised nature of work. Delta Park was unusual
for the time in adopting a potentially outdated modernist style for most of the buildings,
although only one, 200 Delta Park, was actually built as shown. The original site plan
as depicted on the model included hotels and a leisure centre, all intended to cater for
a new type of worker who placed a high value on wellbeing, with Delta Park offering a
highly manicured setting that was designed to create a sense of 'collegiate sociability.'[92]
New worker values, new technologies, new industries, and new locations came to define
the growth of out-of-town development in the 1990s, with good communication and
transport links seen as being vital to the workplace of the future.

The desire for easy transport access is perhaps best demonstrated by the final model
in this chapter, Thorp's 1992 model of Aukett Associates' design for Causeway 25, an
unbuilt development adjacent to the M25 near Staines (Figure 3.23). Michael Aukett
was one of Britain's leading business park architects, having worked on the development of both Stockley Park and Solent Business Park, and was shortlisted for the Stirling
Prize for his design of Proctor & Gamble's headquarters in Weybridge. Having spent

**FIGURE 3.23** Model of Causeway 25. Architect: Michael Aukett. Made by Thorp, 1992. Courtesy Thorp Archive, AUB.

time studying science park campuses in the United States, Aukett was well versed in the techno-corporate architecture such sites demanded and his design for Causeway 25 was no exception. The petal-shaped building was designed to fit into an awkward site nestled within a curving off-ramp that connected the A30 with the A308 on an elevated roadway parallel to the M25. Containing four floors and a substantial atrium, the building was orientated towards a small open-air car park and an ornamental pool with additional parking underground, while access was to be provided via a pair of new roads that would pass under the Glanty Loop off-ramp. Located within metres of Britain's busiest stretch of motorway, this was an extremely well-connected site, although perhaps not the most attractive one, squeezed as it was into such an unlikely position. Thorp's model captures this connectivity through the inclusion of a large number of vehicles, highlighting to a potential occupier just how accessible the building would be. This was the overriding element of the design that was on display in the model, with the building itself rendered fairly simply while the landscaping and roads were more realistically detailed. As a vision for a statement headquarters building, Causeway 25 was all about location, and while the project was never completed, the overall plan and road access design was carried over almost exactly into an entirely different later proposal for the site designed by John Seifert (son of Richard Seifert) that was built in 1998.

By the 1990s, how architects imagined the future of the office was largely centred on communication, in terms of both physical access and technology, but they had also embraced the importance of hybrid forms, with one vision from 1994 predicting that the office of tomorrow would be a mix of 'Oxford college, marketplace, home workshop, gentleman's club, and hotel.'[93] With the disruptive influence of the internet looming on the horizon, it was also clear that the pace of change would continue to accelerate and that the distinction between different types of workplace would inevitably become less apparent. The models of both offices and industry that Thorp made in the closing years of the twentieth century, with change by then a constant, were in that respect no different to any that they had made before, with all the models featured in this chapter demonstrating that the future of where we might work was largely imagined in response to broad economic and political changes rather than discrete architectural ideas, with architects and planners developing new forms of buildings and new choices of location that embraced flexibility in order to adapt to futures that were evolving faster than they could predict. New building types and an increasingly blurred line between the traditional office and the factories and warehouses of light industry characterised Britain's evolution into a post-industrial economy that ultimately facilitated a dramatic migration of employment towards the south-east of England and outwards from town and city centres to the suburban fringe. Those trends were not unique to the world of work, however, and as the next chapter exploring architectural models that captured visions of leisure reveals, shops, hotels, sport centres, and more quickly followed the factory and office out of town.

## Notes

1 Lawrence Weaver, *Exhibitions and the Arts of Display* (London: Country Life, 1925), 81.
2 Joshua B. Freeman, *Behemoth: The History of the Factory and the Making of the Modern World* (New York: W.W. Norton, 2019), xii.
3 James F. Munce, *Industrial Architecture* (London: Iliffe books, 1961), 35.
4 Frederick Gibberd, *Town Design* (London: The Architectural Press, 1962), 180.
5 David Edgerton, *The Rise and Fall of the British Nation* (London: Penguin, 2019), 78.
6 Arthur J. McIvor, *A History of Work in Britain, 1880–1950* (Basingstoke: Palgrave, 2001), 1.
7 Edgerton, *The Rise and Fall of the British Nation*, 200.
8 McIvor, *A History of Work in Britain*, 158.
9 McIvor, *A History of Work in Britain*, 166.
10 Andrew Newell, 'Structural Change,' In *Work and Pay in 20th Century Britain*, eds. Nicholas Crafts, Ian Gazeley and Andrew Newell (Oxford: Oxford University Press, 2007), 40.
11 Ian Gazeley and Andrew Newell, 'Introduction,' In *Work and Pay in 20th Century Britain*, eds. Nicholas Crafts, Ian Gazeley and Andrew Newell (Oxford: Oxford University Press, 2007), 1.
12 John, Singleton, 'The British Economy,' In *20th Century Britain: Economic, Cultural and Social Change*, eds. Nichole Robertson, John Singleton and Avram Taylor (Abingdon: Routledge, 2023), 35.
13 Chris Wrigley, 'Work, the Labour Market and Trade Unions,' In *20th Century Britain: Economic, Cultural and Social Change*, eds. Nichole Robertson, John Singleton and Avram Taylor (Abingdon: Routledge, 2023), 99.
14 Norman Taylor, *Architectural Modelling and Visual Planning* (London: Cassell, 1959), xi; Thomas Hendrick *Model Making as a Career* (London: Percival Marshall, 1952), iii.
15 Edgerton, *The Rise and Fall of the British Nation*, 79.
16 Frank E. Huggett, *Factory Life & Work* (London: Harrap, 1973), 84.
17 John Winter, *Industrial Architecture* (London: Studio Vista, 1970), 85.
18 Helena Chance, *The Factory in a Garden* (Manchester: Manchester University Press, 2017), 44.
19 Gavin Stamp, *Interwar: British Architecture 1919–39* (London: Profile, 2024), 218.
20 Newell, 'Structural Change,' 1.
21 Edgar Jones, *Industrial Architecture in Britain 1750–1939* (London: Batsford, 1985), 207.
22 Huggett, *Factory Life & Work*, 80.
23 Chance, *The Factory in a Garden*, 31.
24 Chance, *The Factory in a Garden*, 45.

25 Kathryn Morrison and John Minnis, *Carscapes: The Motor Car, Architecture and Landscape in England* (London: Yale University Press, 2012), 15.

26 McIvor, *A History of Work in Britain*, 33.

27 Edgerton, *The Rise and Fall of the British Nation*, 40.

28 Jonathan Clarke, 'Development: Speculative Office Development and Public Sector Tenants,' In *Reconstruction: Architecture, Society and the Aftermath of the First World War*, eds. Neal Shasore and Jessica Kelly (London: Bloomsbury, 2023), 89–91.

29 Eileen Chanin, 'The New London,' In *Reconstruction: Architecture, Society and the Aftermath of the First World War*, eds. Neal Shasore and Jessica Kelly (London: Bloomsbury, 2023), 60.

30 Clarke, 'Development,' 94.

31 Chanin, 'New London,' 76.

32 Clarke, 'Development,' 94.

33 Clarke, 'Development,' 94.

34 Clarke, 'Development,' 87.

35 Elain Harwood, *Space Hope and Brutalism: English Architecture 1945–1975* (London: Yale University Press, 2016), 359.

36 Nicholas Bullock, *Building the Post-war World: Modern Architecture and Reconstruction in Britain* (London: Routledge, 2002), 258.

37 Bullock, *Building the Post-war World*, 245.

38 Alan Powers, *Britain: Modern Architectures in History* (London: Reaktion, 2007), 118.

39 David Kynaston, *Modernity Britain* (London: Bloomsbury, 2015), 46.

40 Otto Reiwoldt, *New Office Design* (London: Lawrence King, 1994), 6.

41 Peter Manning, *Office Design: A study of Environment* (Liverpool: Department of Building Science, Liverpool University, 1965), 19.

42 Harwood, *Space Hope and Brutalism*, 359.

43 Alan Delgado, *The Enormous File: A Social History of the Office* (London: John Murray, 1979), 102.

44 Manning, *Office Design*, 98–99.

45 Powers, *Britain*, 95.

46 Santa Raymond and Roger Cunliffe, *Tomorrow's Office* (London: E&FN Spon, 1997), 1.

47 Andrew Laing, 'New Patterns of Work: The Design of the Office,' In *Reinventing the Workplace*, ed. John Worthington (London: The Architectural Press, 1997), 27.

48 Deyan Sudjic, *The 100 Mile City* (London: HarperCollins, 1993), 125.

49 Laing, 'New Patterns of Work,' 31.

50 Powers, *Britain*, 223.

51 Reiwoldt, *New Office Design*, 9.

52 Reiwoldt, *New Office Design*, 9.

53 McIvor, *A History of Work in Britain*, 32.

54 John F. Wilson, 'Big Business and Management in Britain,' In *20th Century Britain: Economic, Cultural and Social Change*, eds. Nichole Robertson, John Singleton and Avram Taylor (Abingdon: Routledge, 2023), 148 and Nicholas Comfort, *Surrender: How British Industry Gave Up the Ghost 1952–2012* (London: Biteback, 2012), 10.

55 Anthony Goss, *British Industry & Town Planning* (London: Fountain Press, 1962), 18.

56 Harwood, *Space Hope and Brutalism*, 347.

57 Comfort, *Surrender*, 17.

58 Tony Hall, *Nuclear Politics* (London: Pelican, 1986), 44.

59 Harwood, *Space Hope and Brutalism*, 342.

60 Craig Martin, *Shipping Container* (London: Bloomsbury, 2016), 20.

61 Sudjic, *100 Mile City*, 111.

62 Christopher Harvie, *Fool's Gold* (London: Hamish Hamilton, 1994), 1.

63 Harvie, *Fool's Gold*, 74.

64 Harvie, *Fool's Gold*, 47.

65 Harvie, *Fool's Gold*, 4.

66 Singleton, 'British Economy,' 36.

67 Edgerton, *The Rise and Fall of the British Nation*, 475.

68 Sudjic, *100 Mile City*, 124.

69 Sam Weatherell, *Foundations: How the Built Environment Made Twentieth-century Britain* (Princeton: Princeton University Press, 2023), 191.
70 Harwood, *Space Hope and Brutalism*, 359.
71 Goss, *British Industry*, 70.
72 Goss, *British Industry*, 122.
73 Wetherell, *Foundations*, 39.
74 Wetherell, *Foundations*, 34.
75 Edgerton, *The Rise and Fall of the British Nation*, 404.
76 Goss, *British Industry*, 65.
77 Wetherell, *Foundations*, 20.
78 Reinhold Hohl, *Office Buildings: An International Survey* (London: The Architectural Press, 1968), 32.
79 Chance, *The Factory in a Garden*, 197.
80 Sudjic, *100 Mile City*, 123.
81 Wetherell, *Foundations*, 166.
82 Alastair Goobey, *Bricks and Mortals* (London: Century Business, 1992), 14.
83 Goobey, *Bricks and Mortals*, 14.
84 Geraint Franklin and Elain Harwood, *Post-Modern Buildings in Britain* (London: Batsford, 2017), 84.
85 Chance, *The Factory in a Garden*, 3.
86 Chance, *The Factory in a Garden*, 196.
87 Wetherell, *Foundations*, 167.
88 Wetherell, *Foundations*, 170.
89 Wetherell, *Foundations*, 176.
90 Wetherell, *Foundations*, 165.
91 Chance, *The Factory in a Garden*, 203.
92 Wetherell, *Foundations*, 171.
93 Reiwoldt, *New Office Design*, 9.

# 4

# LEISURE

Outside of the home and the workplace, the most familiar types of buildings that people encounter in their daily lives are usually those in which they shop, relax, exercise, or are otherwise entertained. During the twentieth century, the function and design of these buildings continually changed in response to shifting ideas about what leisure even was, which activities were considered appropriate for different social classes, and how much time people had to devote to them. The impact on the built environment as huge numbers of holiday camps, cinemas, hotels, sports grounds, shopping centres, and other leisure facilities began to complete for every last penny of disposable income in the working man's (and later working woman's) pocket was profound, and throughout the twentieth century visions of future palaces of pleasure, designed to entice the senses and provide recreation and entertainment in exchange for hard-earned cash, poured from the desks of architects, developers, retailers, and entrepreneurs. As spaces devoted to fuelling the cycle of mass consumption that became so central to Britain's economy during the twentieth century, the architectural models made to communicate these visions therefore had to present convincing tableaus not just of the architectural designs but also the emotional benefits of spending money on what was contained inside.

An early example of this was John Thorp's 1920 model of the shoe retailer Lilley and Skinner's new Oxford Street flagship store (Figure 4.1). Designed by the architect Arthur Sykes, the imposing building adopted a late-eighteenth century style with stuccoed pilasters and a mansard roof to match the existing buildings around it, although this approach was only taken as a result of criticism from local residents of Syke's initial, less sympathetic proposal. The model itself comprised a thin slice of the front of the building to illustrate the facade, and given the impressive level of detail included in the ground floor displays it was likely commissioned either by or for the retailer to demonstrate how they would be able to showcase their wares to passing shoppers. This was, after all, a vision of not just another shoe shop, but as the company itself proclaimed, a vision of what would be the largest shoe shop in the world. Here, shopping for shoes, an act considered by most people to be just a necessity, was being projected as a form of theatre and in Thorp's model it is the goods themselves rather than the architecture of the building that is the focus of attention.

DOI: 10.4324/9781032715728-5

**FIGURE 4.1**  Model of Lilley and Skinner's London store. Architect: Arthur Sykes. Made by Thorp, 1920. Courtesy Thorp Archive, AUB.

The Lilley and Skinner model was a clear sign of what was to come, reflecting not only the interwar trend for larger, brighter, and better furnished shops where shopping was treated as a pleasurable activity rather than a chore,[1] but also the dominance of shopping as the nation's leading leisure activity during the second half of the century. Arcaded shopfronts with entrance lobbies, spacious windows, and island display cases were all seen as the future of retailing at the time,[2] heavily influenced by the opening of Selfridges in 1909 and its importation of North American retail practices.[3] This was an unusual model for Thorp during this period, however, as other than a handful of shopfront models for Mac Fisheries and Dewhurst the Butchers, the company received very few commissions for models relating to shopping until after the Second World War. Neither, despite their phenomenal growth in numbers during the interwar years, do any models of cinemas appear in Thorp's early records, and throughout the twentieth century architectural models of leisure-related buildings generally seem to have been called for only when truly grand projects were being proposed. What were far more common than models of individual shopfronts were models of shopping centres, sports grounds, swimming pools, and leisure centres. These models were usually made to assist architects in selling their ideas to their clients and for those clients to sell their ideas to their investors, and later to the public in advance of planning consultations. As such they had to capture not only the form and detailing of the buildings proposed but also a sense of the activities they would enable. This encouraged a greater use of animation – the inclusion of people, vehicles, and other details to create a specific scene – than was usually present in office or housing models, for example. When presented to the public, models of new shopping centres, lidos, theatres, and sports centres also served as highly symbolic expressions of modernity, particularly during the era of postwar reconstruction, and so the inclusion of relatable details as seen in the Lilley and Skinner model enabled those viewing the models to project themselves into the optimistic futures they were predicting.

In examining eighteen models of buildings dedicated to the pursuit of leisure, this chapter explores how the different visions of the future they portrayed became increasingly commercialised and served to shape the built environment through the development and proliferation of what were often entirely new building types. Defined as the endeavours we choose to engage in for pleasure rather than payment,[4] the concept of leisure initially held overtly masculine associations during the early decades of the century as with only men able to work, leisure, as its opposite, was considered a wholly male activity,[5] with men leaving the home to spend time in social clubs and sports grounds, while women engaged in pastimes and hobbies within the home. The emergence of shopping as a leisure activity challenged this distinction, providing a non-domestic space for women to meet and respectably socialise, with leisure subsequently gaining strong symbolic associations with emancipation and economic prosperity. The different visions of the future of leisure that the models of shopping centres, hotels, sports centres, and holiday camps featured in this chapter evidence therefore highlight not only the inevitable commercialisation of free, non-working time but also the embracing of more family-focused activities that were suitable for all. Made to whet the appetite of not just those who would use the future recreational facilities they described but more often the investors who would ultimately profit from them, architectural models were employed to sell the dream of happy and satisfied consumers, and the range of models discussed reveal rapidly changing cultural tastes, shifting hierarchies of leisure, and the same trends of homogenisation and the move to out-of-town locations observed in the previous chapter relating to work.

The earliest models in Thorp's archive relating to leisure activities stem from the interwar years and it was during this period that the leisure industry as it is recognised today started to emerge, with the commercialisation of leisure closely linked to the rise in living standards that followed the First World War.[6] As the working week reduced from fifty-four hours to forty-eight between 1910 and 1920, the amount of time available for leisure activities grew,[7] while increased wages and lower prices gave people higher levels of disposable income to spend on recreation and entertainment during their free time. After the Second World War the leisure market expanded rapidly with shopping taking its place as the nation's favourite pastime outside of the home. This was symbolised by the building of the Chrisp Street shopping precinct as part of the architectural exhibit of the Festival of Britain, a clear indication of shopping's importance in the New Elizabethan Age.[8] Models of shopping centres quickly became a major source of income for Thorp and other modelmakers working at the time, and while architects and planners were drawing from European ideas of architectural modernism during the postwar reimagining of Britain's war-damaged towns and cities, the real influence, 'culturally, commercially, and architecturally'[9] in terms of the shopping centres and leisure facilities that were placed at their heart came instead from across the Atlantic, where 'visions of affluence, mass consumption, and commercial modernity that were being generated in the USA provided the bedrock of ideas and forms' that shaped the leisure environments of the second half of the twentieth century in Britain.[10]

As was the case with the miniature visions of the future of work examined in the previous chapter, the future of leisure also succumbed to the all-encompassing influence of the motor car, with the desire for convenience instigating an inevitable move out of town; the flight of shops, cinemas, and sports centres from town centres to the suburbs threatening to rob the nation's high streets of the amenities that sustained them, and as so many of the models in this chapter evidence, with their optimistic, playful, and ruthlessly commercial depictions of futures yet to come, this was a vision over which few people had any meaningful control. Fuelled by the British economy's increasing dependence on services, models of the buildings in which leisure was packaged and sold to hungry consumers were in much demand, and by the 1990s Thorp's order book was dominated by more future visions of leisure than any other concern.

## Seaside Dreams

During the interwar years, one leisure activity in particular was represented above all else in the models that Thorp was commissioned to make: the seaside holiday. As noted above, the modern leisure industry began to develop during this period as a result of changes to working hours, pay, and, by the end of the 1930s, the introduction of the Holidays with Pay Act, which established a legal entitlement to paid annual leave. At the same time, technological developments in motor transportation that lead to the growing presence of cars, busses, and coaches on Britain's roads had opened up the possibilities of mass tourism, with the seaside summer holiday at its core.[11] Disposable income almost doubled between 1913 and 1936,[12] and with more money to spend and more time to spend it in, the holiday as a leisure activity became a major source of economic growth with both the middle and working classes flocking to seaside resorts in almost unimaginably large numbers. The seaside had become the nation's 'pressure valve,'[13] where millions headed every summer to enjoy piers and promenades and the curiously British invention of the seafront as a place of leisure rather than work.[14]

Seaside architecture had long been used as a means of defining and expressing the identities of individual resorts,[15] but by the 1930s that architecture had begun to replace the sea itself as the principal focus of the seaside holiday. No longer was the aim to enjoy what nature had to offer but rather the manmade activities in the built environment that had clustered there. 'Pools, promenades and amphitheatres transformed bathers into performers,'[16] as theatrical architecture served to elevate and sanitise the experience by insulating holidaymakers from the natural world and all its inconveniencies. John Thorp's 1935 model of a proposed bathing pool in Bognor Regis demonstrated this fashion particularly well (Figure 4.2). The large rectangular pool was planned to be built jutting out into the sea, following a trend to incorporate such pools into sea defences as had been pioneered in both Blackpool and Hastings,[17] and in doing so would force anyone using the beach to step onto the promenade behind. Three heights of diving board can be seen to the right of the model, while to the left are toilet blocks, changing rooms, and a pavilion, with tiered seating and a perimeter walkway providing spaces to stroll, sit, and relax. Plans for a bathing pool on Bognor seafront had been promoted since 1928, but by the time of Thorp's model in 1935 a much more advanced proposal had clearly been

**FIGURE 4.2**  Model of a proposed bathing pool in Bognor Regis. Architect: unknown. Made by Thorp, 1935. Courtesy Thorp Archive, AUB.

developed. Designed by an unknown architect for the town council, the plans generated considerable local controversy and with an estimated cost of £51,000 to construct, permission was ultimately refused.

Lidos and bathing pools such as the Bognor model illustrated had become hugely popular during the interwar years, offering the potential for 'healthy exercise in the fresh air, sun worship, [and] the mass culture of leisure in which everyone would be a consumer, all wrapped up in the clean forms of modern architecture.'[18] The vision on display in Thorp's model embodied the health and fitness craze that was sweeping Britain at the time, with bathing pools having emerged as the 'preeminent architectural symbol of the British seaside.'[19] Employing innovative building techniques such as the use of reinforced concrete, pools projected the idea of taming nature's wildest element, the sea, and turning it into a 'synthetic creation suitable for modernity.'[20] More than one hundred and eighty such bathing pools and lidos were built during the 1930s,[21] with the proposal for Bognor comparatively restrained when considered alongside Morecombe's £130,000 swimming stadium or Blackpool's open air baths with five hundred dressing rooms and space for three thousand spectators.[22] Featured in adverts by both local councils and railway companies to encourage visitors, pools acted as 'architectural sites of spectacle and display,'[23] and while ultimately unbuilt, the intentions projected by the Bognor model clearly signal a desire to embrace the new age of leisure-based liberal modernity.

A few months earlier another model of seaside leisure had left John Thorp's workshop that outlined an altogether different way of enjoying the seafront, which, as the model makes clear, involved far more sedate and respectable activities than were associated with communal bathing pools. Thorp's 1934 model of a proposed new bandstand in

**FIGURE 4.3**  Model of an early proposal for Eastbourne bandstand. Architect: Leslie Rosevere. Made by Thorp, 1934. Courtesy Thorp Archive, AUB.

Eastbourne (Figure 4.3) depicted one of several that were either planned or constructed along the town's promenade during this period.[24] Designed by Leslie Rosevere, the Borough Engineer, this grand circular structure would have dominated the seafront near Wish Tower and with generous landscaping and a wide, curving approach, this was a vision of wholesome outdoor entertainment where the town's citizens and holidaymakers alike could come together to listen to music in the open air. Proposed as part of a wider seafront improvement programme instigated by the town council, Rosevere's design sought to create an attraction that would encourage people to visit Eastbourne rather than its competitors, but it was deliberately aimed at encouraging a specific type of visitor, namely the middle classes who would be drawn by the appeal of respectable, and fully clothed, recreational activities. Modelled on the inland spar towns in promoting notions of good health and relaxation,[25] class-conscious seaside resorts such as Eastbourne considered the provision of outdoor leisure spaces an important part of their civic duty, and the elegance of the scene depicted in Thorp's model is far apart from the bustling confinement of the Bognor bathing pool. The design outlined in the model was never built as proposed, with an alternative site eventually being chosen one hundred metres further east in a much more restricted location. With clear similarities to Rosevere's earlier plan, the final version that was constructed in 1935 kept the same broad approach but was reduced to a semi-circular amphitheatre without the generous surroundings, but which could nevertheless accommodate three thousand people for performances by the town's municipal orchestra.

While the model of Eastbourne bandstand was conveying a more refined, middle-class vision of civic-funded outdoor culture, three years later Thorp was commissioned to produce a large model of a commercial project that was intended to offer a seaside leisure experience for the masses that was both aspirational and affordable: Prestatyn Holiday

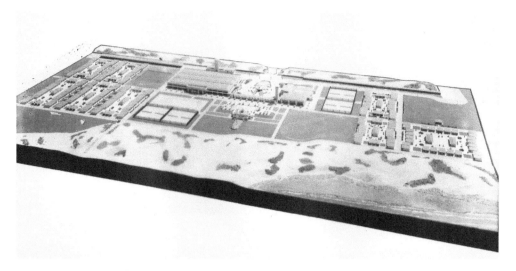

**FIGURE 4.4**    Model of Prestatyn Holiday Camp. Architect: William Hamlyn. Made by Thorp, 1938. Courtesy Thorp Archive, AUB.

Camp (Figure 4.4). A joint venture between the LMS Railway and the holiday company Thomas Cook, Prestatyn was designed by the LMS's chief architect, William Hamlyn, as a progressive and modernist vision of the British holiday of the future.[26] Thorp's model showcased the full layout of the fifty-eight acre site, with the sea and sand dunes depicted in the foreground and holiday chalets on either side arranged around central courtyards that contained the shared washrooms, while in the centre is the massive Sun Court with its surrounding dining room, ballroom, concert hall, and swimming pool. A running track and games pitches can also be seen, while tennis courts and plentiful outdoor seating with shady parasols complete the depiction of a holiday where almost every form of popular leisure at the time was within reach.

Prestatyn was an experiment for both companies, intended to serve as the template for a whole chain of similar camps up and down the country, and it was particularly notable for the quality of its architecture, all rendered in gleaming white with art deco flourishes. The idea was to create an upmarket family holiday camp that for £3 per week offered to bring a high-quality experience within the financial reach of many middle and upper-working-class families. Designed to hold two thousand guests within its nine hundred chalets, Prestatyn also boasted a sixty-foot observation tower and the ship-shaped Prestatyn Clipper bar (Figure 4.5). Here, children could climb the ropes and play deck games outside while parents enjoyed a drink or two indoors.[27]

Holidays camps during the 1930s were designed to appeal to families with both a limited budget and limited holiday time,[28] and with everything included in the price they offered a much more affordable alternative to the traditional seaside boarding house.[29] Prestatyn was the epitome of the holiday camp's position as the most fashionable form of modern and egalitarian leisure, although its promoters were perhaps a little caught up in their own vision when proclaiming that 'as the word camp cannot convey one fraction of [Prestatyn's] amenities, we have christened it the Chalet Village by the Sea.'[30]

**FIGURE 4.5**    Close-up of the model of Prestatyn Holiday Camp showing the Clipper bar in the foreground. Courtesy Thorp Archive, AUB.

While targeted at the mass leisure market, guests were expected to dress for dinner,[31] and the Clipper bar, with its ocean liner aesthetic, sought to impress ideas of luxurious modernity.[32] Opening in June 1939, and with Harry Warner, Billy Butlin, and Fred Pontin already building their own holiday camp empires at the time, Prestatyn offered a more aspirational experience that included running water and electricity in every chalet. The speed at which this particular vision of leisure was adopted was remarkably swift, as while the first holiday camp for young men had opened on the Isle of Man in 1894, the first family-oriented camp, Butlin's in Skegness, was only completed in 1936, and so just two years later Thorp's model was illustrating how Thomas Cook and the LMS were attempting to access this new and highly lucrative market.

Prestatyn, as with most holiday camps at the time, sought to bring together the cultural trends of the age – health and exercise, art deco, modernism, and Hollywood glamour – and repackage them for the mass market,[33] and it was this commercialisation of leisure that makes the vision behind the model of Prestatyn Holiday Camp so indicative of the types of models that Thorp would be commissioned to make through the remaining decades of the century. Unlike the bathing pool and bandstand models of just a few years before, Prestatyn was an example of privatised leisure where everything was available, but for a fee. Prestatyn was also the only vision of the three that progressed beyond model form, a sign of the commercialisation of leisure that was to come, and which would accelerate spectacularly following the Second World War as the retreat from nature and the desire for artificially sanitised leisure experiences helped to fuel a demand for models of a radically new architectural form.

## Visions of Affluence

Throughout the 1950s and 1960s, architectural models of a new type of urban environment began to be displayed to the public in town halls, community centres, and market-places in dozens, if not hundreds of towns across the country: the shopping centre. With Britain rapidly becoming a full blown consumerist society,[34] a new affluence had emerged with car ownership jumping from two million in 1950 to eleven million in 1964 and the presence of household utilities in the nation's homes such as refrigerators, freezers, and washing machines more than trebling.[35] Britain wanted to go shopping and planners, architects, and property developers responded with bold new visions of how shopping could be modernised and rationalised, all projected through the lens of modernist architecture. Town planners enthusiastically positioned open-air shopping precincts and later enclosed shopping centres as the centrepieces of their dreams to rebuild and modernise Britain's war-damaged towns and cities, and while shopping as an activity had accounted for only a handful of models in Thorp's order book before the Second World War, in the decades that followed highly detailed masterplan models of proposed shopping centres became a lucrative line of business for the company. As town and city centres were comprehensively redeveloped, shopping centres became seen as core commercial amenities alongside public buildings such as civic centres and libraries, and the architectural models made to communicate their designs had to reflect not just changing social and cultural ideas relating to leisure, but also entirely new architectural concepts as well.

By the late 1960s, the momentum for shopping centres as a means of meeting the demands of the newly affluent society seemed unstoppable, with architects and property developers queuing up to present grand ideas to local councils to help them realise their future-leaning ambitions. In 1967, Thorp was commissioned to make a model of a proposed new shopping centre in Chelmsley Wood that demonstrated the radical and wholly artificial nature of how the future of shopping was imagined at the time (Figure 4.6). Designed by Ian Fraser for Town & City Properties, the plan was for twin parades of shops on two levels with blocks of flats overhead, entirely isolated from the rest of the community by an enormous expanse of car park. Pedestrian access was to be via a slender raised walkway, based on the assumption that most people would arrive by car. Chelmsley Wood was an entirely new community being built by Birmingham City Council that was planned to be Europe's largest new housing development with over fifteen thousand homes, and the shopping centre as proposed in the model was intended to offer seventy shops undercover with housing included in the scheme in order to prevent the area from becoming lifeless in the evenings. This design was never built, however, with a much smaller precinct built in 1971 that contained point blocks of flats placed next to the shopping area rather than over it, and with far fewer shops included overall.

Drawing from Dutch ideas about separating shoppers and cars, pedestrianisation was seen by most postwar town planners as a means to not just rebuild but to improve, creating modern and highly efficient open-air commercial zones, such as were built in Coventry and Harlow shortly after the war.[36] In the late 1950s, British architects and planners then began to tour the United States to study the newly emerging form of the covered shopping mall, the first of which, the Southdale Centre in Minnesota, designed by Victor Gruen, opened in 1956,[37] and were evidently convinced that the future lay in controlled, artificial environments where shopping was projected as a leisure pursuit

**FIGURE 4.6**    Model of an early proposal for Chelmsley Wood Shopping Centre. Architect: Ian Fraser for Town & City Properties. Made by Thorp, 1957. Courtesy Thorp Archive, AUB.

rather than as a chore to gather life's essentials.[38] For architects, the design of enclosed shopping centres such as proposed for Chelmsley Wood meant embracing an entirely new urban form. What a shopping centre should look like was not entirely clear, and when the Arndale Centre in Poole was proposed in 1963, the developers offered to fly the Town Clerk and Borough Architect to Toronto as that was the only comparable development they could show them, so new was the concept at the time.[39] Innovative approaches to spatial planning were also adopted to predict how many shops a centre would require and where they should be placed,[40] and by the 1960s almost every town in Britain wanted an enclosed shopping centre to attract trade and improve their regional standing.[41] A 1965 model of the unbuilt proposal for the Castle Vale Shopping Centre made for Samuel Properties perhaps best captures the role that shopping centres played in this regard and their importance to the nation's economy at the time (Figure 4.7). With the centre entirely enclosed and accessed only by road, this was a dream of commercialised modernity that positioned the shopping centre as a leisure destination designed to be enjoyed solely from the inside, and with little consideration given to their exteriors, shopping centres, as with the plan for Castle Vale, tended to be monolithic and overpowering, with almost no regard for the existing environment around them.[42] That the Castle Vale estate, and the less ambitious shopping centre that was eventually built in place of what was depicted in Thorp's model, was developed on the site of the British Industries Fair at Castle Bromwich (see Chapter 3) was also a rather symbolic indication of the future of Britain's economy, with an exhibition centre dedicated to industry demolished to make way for department stores and a bowling alley.

**FIGURE 4.7**   Model of an early proposal for Castle Vale Shopping Centre. Developer: Samuel Properties. Made by Thorp, 1965. Courtesy Thorp Archive, AUB.

The ambition of local councils to build prestigious new shopping centres to replace their existing town centres formed a central part of the postwar zeal for comprehensive redevelopment (as seen in Chapter 1), and in 1971 Thorp produced a detailed model of an unbuilt proposal for the redevelopment of Kingswood Central Area, designed for Kingswood Urban District Council by Arndale Developments in collaboration with the Bristol architects Power, Clark & Hiscocks (Figure 4.8). Compared to the impenetrable structures proposed for both Castle Vale and Chelmsley Wood, the form of the Kingswood shopping centre highlights an evolution of design philosophy that had emerged in the late 1960s, depicting a new vision of the future of shopping centres that incorporated large expanses of glazed roofing to allow natural light onto the concourse and much more clearly defined pedestrian entrances complementing the four multi-storey car parks around the perimeter. Kingswood Council had been pursuing plans for the redevelopment of the town centre since 1968, and what may not be immediately clear from the model is that the proposals as depicted involved the complete demolition of the existing high street, the route of which can be seen as a pedestrianised walkway running from top to bottom, the road itself diverted to the right on a new dual carriageway. While the model skilfully makes the development appear particularly inviting, the scale of the destruction it would have involved was seen as unpalatable in an era when conservation concerns were starting to be raised, and the much smaller Kings Chase shopping

**FIGURE 4.8** Model of a proposal for the Kingswood Central Area Redevelopment. Developer: Arndale Developments and Kingswood Urban District Council. Made by Thorp, 1971. Courtesy Thorp Archive, AUB.

centre was eventually built to one side of the existing high street instead. The desire for such shopping centres showed no signs of abating, however, fuelled by an 'almost wishful repetition of the mantras of prosperity and affluence,'[43] with new developments seen as highly aspirational spaces where shoppers could 'seek comfort in their gleaming hallways.'[44] Physically turning away from the weather, urban decay, and crime, the Kingswood proposal, and many others like it, offered a total concept that was designed to meet everyone's shopping needs. Arndale, the developer, had elevated this approach almost to an art form by this time, introducing a whole new experience of mass leisure drawn from North American forms,[45] and through its expansive building programme 'provided the modern commercial landscapes through which the affluent society was encountered, accommodated, and made concrete.'[46] Arndale's shopping centres were seen as inseparable components of urban renewal schemes, providing the private capital to revitalise ageing town centres and create luxurious and convenient indoor spaces that were fit for the future. By the end of the 1970s more than two-thirds of towns in Britain either had a substantial enclosed shopping centre or were in the process of building one,[47] completely transforming the social and economic makeup of urban Britain.[48]

The leisure demands of the postwar affluent society were not just restricted to shopping, however, and while Thorp was kept particularly busy with models of shopping centres during the 1960s, a number of equally striking models of proposed hotels that the company produced reflected a radical shift in attitudes towards holidays and tourism compared to

**FIGURE 4.9**  Photomontage of a model of an early proposal for the PENTA hotel in Kensington. Architect: Richard Seifert and Partners. Made by Thorp, 1969. Courtesy Thorp Archive, AUB.

the holiday camp models of the interwar years. In 1969 Thorp created a series of photomontages that carefully placed different views of their model of Richard Seifert's design for the PENTA hotel on Cromwell Road in London within photographs of the existing street scene. Quite what Seifert was hoping to achieve by commissioning these remains unknown, as the only certainty was surely that the images would illustrate how his proposal was spectacularly out of keeping for the surrounding area (Figure 4.9). Seifert's enormous forty-storey hotel would have utterly dominated the skyline, its curving form intended to reference the tail of an aircraft. Showcasing the building's gleaming white concrete and

**FIGURE 4.10** Photomontage of the early PENTA model with the Kensington Air Terminal to the right. Courtesy Thorp Archive, AUB.

glass exterior, Thorp's model dramatically outlined the impact the design would have had on the local area, complete with a raised pedestrian walkway over the main road. This was an air bridge to the West London Air Terminal, where passengers due to depart from the rapidly expanding Heathrow Airport could check in and be relayed to the airport by bus. The terminal itself can be seen in the centre right of the aerial photomontage (Figure 4.10), and it was the terminal's presence that the hotel intended to exploit.

PENTA was a consortium of five major airlines that included BOAC, BEA, Lufthansa, Swissair, and Alitalia, and intending to take a slice of the lucrative hotel market, the PENTA group of companies were keen to invest in affordable hotel rooms so they could ensure that passengers who were booking cheap rate flights with them would have budget accommodation when they arrived.[49] Seifert's PENTA hotel in London was therefore intended as much for foreign tourists arriving as it was for British tourists flying abroad, and this initial design with over two thousand rooms was planned to be the largest hotel in the world. The government had begun to encourage the building of hotels in place of offices as early as 1964, a process that was further boosted by the 1969 Development of Tourism Act which provided financial incentives to fund the creation of one hundred thousand new hotel rooms across the country,[50] and Seifert's contribution on Cromwell Road was a direct result of this funding that put forward a striking architectural vision intended to take advantage of the ballooning demand for international tourism and the packaged holiday which had emerged as popular new forms of mass leisure.[51] Perhaps unsurprisingly, this initial design was rejected, and while it is possible to see elements of the tail-shaped concept in the overall massing of the much smaller hotel that was eventually constructed, the more ordinary, blocky tower that was built lacked the daring confidence that Thorp's model of the earlier version conveyed. With even the completed building described at the time as a 'monster apparition' and 'a terrifying interruption of the weave of this part of London,'[52] quite how the original proposal was received can only be imagined.

FIGURE 4.11    Model of the Plymouth Holiday Inn. Architect: A.J. Hines. Made by Thorp, 1970. Courtesy Thorp Archive, AUB.

The following year another hotel model emerged from Thorp's workshop of a project that, unlike Seifert's scheme, was actually completed: the Plymouth Holiday Inn (Figure 4.11). Designed in 1972 by the Bristol-based architect A.J. Hines, the model captured the hotel's brutalist nature with its depiction of the building's large concrete panels and blocky entranceway. The twelve-storey building was planned to contain 211 rooms with an on-site restaurant, swimming pool, and underground parking, and was situated adjacent to the historic Hoe public park. Having also taken advantage of the Development of Tourism Act, which provided grants of either twenty percent of the capital cost of building a hotel or £1000, whichever was the smaller amount, this was Holiday Inn's first British hotel. Founded in Memphis in 1952, by 1970 the company had more than one thousand hotels in the United States alone and the Plymouth hotel was part of their international expansion. Offering simple, clean, and reliable accommodation for the masses, the Plymouth Holiday Inn included televisions and coffee makers in every room, and was designed to cater for travelling families on short holidays. Faintly praised as 'comfortable, clinically efficient and characterless,'[53] hotels of this kind were soon common sights across the country, and with more than eight million foreign visitors arriving in Britain on holiday each year by the time the Plymouth hotel opened, the hospitality industry had become larger than the motor and aircraft industries combined.[54] For Plymouth, having endured the almost complete reconstruction of the city centre after heavy bombing in the Second World War, the Holiday Inn was seen as another sign of the city's leisure-based renaissance, with new shopping centres, a theatre, and further hotels all opening at the same time, the dream of affluence thriving as postwar Britain looked confidently into the future.

### Sport and Recreation

Alongside the seemingly endless demand for models of highly commercial developments of hotels and shopping centres in the 1960s and 1970s, changes to what were ostensibly more traditional forms of leisure – sport and exercise – also provided a significant amount of work for Thorp's modelmakers. Over a twenty year period from the late 1960s to the late 1980s, the models recorded in Thorp's archive evidence major changes to how the buildings in which those activities took place were designed, with an increasing tilt towards commercialisation and entertainment. Sports centres quickly transformed into leisure centres while lidos and bathing pools similarly became leisure pools. The architectural models of these buildings changed accordingly, using increasing amounts of animation and focusing less on new architectural forms and more on the wonders that they were projected to contain. With sport having been seen as a traditionally male activity, the rebranding of swimming, tennis, and even team sports as forms of leisure shifted the balance to be more welcoming towards women and families, offering not just healthy exercise but a whole range of entertaining distractions. Increasingly targeted at a younger demographic, the architects behind the sports and leisure complexes of the latter decades of the twentieth century responded with ever more theatrical environments in which to play, relax, and socialise.

Spectator sports also generated several expensive commissions for Thorp as proposals for new stadia were put forward, one of the earliest being Osborne V. Webb and Partners' design for the National Stadium at Cardiff Arms Park, the home of Welsh Rugby Union

**FIGURE 4.12** Model of the National Stadium at Cardiff Arms Park. Architect: Osborne V. Webb and Partners. Made by Thorp, 1967. Courtesy Thorp Archive, AUB.

(Figure 4.12). Thorp's 1967 model, photographed, as with so many of the company's models from this period, by Henk Snoek, outlined the architects' clever solution to the problem of needing to fit two entirely different rugby grounds into a compact site on the banks of the River Taff. First considered in 1962, the plan was to build a brand new stadium for the Rugby Union club that would hold seventy-five thousand spectators with a smaller stadium for the Rugby League club next door.[55] The architects' innovative solution was to propose a double-sided structure whereby two separate grandstands could be suspended back to back. This can be seen in the centre of the photograph, with the common entranceway to the right. The Rugby Union stadium is clearly the larger of the two, with its distinctive cantilevered roof curving neatly around the tiered seating, although a capacity of only fifty-eight thousand spectators was achieved upon construction rather than the proposed seventy five. Today, the stadium design appears relatively unremarkable but at the time this was an unusually daring vision. Osborne V. Webb and Partners had few references to draw from in terms of postwar stadia of this size in Britain, with the 1923 Empire Stadium in Wembley and Hillsborough's 1961 North Stand studied in order to make comparisons.[56] The Cardiff Arms Park project put forward a bold vision of not only the future architecture of national sporting venues but also of Welsh Rugby itself, proudly celebrating the importance of the sport to the nation. Construction of the

**FIGURE 4.13**   Model of Kelsey Kerridge Sports Centre, Cambridge. Architect: Geoffrey Cresswell. Made by Thorp, 1968. Courtesy Thorp Archive, AUB.

twin stadia began in 1968 and was not completed until 1984, such was the complexity and cost of the project. With Thorp's model including tiny figures on the main pitch to give a sense of scale, the sheer size of the building can be seen, illustrating how significant an investment this modern and architecturally striking venue was to be.

The majority of the sport-related commissions that Thorp made during the second half of the twentieth century were not for spectator sports, however, but rather for spaces in which ordinary people could turn up and take part themselves, and in 1968 the company was commissioned to make their first model of what was then an entirely new type of building, a sports centre (Figure 4.13). The model, of the Kelsey Kerridge Sports Centre in Cambridge, showed cars arriving at the drop-off point at the front, long windows on the upper floors, and a multi-storey car park at the far end. The design of the scheme, on Queen Anne Terrace opposite Parkers Piece, was led by the city surveyor, Geoffrey Cresswell, and it was intended to provide a convenient civic amenity where people could play indoor sports such as squash and badminton. When completed in 1975, the centre demonstrated the municipality's commitment to the dream of sport for all, and across Britain hundreds of similar facilities were being built by local authorities keen to embrace the same vision.[57]

The idea of the sports centre developed following the publication of the 1960 Wolfenden report into sport and community that called upon local authorities to improve access to indoor sports.[58] The earliest was already under construction in Harlow, which opened in 1964 to become the first indoor community sports centre in Britain, with similar projects in Bracknell, Billingham, and Poole soon following. The popularity of indoor sports had grown during the 1950s and the new secondary schools being built (see Chapter 5) were already incorporating sports halls rather than traditional gymnasiums. Essentially multi-purpose halls designed to accommodate as many different indoor sports as possible, sports centres also included swimming pools where budgets and space allowed. As an entirely new form for architects in Britain to work with, inspiration was drawn from French and West German examples as well as the designs of the new school sports halls being built here in Britain. As the model of the Cambridge sports centre shows, the exteriors of such facilities were generally stark and utilitarian, following the same inside-out approach that shopping centres had adopted, although unlike these within sports centres little consideration was initially given to socialising and relaxation.[59] Architects nevertheless began to merge both commercial and civic perceptions of leisure to create 'an innovative and ambitious typology'[60] that employed the latest technological developments in both structural design and environmental systems control.[61]

Sports centres subsequently underwent a massive expansion during the 1970s, standing as symbolic representations of British aspirations of affluence during a period of intense social and economic change.[62] In providing classless spaces that were seen as having an important role in social regeneration, sports centres provided an entirely different environment to spend leisure time in, but by the mid-1970s the visions of their future form had already begun to evolve, with one 1976 prediction suggesting a departure from offering purely sporting activities to include more relaxing pastimes such as were offered by arts venues and museums.[63] By the 1980s this transition had taken place, and as Thorp's 1987 model of Bracknell Leisure Pool, designed by Sargent and Potiriadis, reveals, the scale of change was far greater than anyone could have predicted (Figure 4.14).

At first glance, this 1:100 scale interior model would appear to have little in common with the bland exterior model of the Kelsey Kerridge Sports Centre, but the seeds for this playful environment had been sown just a year before the earlier model was made with the completion of one of the first sports centres in Britain, Billingham Forum. Built between 1962 and 1967, Billingham had included not just a sports hall and a swimming pool, but a theatre, skating rink, restaurant, and bar, offering something for everyone in a more relaxed setting that appealed to families.[64] During the 1970s sports centres increasingly began to be referred to as leisure centres, the change of title indicating a shift away from notions of health and fitness and towards more 'nebulous concepts of happiness, free time, and even fun and glamour.'[65] Sport was seen as a specific activity for the dedicated while leisure was far more generalised and for all, and architects began to adopt a tropical feel to the design of swimming pools with wave machines and bars that offered 'relaxed leisure for all the family.'[66] Bletchley pool opened in 1974 with lagoons, palm trees, and deck chairs, but nothing reached the same heights of fun and whimsy than what Peter Sargent and Mark Potiriadis achieved with their vision for Bracknell Leisure Pool. Unmissable in the photograph of the model is the pirate ship complete with sails, while the sun loungers on the curving terraces are more reminiscent of a tropical holiday than a municipal swimming pool. The building itself is reduced to a background for the theatrics presented inside, with the model reflecting the architects' clear intention of recasting the swimming pool as a relaxing space rather than a formal and competitive one, and the use of figures in yoga poses and realistic model palm trees helped to convey

**FIGURE 4.14**   Interior model of Bracknell Leisure Pool. Architect: Sargent and Potiriadis. Made by Thorp, 1987. Courtesy Thorp Archive, AUB.

the informal setting of the scene and emphasise how this was to be a family space that was more about fun than exercise.

The trend for sports centres to become leisure centres and adopt a more casual approach to exercise and recreation took a further step towards pure entertainment with the appearance of leisure parks in the late 1980s, and in the same year that the Bracknell model was made, Thorp was commissioned to make a large model of a speculative concept for a truly grand example of this brand new type of building for the architects Simons Design (Figure 4.15). Here, the sporting elements of the leisure centre were almost entirely replaced by other forms of entertainment, and unlike the models of Cambridge or Bracknell, this was a concept for a privately-financed venture intended to extract as much money from its visitors as possible. The most notable feature of the model is the car park, emphasising an out-of-town location which promises convenient access. Made with part of the roof removed, the model showcased the range of activities that were proposed, with a swimming pool, skating rink, snooker hall, bowling alley, children's zone, multiscreen cinema, maze, restaurant, and games arcade. At the time, this was an entirely new proposition, with the Tower Park leisure complex in Poole one of the first in Europe when it opened in 1989. The inclusion of a multiscreen cinema was a further importation of a North American trend,[67] and cinemas were increasingly used as the main anchors within leisure developments with a range of different activities positioned alongside.

The concept put forward in Thorp's model for a hypothetical location projected this trend on a much larger scale, predicting what became known as Urban Entertainment

**FIGURE 4.15**   Model of a hypothetical leisure complex. Architect: Simons Design. Made by
Thorp, 1987. Courtesy Thorp Archive, AUB.

Centres where a critical mass of activities would allow customers to 'optimise their leisure time.'[68] In many ways this was not too dissimilar to the ethos of the interwar holiday
camps, although in this case you had to pay for everything you wanted to do separately.
With a fairly bland exterior and expansive roof, the design outlined in the model drew
heavily from North American out-of-town shopping malls, focusing all attention on the
interior, while the long signposted approach evoked the entrance to a theme park, which
was essentially what this was, just indoors. Aiming for spectacle in the creation of a
'lively sense of place,'[69] this was a vision of commercialised leisure taken to the extreme.
Gone were the ambitions of promoting exercise or reinvigorating a community and by
the end of the 1980s the design of such buildings had become focused on 'maximising
customer spend.'[70] This, and the move to the edge of town, heralded the future of not just
the leisure centre but also leisure in its broadest sense, as by the end of the century the
cinema, the supermarket, and the shopping centre had also moved out of town as a result
of an unwavering belief that convenience and size would boost their appeal.

### The Rise of the Retail Park

By the time the leisure park model for Simons Design was made in 1987, the overwhelming majority of commissions for models Thorp received relating to the pursuit of leisure
were for proposals in out-of-town locations, particularly in terms of shopping. With more

**FIGURE 4.16**   Model of The Galleria, Hatfield. Architect: Michael Aukett Associates. Made by Thorp, 1987. Courtesy Thorp Archive, AUB.

than four hundred enclosed shopping centres having been built in town centres across the country,[71] property developers and retailers had begun to look for new and better ways to attract customers, with supermarkets having started to drift towards suburbia in the early 1970s, the big box DIY and electrical retailers following in the late 1970s, and by the mid-1980s high street chains had similarly become enticed by the vast regional shopping centres and retail parks that were beginning to be built.[72] Planners, despite their instinctive opposition to out-of-town retail development, proved unable to halt the flight from town centres, and 'liberated from their urban context,'[73] new forms of retail buildings emerged. The most eye-catching of these were the regional shopping centres, a further North American import that was pioneered in Britain with the opening of the Brent Cross shopping centre in 1976 and followed by Merry Hill in 1985, the Metrocentre in 1986, and both Lakeside and Meadowhall in 1990. Architectural models of all of these were produced, but not by Thorp, as by the 1980s more than a dozen other architectural modelmaking companies were in business, with Nick Quine at AMI making the original model of the Trafford Centre, for example. Thorp did make the architectural model for a particularly experimental out-of-town shopping centre, however, Hatfield Galleria, or the A1 Gallerias as it was known at the time of the proposal in 1987 (Figure 4.16).

Designed by Michael Aukett Associates, no strangers to out-of-town development (see Chapter 3), Hatfield Galleria was a relatively small out-of-town shopping centre with one hundred and thirty units covering 380,000 square feet. The project was the brainchild of the British developer The Carroll Group, which sought to take North American mall design and management principles and adapt them to suit British tastes, with The Galleria designed to be as much a social venue as it was a shopping destination.[74] The building was unusual in that it was built over the A1(M) motorway in a cut and cover tunnel, making it highly visible to drivers passing underneath. The site was divided into two halves with a retail area and a leisure complex connected by a pedestrian walkway. The main retail centre was dominated by a large glazed courtyard that was inspired by Hatfield's aviation heritage to resemble an aircraft hangar, and in a departure from British shopping centre design at the time the developer forwent the traditional anchor store and dispersed the catering around the whole site rather than installing a dedicated food court. This was a very different vision to the larger centres such as Merry Hill and the Metrocentre, with the huge atrium replacing the anchor store as a focus of activity and intended to house fashion shows, community events, and exhibitions. With a strong leisure element, The Galleria also included a nine screen cinema, a skating rink, a crèche, restaurants, a hair salon, and a sports hall.[75] Photographed from the complex's southern end, Thorp's model shows the A1(M) heading into a tunnel under the main atrium, with a convenient bus stop right outside. To the rear is the leisure complex, connected by a covered walkway running alongside the multi-storey car park. The dominant feature of the development is clearly the atrium, which in calling back to the central light wells of early department stores, was a North American design that was rarely adopted in Britain, with Hatfield Galleria positioned as a bold and innovative attempt to introduce the concept over here.

The merging of shopping centres and leisure parks had been predicted as early as the 1970s, with libraries, nightclubs, dance halls, and other community activities being incorporated into their designs to extend their social reach,[76] while shopping centres became seen as places to spend the day as a leisure experience even if you had nothing you needed to buy. Planners had long resisted out-of-town retail development, however, with the first planning application for an out-of-town shopping centre at Haydock Park having been refused in 1964 due to concerns about the impact on neighbouring town centres,[77] although the Pilkington Glass Age Development Committee had proposed a six hundred metre long shopping centre in the West Midlands even earlier in 1955.[78] Brent Cross took fifteen years to gain planning approval, but by the 1970s pressure from both developers and retailers was beginning to mount as the logic for out-of-town retailing became clear. In 1970 Lord Sainsbury outlined a vision of the future of shopping where customers would drive into large convenient car parks to find a wide range of shops all big enough to stock their maximum ranges, with play areas for children, restaurants, and cloakrooms provided, all on the edges of towns.[79] By the 1980s, planners had finally lost the battle, and when Marks and Spencer moved into the Meadowhall Centre in Sheffield and scuppered a longstanding plan for a regional shopping centre in Rotherham, it was observed that 'the board of M&S in Baker Street made as important a contribution to retail planning in South Yorkshire as did local or central government.'[80]

Despite continued objections from planners, the growth of out-of-town retail development continued apace throughout the 1980s and 1990s, and while in 1980 just five percent of retail sales were taking place out of town, by 1991 this had soared to seventeen percent.[81] Most of this growth was not in the large regional shopping centres, which central government finally began to curtail in the 1990s, but in more modestly sized retail parks and grocery superstores. Often constructed on brownfield sites in well-connected locations near major roads, retail parks and out-of-town supermarkets, as yet more new forms to grace the built environment, became the 'enablers of super-sized consumerism,'[82]

**FIGURE 4.17**    Model of Sainsbury's Bury St Edmunds. Architect: J Sainsbury Development Division. Made by Thorp, 1986. Courtesy Thorp Archive, AUB.

and during the final two decades of the twentieth century, commissions for models of out-of-town supermarkets became the single most lucrative line of business for Thorp, with at least thirty models for Sainsbury's alone made between 1984 and 1995, for example. Thorp's 1986 model of the then-proposed new Sainsbury's in Bury St Edmonds was typical of these (Figure 4.17). Made at 1:500 scale, the model presented what was then an ideal vision of an out-of-town supermarket with a large and welcoming store positioned at the junction of two major roads with an extensive car park at the front and separate delivery access at the rear. Highly visible to passing drivers, this was the shopper's dream, spacious and convenient.

The Bury St Edmonds store, which opened as planned in 1987, offered long opening hours into the evening, free parking, a coffee shop, and with its own in-store bakery was more than four times larger than the older store in the town centre. Lord Sainsbury's 1970 vision had been realised and perhaps sooner than he might have expected. Out-of-town supermarkets had been operating in the United States since the 1950s, and with France developing the hypermarket concept in the 1960s, Britain quickly followed suit during the 1970s. Their subsequent growth in Britain was spectacular, with the number of out-of-town superstores rising from just four in 1965 to more than one thousand in 1996.[83] The move out of town to sites such as Bury St Edmonds was largely driven by the growth in ownership of both cars and refrigerators, which together instigated a shift in consumer behaviour to favour a weekly food shop as people could drive to a larger supermarket and stock up on food that would keep for longer when refrigerated.[84] Offering plentiful parking as close to the shop as possible became vitally important for

**FIGURE 4.18**   Model of Tesco Windsor. Developer: Tesco. Made by Thorp, 1991. Courtesy Thorp Archive, AUB.

supermarket chains and so an urgent search for suitable new sites on the edge of towns began.[85] Sainsbury's opened an experimental out-of-town store in Peterborough in 1972 that at 25,000 square feet was the largest supermarket in the country at the time,[86] while a second in Cambridge in 1974 became the template for their future superstores. Tesco quickly followed with a hypermarket near Manchester in 1976, and by the 1980s was opening two out-of-town superstores every single week.[87]

The external appearance of out-of-town supermarkets became crucial in making what were essentially large sheds more attractive to both shoppers and planners alike.[88] Asda's South Woodham Ferrers store, designed by Alcock in 1978 and intended to mimic the architectural style of a traditional tithe barn with handmade bricks, pitched roofs, dormers, and archways, established a style known as 'Essex Barn' that dominated supermarket design for the next fifteen years.[89] Tesco, in particular, embraced this approach as a means of satisfying the demand of local planners, as their pitched roof designs with clock towers offered much smarter buildings than the disused industrial sites they were hoping to replace.[90] Thorp's 1991 model of Tesco's proposed Windsor store demonstrates this style to great effect, with the complex pitched roofline simply for show, hiding what was still a flat box underneath (Figure 4.18). Compared to the models of postwar shopping centres featured earlier in this chapter, a significant investment in the exterior is evident, projecting an image of a retailer that was considerate of the communities they sell to by taking care to improve the built environment for all. With no less than two separate clock faces, the Windsor store was also a firm sign of things to come, with twenty-three out of

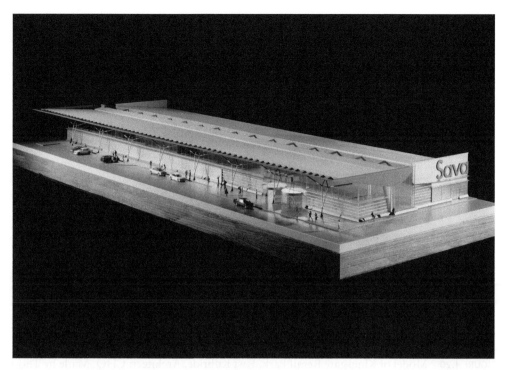

**FIGURE 4.19**   Model of an early proposal for Sydenham Savacentre. Client: J Sainsbury Development Division. Made by Thorp, 1994. Courtesy Thorp Archive, AUB.

the twenty-four Tesco stores that opened in the following year featuring similar clocks,[91] a rather curious architectural quirk that can be found in many of the more than three hundred supermarkets of all brands that opened over the following five years.[92]

Sainsbury's soon tired of the Essex Barn style and from the mid-1980s began to commission well-known architects to design sleek high-tech stores that projected an entirely different vision of how the supermarket of the future should look. Following ABK's design for the Canterbury Sainsbury's in 1984 and Nicholas Grimshaw's Camden store in 1988, Sainsbury's in-house Development Division won twenty-four architectural awards,[93] and in 1994 Thorp was asked to make a model for Sainsbury's that showcased a radically different architectural treatment for their Savacentre hypermarket concept (Figure 4.19). Whether this design was completed in-house or was the work of an external architectural practice remains unclear, and while this particular proposal was never built it appears to be an early concept for the Sydenham store. Clearly inspired by the frontage of Norman Foster's Stanstead Airport, the design featured a prominent wing-shaped canopy supported by tree-like structural columns with the roof rendered in an eye-catching bright blue. The model, although detailed with realistic figures and cars, is far more abstract in composition than any of the other supermarket models Thorp made, evidencing a more artistic and less commercial approach that was more suited to models of cultural and civic buildings at the time. This was likely a nod towards Sainsbury's desire to be recognised within the architectural press for the quality of its buildings, and the model certainly projected a more refined sense of architectural design.

**FIGURE 4.20**    Model of Kingsgate Retail Park, East Kilbride. Architect: CHQ. Made by Thorp, 1993. Courtesy Thorp Archive, AUB.

By the 1990s, the steady stream of commissions for models of out-of-town supermarkets had expanded to include models of retail parks, which following the relaxation of planning constraints to encourage the redevelopment of edge-of-town industrial sites, had begun to spread across Britain's urban landscape. In 1993, Thorp's model of the proposed Kingsgate retail park in East Kilbride illustrated the natural progression from out-of-town supermarket developments to full-blown retail parks that was taking place (Figure 4.20). With a Sainsbury's supermarket at the top left of the model, ten other large retail units were planned alongside, with a petrol station and two fast food outlets near the entrance. It is the car park that dominates the model, however, with 1500 spaces shown and the model suggesting that there would always be a free space right outside every front door. Bringing together the convenience of a weekly food shop in a supermarket and big ticket electrical, furniture, and DIY stores, retail parks were highly attractive to both shoppers and retailers alike, offering convenient access and low rent due to cheap land prices. This was a vision of the easy shop, where it was possible to drive in, find a space, pick up what you wanted, perhaps eat a burger or pizza for lunch, fill up with petrol, and then drive home. Ease and convenience ruled, with the entire experience centred on the individual. There was no community to be served here and none of the civic amenities that would be found mixed among the traditional high streets that shoppers were increasingly abandoning.

Just one year after the Kingsgate model was made, a further vision of out-of-town retailing emerged that projected an even more significant migration from the high street to the retail park, as captured in Thorp's 1994 model of a proposed joint venture between Sainsbury's and Marks and Spencer (Figure 4.21). Here the intention was for a shared retail

**FIGURE 4.21**   Model of a proposed M&S/Sainsbury's retail complex in Chingford. Developer: Taylor Group. Made by Thorp, 1994. Courtesy Thorp Archive, AUB.

development that contained a standalone department store next to the supermarket, an attempt by both companies to leverage each other's brand appeal. The model is noticeably more realistic in its placement of cars, presenting a busy day with the car park almost full. The Sainsbury's opened as planned but the Marks and Spencer shown on the model was never built, although it was not long before the department store chain opened on similar retail parks that provided the opportunity to create much larger stores than they could possibly build in existing town centres. What this final model illustrates is just how pervasive the out-of-town dream had become by the end of the twentieth century, with a new wave of high street names beginning to follow the electrical and furniture stores to the mass of retail parks growing on the edges of Britain's towns and cities, leaving the nation's traditional high streets at a 'crossroads of decline and regeneration.'[94] Leisure, as with so many of the visions of work seen in the previous chapter, had ultimately been seduced by the convenience of lower land prices and plentiful parking, the culmination of a steady march towards the commercialisation of free time that Thorp's models of shopping centres, sports centres, holiday camps, and hotels witnessed as the twentieth century advanced.

**Notes**

1   John Stobart, *Spend Spend Spend: A History of Shopping* (Stroud: The History Press, 2008), 173.
2   Stobart, *Spend Spend Spend*, 164.

3 Erika Diane Rappaport, *Shopping for Pleasure* (Princeton: Princeton University Press, 2001), 143.
4 Peter Borsay, *A History of Leisure* (Basingstoke: Palgrave Macmillan, 2006), 2.
5 Jeffey Hill, *Sport, Leisure and Culture in Twentieth-century Britain* (Basingstoke: Palgrave, 2002), 8.
6 Borsay, *A History of Leisure*, 25.
7 Stephen Jones, *Workers at Play: A Social and Economic History of Leisure, 1918–1939* (London: Kegan Paul, 1986), 15.
8 Stobart, *Spend Spend Spend*, 203.
9 Alistair Kefford, 'The Arndale Property Company and the Transformation of Urban Britain, 1950–2000,' *Journal of British Studies*, July 2022, 571.
10 Kefford, 'The Arndale Property Company and the Transformation of Urban Britain, 1950–2000.'
11 Hill, *Sport, Leisure and Culture*, 79.
12 Peter Scott, 'Leisure, Consumption and Consumerism,' In *20th Century Britain: Economic, Cultural and Social Change*, eds. Nichole Robertson, John Singleton, and Avram Taylor (Abingdon: Routledge, 2023), 115.
13 Kathryn Ferry, *The British Seaside Holiday* (Oxford: Shire, 2009), 7.
14 Madeline Bunting, *The Seaside* (London: Granta, 2023), 7.
15 Fred Gray, *Designing the Seaside* (London: Reaktion, 2006), 7.
16 Gray, *Designing the Seaside*, 184.
17 Allan Brodie, *The Seafront* (Swindon: Historic England, 2018), 28.
18 Ferry, *British Seaside Holiday*, 73.
19 Gray, *Designing the Seaside*, 181.
20 Gray, *Designing the Seaside*, 184.
21 Brodie, *The Seafront*, 126.
22 Ferry, *British Seaside Holiday*, 74.
23 Gray, *Designing the Seaside*, 182.
24 Brodie, *The Seafront*, 97.
25 Paul Rabbitts, *Bandstands* (Swindon: Historic England, 2018), 35.
26 Kathryn Ferry, *Holiday Camps* (Oxford: Shire, 2010), 19.
27 Ferry, *British Seaside Holiday*, 58.
28 Lucy Lethbridge, *Tourists* (London: Bloomsbury, 2022), 214.
29 Ferry, *British Seaside Holiday*, 55.
30 Ferry, *Holiday Camps*, 13.
31 Juliet Gardiner, *The Thirties: An Intimate History* (London: Harper Press, 2010), 601.
32 Ferry, *Holiday Camps*, 20.
33 Ferry, *Holiday Camps*, 13.
34 David Kynaston, *Family Britain* (London: Bloomsbury, 2010), 664.
35 Giles Emerson, *Sainsbury's: The Record Years, 1950–1992* (London: Haggerston Press, 2006), 59.
36 Stobart, *Spend Spend Spend*, 203.
37 Sam Weatherell, *Foundations: How the Built Environment Made Twentieth-century Britain* (Princeton: Princeton University Press, 2023), 74.
38 Elain Harwood, *Space Hope and Brutalism: English Architecture 1945–1975* (London: Yale University Press, 2016), 35.
39 John Hillier and Martin Blythe, *Poole's Pride Regained, 1964–1974* (Poole: Poole Historical Trust, 1996), 33.
40 Weatherell, *Foundations*, 63.
41 John Grindrod, *Concretopia* (Brecon: Old Street, 2013), 197.
42 Stobart, *Spend Spend Spend*, 207.
43 Otto Saumarez Smith, *Boom Cities* (Oxford: Oxford University Press, 2000), 74–75.
44 Matthew Newton, *Shopping Mall* (London: Bloomsbury, 2017), 17.
45 Kefford, *Arndale*, 565.
46 Kefford, *Arndale*, 565.
47 Stobart, *Spend Spend Spend*, 207.
48 Kefford, *Arndale*, 564.
49 Mary Cathcart Borer, *The British Hotel through the Ages* (Cambridge: Lutterworth Press, 1972), 252.

50 Harwood, *Space Hope and Brutalism*, 412.
51 Borer, *British Hotel*, 248.
52 Lance Wright, 'Hotels,' *The Architectural Review*, September 1972, 132.
53 Borer, *British Hotel*, 249.
54 Harwood, *Space Hope and Brutalism*, 411.
55 David Parry-Jones, *Taff's Acre: A History and Celebration of Cardiff Arms Park* (London: Willow Books, 1984), 17.
56 Parry-Jones, *Taff's Acre*, 28.
57 Hill, *Sport, Leisure and Culture*, 171.
58 Otto Saumarez Smith, 'The Lost World of the British Leisure Centre,' *History Workshop Journal*, Autumn 2019, 193.
59 Anthony Wylson, *Design for Leisure and Entertainment* (London: Newnes-Butterworths, 1980), 69.
60 Smith, 'British Leisure Centre,' 182.
61 Smith, 'British Leisure Centre,' 182.
62 Smith, 'British Leisure Centre,' 182.
63 Gerald Perrin, 'Sports Centres and Swimming Pools,' In *Planning: Buildings for Administration, Entertainment and Recreation*, ed. Edward Mills (London: Newnes-Butterworths, 1976), 6:1.
64 Wylson, *Design for Leisure and Entertainment*, 69.
65 Smith, 'British Leisure Centre,' 182.
66 Wylson, *Design for Leisure and Entertainment*, 69.
67 Hill, *Sport, Leisure and Culture*, 71.
68 Natalie Doury, 'Successfully Integrating Cinemas into Retail and Leisure Complexes: An Operator's Perspective,' *Journal of Leisure Property* 1, no. 2, 2001, 121.
69 Doury, 'Successfully Integrating Cinemas into Retail and Leisure Complexes,' 124–125.
70 Doury, 'Successfully Integrating Cinemas into Retail and Leisure Complexes,' 122.
71 Elain Harwood, 'Markets, Arcades, Precincts and Shopping Centres,' In *100 20th Century Shops*, eds. Susannah Charlton and Elain Harwood (London: Batsford, 2023), 38.
72 Stobart, *Spend Spend Spend*, 224.
73 Kathryn Morrison, *English Shops and Shopping* (New Haven: Yale University Press, 2003), 291.
74 Paulette Pipe, 'Great Expectations,' *DR: The Fashion Business*, 24 November 1990, 58–59.
75 Pipe, 'Great Expectations,' 58–59.
76 Clive Darrow, 'Introduction,' In *Enclosed Shopping Centres*, ed. Clive Darrow (London: Architectural Press, 1972), 12.
77 Peter McColdrick and Mark Thompson, *Regional Shopping Centres* (Aldershot: Avebury, 1992), 14.
78 Morrison, *English Shops*, 295.
79 Emerson, *Sainsbury's*, 104.
80 McColdrick and Thompson, *Regional Shopping Centres*, 2.
81 Phil Ruston, *Out of Town Shopping: The Future of Retailing* (London: The British Library, 1999), 55.
82 John Grindrod, *Iconicon* (London: Faber and Faber, 2022), 168.
83 Ruston, *Out of Town Shopping*, 163.
84 Stobart, *Spend Spend Spend*, 216.
85 Emerson, *Sainsbury's*, 84.
86 Emerson, *Sainsbury's*, 113.
87 Sarah Ryle, *The Making of Tesco* (London: Bantam Press, 2013), 120.
88 Stobart, *Spend Spend Spend*, 216.
89 Andrew Kirby, 'The Architectural Design of UK Supermarkets: 1950–2006' (PhD diss., UAL, 2008), 13.
90 Ryle, *Tesco*, 124.
91 Morrison, *English Shops*, 289.
92 Ruston, *Out of Town Shopping*, 8.
93 Emerson, *Sainsbury's*, 206.
94 Morrison, *English Shops*, 1.

# 5

# CITIZENSHIP

In 1984, Thorp was commissioned by Hart District Council to make a model of the then-proposed Fleet civic centre. The council, which had been formed during the 1974 local government reorganisation, was in need of a new home and the model was intended to share its vision of a new centralised development close to the main shopping street (Figure 5.1). Thorp's model, made at 1:200 scale, showed the four-storey council office building situated next to a combined library, theatre, and community space, well served by ample parking. Grouped together here were some of the most visible services that the citizens of Hart District Council relied on, a proud statement of the council's leadership and ambition, but the new civic centre, designed by the architectural practice Leslie Jones, was just one of many different public buildings Fleet's residents might encounter during their daily lives. These could include schools, police stations, courtrooms, hospitals, job centres, and perhaps even public museums or galleries alongside the local government offices and libraries depicted in Thorp's model, all serving as instruments of the state and the physical means through which the nation's public services were accessed.

Following the more commercial visions of the future of Britain's built environment featured in the previous two chapters relating to work and leisure, this chapter examines the more ideological and political ideas captured by architectural models of public buildings. Tracing an expansion of public services during the twentieth century, it considers how architects were tasked with reimagining the buildings and spaces in which 'cultures of democracy and civic society'[1] were expressed in response to shifting expectations of the welfare and community services that individuals wanted the state to provide. These visions, as always, were explored and projected through architectural models, with Fleet Civic Centre just one of the many such models made by Thorp during the twentieth century, and by examining eighteen of these models this chapter examines how changing visions of the future of Britain's public buildings were shaped by different social and political attitudes towards citizenship, government, health, education, and law. In exploring the buildings and spaces in which the institutions of state carried out their activities in support of the communities they served, both practical and symbolic functions are observed, with public buildings having long acted as highly visible manifestations of the

DOI: 10.4324/9781032715728-6

**FIGURE 5.1**    Model of Fleet Civic Centre. Architect: Leslie Jones. Made by Thorp, 1984. Courtesy Thorp Archive, AUB.

benefits of democratic citizenship,[2] providing not just the services that citizens demand of the state, but symbolic reminders of the state's generosity in committing to them. Countless town halls, schools, hospitals, and many other public buildings were first imagined and then built as confident architectural statements and most of the models outlined in this chapter similarly adopt this symbolism, communicating deeply embedded messages of utopian optimism, social progressiveness, and civic pride. This chapter also takes a broad view of what constitutes a public building, encompassing both buildings owned by the state on behalf of the public and privately owned buildings that offered services to the public. This allows for the inclusion of private hospitals, cathedrals, and university campuses, all of which played active roles in providing the benefits of citizenship during the twentieth century in Britain.

As was the case in the first two chapters dedicated to models of place and home, the expansion of the state's role in providing public services was again largely in response to the growing horror expressed during the late nineteenth century at the health and living conditions of many of the poorest in society, but also the increased formalisation of local government and the consolidation of municipal democracy during the same period.[3] Investigations into the causes and effects of poverty had highlighted the failure of existing social support structures such as the Poor Laws,[4] and through the early twentieth century an ideological shift away from expecting individuals to rely on self-help and the charity of others began to favour increased state spending in order to improve the lives of every citizen.[5] Underlying this change was a belief that society could be shaped to the will of those in charge,[6] and following the sacrifice of so many lives during both World Wars, the idea that those in charge should shape society for the betterment of everyone became the underlying principle of the welfare state. The built environment became a crucial factor in enabling those aspirations to be realised,[7] and as the state and the public services it offered grew in size, so too the need for additional buildings in which to carry out its duties increased, and with local governments handed the responsibilities for administering many public services during the early twentieth century,[8] notions of welfare, citizenship, and democratic government became inexorably entwined.

The architectural models featured in this chapter therefore capture just some of the ideas and debates that were explored as architects responded to the demands those changes placed on the built environment, recording the original optimistic and socially beneficial dreams of projects that in most cases were actually built. Commissioned to communicate different visions of future public buildings and spaces, many of the models served as confident statements of civic and institutional pride, triumphant reminders of the progressive nature of the welfare state, and, at the end of the century, of the era of creeping privatisation that followed.

## Healthy Communities

The types of models of future public buildings and spaces that John Thorp made in the early decades of the twentieth century reflected the overriding desire of the age – to improve the health of the nation and tackle both the causes and consequences of poverty. This proved to an enormously influential ambition that did much to shape Britain's built environment at the time, as previous chapters have already outlined. An 'outpouring of work on poverty, economic insecurity and the living standards of the poor,'[9] served to influence utopian dreams of better quality living for all, with Thorp's order book reflecting contemporary attempts to service those dreams not only through the provision of housing and the rethinking of the organisation of Britain's towns and cities, but in the design and construction of buildings and spaces dedicated to public health and wellbeing. The building of hospitals is something that is perhaps more readily associated with the postwar era and the founding of the National Health Service, and yet there are just as many examples of hospital models in Thorp's records dating to before the Second World War as there are in the decades that followed. These early models were usually directed towards a very different audience to those of postwar models of NHS hospitals, however, being very much for internal stakeholder consumption rather than the general public as most of the hospitals concerned were not state funded, and so the models were often prepared for the benefit of patrons, benefactors, and medical professionals instead (Figure 5.2).

At the start of the twentieth century the provision of healthcare was split between voluntary hospitals funded by charitable donations, local authority hospitals set up to deal with infectious diseases, and Poor Law infirmaries for those in poverty and in need of medical care. With no centrally coordinated approach to caring for the nation's health, and varying standards of care depending on where you lived and your financial means, inequality of provision was rife. This began to change through the welfare reforms of the 1906 Liberal government that started to imagine a future in which a high standard of healthcare would be available to every citizen. With the transfer of the Poor Law guardianships to local authorities in 1909 and the introduction of the 1911 National Health Insurance Act which offered sickness benefits for all wage earners between the ages of sixteen and seventy, the dream of universal healthcare slowly began to take hold.

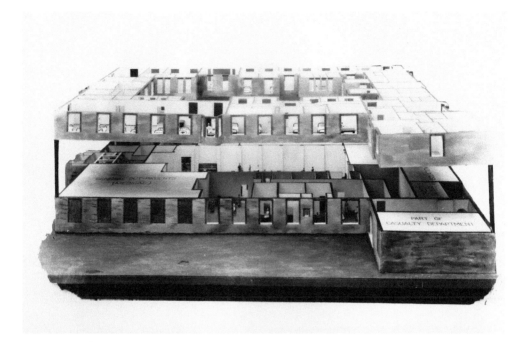

**FIGURE 5.2**    Explanatory model of an unknown hospital wing. Architect: unknown. Made by John Thorp, c1915. Courtesy Thorp Archive, AUB.

In 1900 John Thorp was commissioned to make a series of hospital models for display at that year's Paris Exposition to showcase an important step towards this grand utopian vision – the first state-funded hospitals for infectious diseases to be built in London. The Paris Exposition, with its turn of the century optimism, was filled with visions of the future application of scientific advances and new technologies and was, therefore, the ideal venue to present Britain's latest ideas about how hospitals of the future should be both designed and funded. One of the models was of a temporary hospital in Tottenham while the others were of Brook Hospital in Shooter's Hill, designed by the architect Thomas Aldwinckle to the specification of the Metropolitan Asylums Board (MAB). Thorp's models, given that they were to proudly communicate the MAB's vision of the future of hospital design to the rest of the world, were large and lavish creations (Figure 5.3), and with potentially millions of people likely to see the models while on display at the Exposition, John Thorp designed them with more than just the normal professional audience in mind, adding explanatory labels in both English and French (Figure 5.4). Costing £300 (some £24,000 today), the largest model was six feet square and made using Thorp's tried and tested construction method of cladding timber shapes with carefully painted card facades. Billiard felt was used for the grounds with sponges cut to shape and painted to represent trees. The purpose of the models was to clearly illustrate not only the design principles Aldwinckle and the MAB had established but also the fact that this was a hospital for all, funded through taxation. This was an ambitious vision of the future of healthcare that was far removed from the voluntary hospitals and workhouse infirmaries of the previous century that reflected a shift away from the virtues of self-help and towards a growing expectation that basic medical care should be provided by the state.[10]

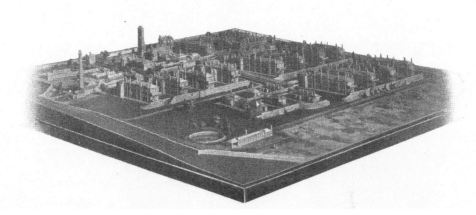

**FIGURE 5.3**    Model of Brook Hospital. Architect: Thomas Aldwinckle. Made by Thorp, 1900. Courtesy Thorp Archive, AUB.

**FIGURE 5.4**    Model of one of Brook Hospital's wards. Architect: Thomas Aldwinckle. Made by Thorp, 1900. Courtesy Thorp Archive, AUB.

The Metropolitan Asylums Board had been established in the 1860s to provide treatment to Londoners suffering from infectious diseases such as smallpox, cholera, and influenza,[11] and in 1891 the Board's responsibilities were expanded through a legal obligation to provide that care free of charge, generating an urgent need for the building of massive new hospitals to cope with demand. Brook was the latest of these and was intended to serve as a template for future hospital designs. Due to the limited diagnostic and therapeutic capabilities available at the start of the twentieth century, hospitals largely relied on the quality of their nursing and the avoidance of further infection as the most effective means of giving their patients the best chance of recovery.[12] This encouraged the design of hospitals to favour good ventilation in large wards positioned to maximise natural sunlight, with the established hospital layout comprising a series of pavilions linked by a covered walkway at ground level.[13] As can be seen in Thorp's model, Aldwinckle followed this same basic approach for his design of Brook Hospital, but in drawing from an exhaustive report by the MAB into the future requirements of its hospitals, set about designing the complex firmly based on the principles of infection control. Two entrances, one for patients and one for staff, kept the infectious isolated upon their arrival, with the two-storey blocks of wards, nurses' homes, laundries, and other facilities kept well apart from one another and linked by separate covered walking routes for staff and patients. Built at a cost of £300,000, Brook Hospital contained nearly five hundred beds for scarlet fever patients and one hundred for those with typhoid or diphtheria.[14] All rooms were kept at the same temperature to prevent draughts, and with the entire site covering twenty-one acres, it was the largest hospital of its kind.

On display in Paris, Thorp's models would have been seen by an enormous number of the nearly fifty million people who visited the exposition, with the MAB's vision of the future of publicly funded healthcare being shared with the widest possible audience. While their making for public consumption was unusual compared to the majority of hospital models Thorp made during the early decades of the twentieth century, they all nevertheless shared a common purpose to communicate messages not only about the design of particular buildings but also the changing approaches to medicine and healthcare behind them. Often labelled with helpful annotations, these models were designed to outline the future benefits of new technologies, treatments, or organisational processes to the people who were either funding them or likely to use them. A later model made by Thorp of St. Mary's Hospital in London in the early 1920s demonstrates this well, with the sectional model of a new building clearly labelled to outline how the spaces were going to be used (Figure 5.5).

**FIGURE 5.5**    Model of St. Mary's Hospital. Architect: unknown. Made by Thorp, c1920. Courtesy Thorp Archive, AUB.

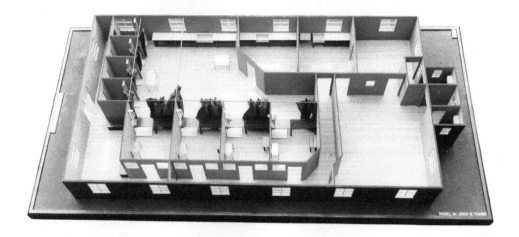

**FIGURE 5.6**   Model of a VD ward. Architect: unknown. Made by Thorp, c1920. Courtesy Thorp Archive, AUB.

As with many of the voluntary hospitals at the time, St. Mary's was at the forefront of both medical science and teaching, constantly developing new techniques and therapies. St. Mary's was very much a scientific institution[15] and Thorp's model projected what was then a state-of-the-art proposal for how hospitals should be designed that placed a much greater emphasis on medicine and surgery over nursing, a very different vision than was on display in the earlier Brook Hospital model. With hospitals having previously been seen as places for the poor, the wealthier middle and upper classes had usually received medical treatment in their own homes, but following the introduction of more sophisticated surgical procedures with better success rates, during the interwar years hospitals increasingly became accepted as the more appropriate locations for operations to be carried out.[16] Voluntary hospitals such as St. Mary's began to expand due to the influx of donations from wealthier patients who were now using their services and the design of future hospitals started to take into consideration the expectations of their new clientele.[17] With the organisation of hospitals shifting away from purely focusing on caring for the medical needs of the poor to providing treatment to people from all social classes and economic circumstances, a greater demand for comfort and privacy was quickly recognised.[18] As a result, during the interwar years the entire image of how hospitals should be used and by whom began to change. These changes in the use of hospitals can be seen in the highly detailed interior of the model of the proposed new building, with smaller ward rooms on the ground floor reflecting the greater desire for privacy, while on the upper floor a pair of operating theatres and sterilising rooms are arranged either side of the x-ray room, highlighting the increased sophistication of the surgeries to be conducted. Another model of a ward building for sufferers of venereal disease made around the same time also demonstrated the advance of not just medicine but attitudes towards privacy and confidentiality, featuring individually curtained treatment bays for what would have been the most intimate of examinations (Figure 5.6).

New ideas relating to healthcare at the time also extended beyond the building of hospitals and following the 1920 Dawson report on the future provision of medical services

**FIGURE 5.7**   Model of a hypothetical playing field. Client: National Playing Fields Association. Made by Thorp, 1937. Courtesy Thorp Archive, AUB.

the importance of preventative measures alongside curative ones was recognised in a recommendation that hospitals should also offer playing fields for outdoor recreation.[19] While the space constraints of urban hospital sites meant this was a fairly impractical suggestion, their inclusion in the report nevertheless reflected a wider recognition of their importance as valuable assets in improving the overall health of the British public. As a result, Thorp's list of commissions during the interwar years began to include an increasing number of models of recreation grounds and playing fields that were responding to a growing interest in the benefits of clean air and exercise (as already seen in Chapter 4), and in 1937, John Thorp was commissioned by the National Playing Fields Association to make a series of models to outline what they imagined the nation's future playing fields should contain. The largest model, of a purely hypothetical playing field, included an athletics track, football, rugby, and hockey pitches, tennis courts, changing rooms, and a car park (Figure 5.7). With its realistic planting and detailed depiction of the pitches, this was a vision of the association's ambition for all local authorities to provide a minimum of five acres of public space for every one thousand people in their communities to ensure everyone had a recreation ground within a reasonable distance of their home. A second model of the proposed King George's Field in Leeds (later known as Red Hall playing fields) included a children's playground in addition to the running track, ten football pitches, and twelve tennis courts (Figure 5.8), and was likely made to highlight the benefits of bidding for one of the hundreds of grants offered between 1937 and 1940 to support the building of playing fields in memory of King George V. Open to local authorities and community groups, the initiative created an additional four thousand acres of community recreation grounds across the country.

The visions of a more athletic, outdoor future that both models portrayed stemmed from the startling revelations about the nation's health and fitness that emerged during the First World War when more than forty percent of army recruits were rejected for not meeting even the most basic physical standards.[20] By 1935 one report claimed that

FIGURE 5.8   Model of King George's Field, Leeds. Client: National Playing Fields Association. Made by Thorp, 1937. Courtesy Thorp Archive, AUB.

ninety-one percent of teenage boys in Britain were not engaging in any physical activities whatsoever,[21] and in response a concerted drive to improve the health and fitness of the nation began. Part of the problem was identified as being the rapid encroachment onto community green spaces by the expanding mass of suburban housing development that was sweeping the land (as seen in Chapters 1 and 2), and in 1925 the National Playing Fields Association had been formed with the aims of protecting these green spaces and promoting the benefits of outdoor recreation, with access to facilities for sport and recreation seen as part of the newly articulated bargain between the public and the state in which health was seen as a fundamental right of citizenship.[22] Both models were projecting visions of an idealised future in which every citizen had access to outdoor recreation spaces and were firmly directed at the institutions and individuals who were able to fund them, the King George's Fields Foundation having raised half a million pounds in donations from wealthy benefactors. These models were therefore highly political in nature, aimed at stakeholders who were able to further the association's cause.

The broader dream of improving public health during the early twentieth century, whether through the provision of facilities to encourage outdoor exercise or through the advancement of hospital design was a largely uncoordinated affair, however, involving contributions from local authorities, voluntary organisations, and pressure groups. Through these interventions, the dreams underpinning the Liberal welfare reforms nevertheless began the gradual march towards the postwar welfare state. As more responsibilities were consolidated under the control of local authorities, including the transfer of the Poor Law guardianships and the increased administration of hospitals and schools, the role of the state in overseeing the provision of community and welfare services began to grow, accompanied by an increased desire to use architectural models that spoke less to internal stakeholders and more directly to the public in order to communicate the grand achievements and future ambitions of the municipal democracies that were leading their citizens into this bold new era.

## Projecting Civic Pride

By the 1930s, the expansion of the reach and power of local authorities, 'with an extraordinary list of responsibilities for the planning and provision of services,'[23] had begun to have a significant influence on the built environment. A golden age of civic pride had arisen in which architecture was to play a vital role through the creation of impressive and highly symbolic public buildings such as libraries, civic centres, and town halls. Architectural models, which by this point had become almost universally recognised as a highly effective means of communicating such visions to the public, enabled local authorities to showcase their future plans not only through the models themselves but through the widespread circulation of photographs of them in newspapers and illustrated magazines, the growth of which during the interwar years had helped to further stimulate the demand for highly realistic models to provide visual content.[24] These photographs helped to connect local people with the ambitions of their elected representatives, meeting an increased democratic responsibility of civic authorities to outline how they were spending the public's money.

For architects working in the 1930s, opportunities to reimagine the town hall and other municipal buildings allowed them to put forward new visions of 'the most important urban markers of democratic citizenship.'[25] Public buildings at the time reflected a 'combined cult of heroism, monumentality and empire,'[26] and with existing Victorian town halls having been designed to dominate central public spaces to compete with 'church and cathedral spires for both supremacy of the urban skyline and the control of their citizen's lives,'[27] the main challenge for architects designing municipal buildings in the interwar years was how to combine an expression of local historic identity with a broader sense of modern civic dignity,[28] and as Thorp's model of Philip Dalton Hepworth's 1937 proposal for Walthamstow Town Hall demonstrates, many of the solutions put forward achieved this with tremendous elegance (Figure 5.9).

The need for major new civic buildings had emerged following a significant change to how the very notion of citizenship and the responsibilities of both individual and state were reframed following the First World War. Soldiers returning from the battlefields of France expected not only better community services and infrastructure but also a greater democratic influence on the decisions being made in their local area.[29] This created an intense pressure 'to match equal political status with a more equal distribution of economic resources.'[30] Essentially, people wanted more from the state in return for their sacrifices and for the benefits of citizenship to be shared more equitably. Following the expansion of the franchise in 1918 and 1928, the demands of mass democracy meant that the size of both central and local government grew rapidly, with the number of civil servants more than doubling. Between 1918 and 1928 state expenditure rose from twelve percent of GDP to twenty nine percent,[31] and with education, health, child services, the poor laws, slum clearance, and social housing all falling under the control of local authorities in the early twentieth century, between 1919 and 1939 annual council expenditure tripled to more than £400 million.[32] As a result of this expansion a raft of new civic buildings were built that conformed to an extended vision of municipal

**FIGURE 5.9**   Model of Walthamstow Town Hall. Architect: Philip Dalton Hepworth. Made by
Thorp, 1937. Courtesy Thorp Archive, AUB.

architecture that embraced the growing role of the state by celebrating the democratic
authority of the institutions they housed. These were to be highly symbolic buildings
designed to proudly display the independence of local government and communicate
ideas of prosperity, dignity, and modernity.[33] Major projects such as Walthamstow Town
Hall, Swansea Guildhall, and Southampton Civic Centre set out very different ideas of
how future municipal buildings should be designed, and the newly formed Walthamstow
Council in particular, having been established in 1929, immediately saw an opportunity
to project a much more democratic vision for its own town hall, holding a public competition in 1932 that Hepworth ultimately won.[34]

Hepworth's original design was a rather unremarkable classical scheme in the spirit
of Sir Christopher Wren, who during the interwar years was revered as an example of
'prolific public service and professionalism.'[35] Such was his influence that almost all of
the sixty six entries to the competition followed the conventions of classical architecture
rather than aligning themselves to the rising tide of modernism.[36] By the time that Thorp's
model was made in 1937, Hepworth's design had evolved as a result of working closely
with the progressive and left leaning council into something that was not quite modernist, but which was also not quite classical, drawing from Swedish architectural influences
in creating what has been described as one of the twentieth century's most dignified solutions to the design of town halls.[37] Adhering to the growing popularity of the civic centre
concept, the competition brief had specified a town hall, library, and law courts to be
included, which Hepworth arranged around a formal pool with tree-lined landscaping
to provide plenty of public open space. As the highly detailed model shows, the three
buildings were to be built from Portland stone with flat roofs and very little external
ornamentation. In place of carved letters and Latin inscriptions, the few statues and
relief panels included were designed to depict concepts of work, education, and fellow-
ship, embodying the intended values of the institution.[38] This was a vision of classicism

**FIGURE 5.10**   Model of Council House, Bristol. Architect: Vincent Harris. Made by Thorp, 1938. Courtesy Thorp Archive, AUB.

'stripped of almost all decoration,'[39] democratised to appeal to every citizen. Reflecting an increasing desire for less decorative, more monumental interpretations of classical architecture, Hepworth's design embraced a Scandinavian simplicity that demonstrated a 'modern civic vernacular rich in symbolism and craftsmanship,'[40] and Thorp's model, widely featured in both local and national newspapers at the time of its unveiling, clearly communicated the bold future intentions of this newly formed council, with its precision and attention to detail helping to make a confident statement about the institution's independence, authority, and sense of pride.

Just one year later Thorp produced an equally striking model of the proposed Bristol city hall, then known as Council House (Figure 5.10), which displayed a similarly transitional design that again leaned towards a functionalist approach by keeping the formality of neo-Georgian architecture but without the towers so typical of earlier civic buildings. Originally planned as a construction project to help relieve rising unemployment in the city,[41] Council House was designed by Vincent Harris, who had already made his name with grand public buildings such as Glamorgan County Hall in Cardiff and Manchester Central Library. For Bristol, Harris clad an internal concrete structure with a red brick and Portland stone facade, the twin pavilions at either end framing the approach to the main entrance in order to emphasise the building's imposing scale. With the model demonstrating how the building's curved form would hug an ornamental pool on the edge of College Green, the inclusion of four cars helped to convey a message of modernity while the figures walking along the permitter highlighted the monumentality of the design, which was intended to act as an unmissable landmark to inspire a strong sense of pride in the city's democratic institutions. Photographs of the model were featured in all the local newspapers where it generated a great deal of excitement about its impressive statement of civic authority, and with the Second World War delaying the completion of the project until 1952, the proposal illustrated by Thorp's model displays subtle differences to what was actually built.

Alongside town and city halls, libraries provided another important opportunity where the provision of a valued public service could be accompanied by a strong reminder of the institutions that were responsible for them. Recognised as an 'emblematic part of the public realm,'[42] during the 1930s a number of impressive library buildings were built by both local authorities and the larger universities to serve as unmissable symbols of civic and institutional pride. In 1930, John Thorp was commissioned to make a model of Giles Gilbert Scott's design for Cambridge University Library which was very much in this vein, offering a bold and forward-thinking vision of how libraries of the future should be designed that balanced a traditional architectural style with the latest construction materials and techniques (Figure 5.11). Scott's proposal, as Gavin Stamp once noted, was emblematic of British civic architecture of the time in that its style was quite hard to define. Monumental in scope, embracing modernity rather than modernism, and extending a 'stylish eclecticism,'[43] the design also drew from the North American skyscraper tradition, likely as the bulk of the funds to build the library had come from the American philanthropist John D. Rockefeller, and it was at his insistence that the entrance was topped by a grand and imposing tower. As the main patron, the highly detailed model was likely built to outline the final design to Rockefeller himself and to serve as a visible reminder of his generosity before the building was completed.

In conjunction with the university's librarian, Alwyn Scholfield, Giles Gilbert Scott placed efficiency central to the design, intending that the staff should be able to retrieve any book within just a few minutes. As Thorp's model showed, from the exterior the placement of the windows gave the impression that the main building only had three floors when in fact there were to be seven and Scott designed the building so that the

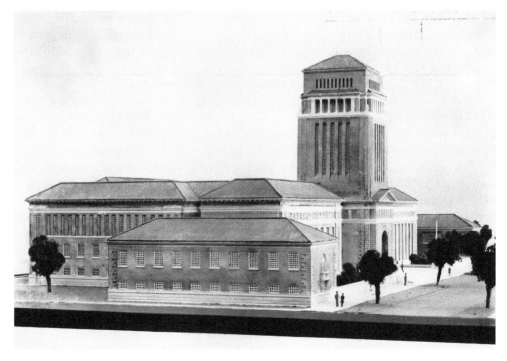

**FIGURE 5.11**  Model of Cambridge University Library. Architect: Giles Gilbert Scott. Made by Thorp, 1930. Courtesy Thorp Archive, AUB.

metal bookcases formed part of the steel structure that carried the weight of the roof and floors.[44] The one hundred and sixty feet high tower was to be used as storage and although the library was still designed to rely on books being requested at a desk rather than adopting an open access approach where you could browse the shelves yourself, this was nevertheless a very modern take on how the operation of future libraries should be organised and a bold architectural statement that emphasised the university's national and international standing. It was also, of course, designed to emphasise Rockefeller's national and international standing as well.

The rise of such grand municipal buildings in the 1930s, particularly town halls in continuing the Victorian approach of competing with churches and cathedrals to dominate their surroundings, did not go unchallenged by either the Anglican or Catholic churches, however, and in 1934, John Thorp's son, Leslie, lead the construction of one of the largest and most impressive architectural models of a single building ever made in Britain, that of Edwin Lutyens' unrealised design for the Metropolitan Cathedral of Christ the King in Liverpool (Figure 5.12). Had the cathedral been completed it would

**FIGURE 5.12**  Model of the unbuilt proposal for the Metropolitan Cathedral of Christ the King in Liverpool. Architect: Edwin Lutyens. Made by Leslie Thorp, 1934. Courtesy Thorp Archive, AUB.

have been the largest public building ever constructed in Britain, a riposte not only to secular municipal authority but also to Giles Gilbert Scott's Anglican cathedral which was already under construction in the city. The Catholic Archbishop of Liverpool, Richard Downey, had first approached Lutyens to design a new cathedral in 1929, and when unveiled to the public in model form at the 1934 Royal Academy Summer Exhibition in London, it was clear that his intention was to build something so extraordinary that Lutyens' himself estimated that it would take two hundred years to build. Lutyens was the leading architect of the age, known for his palatial public buildings that included the enormous Viceroy's House in New Delhi as well as monuments such as the Cenotaph in London. Developed from his 1932 design for the Thiepval Memorial in France, Lutyens' proposal was incredibly daring, standing at more than five hundred feet tall, and with a dome one hundred and sixty feet across and three hundred feet high, the cathedral would have been larger than St. Paul's in London and taller than St. Peter's in Rome.

The model was intended to help raise the funds needed to construct such an enormous structure and it took over a year to build with a team of twelve modelmakers putting in over 200,000 hours' work at a cost of £5000, some £250,000 today. To support Leslie, five additional modelmakers were employed specifically to work on the model so as not to paralyse the rest of the business and enable other commissions to be completed. Made from solid timber at a scale of ¼ of an inch to 1 foot, approximately 1:50 scale, Leslie finished turning the giant dome by hand on a specially adapted lathe. The completed model was breathtaking, seventeen feet long and eleven feet high, conveying the full power and drama of Lutyens' design. Too large to be exhibited in the exhibition's architecture room, it was placed in the central hall where it dominated the entire space. Recalling the scale and importance of the Great Model of St Paul's built for Christopher Wren by the joiners William and Richard Cleere in 1675, Leslie Thorp's model was a resounding success that generated an outpouring of funds that enabled the construction of the crypt to begin, although progress was swiftly curtailed by the outbreak of the Second World War and in the age of austerity that followed Lutyens' enormously expensive design was abandoned, with a modernist design by Frederick Gibberd eventually built on top of Lutyens' crypt and which was consecrated in 1967. The model of Lutyens' design still survives today in the Liverpool Museum, and had his grand vision been completed few state-funded public buildings would ever have matched it in terms of scale and monumentality, a clear sign from the Catholic Church that secular, civic intuitions, in Liverpool at least, did not hold a total monopoly on ambitious expressions of power and pride.

## Welfare for Tomorrow

Following the Second World War, as every chapter in this book makes abundantly clear, the use of architectural models skyrocketed as architects, planners, and engineers set about communicating their plans for the rebuilding and modernisation of almost every aspect of the built environment. Nowhere was this more prevalent than in the provision of public buildings, with the requirements of new schools and hospitals driving an intense period of exploration as architects put forward countless visions of future buildings that would be fit to serve the modern demands of the nation's communities. Thorp, entering its eighth decade of business during the early 1950s, was at the centre of the modelmaking boom that followed, although in terms of models of public buildings its dominance was challenged by the growth of in-house modelmaking workshops within local authority architects' departments. The challenge facing architects (and, by extension, modelmakers) at the time was the enormous task of providing the infrastructure for what William Beveridge's 1942 report on Social Insurance and Allied Services had proposed: the welfare state. In putting forward an ambitious plan for social security and universal healthcare and education, Beveridge was clear that this was nothing less than what people were owed after their wartime sacrifices.[45]

Architectural models were used extensively to explain to the public what was being proposed and to outline the enormous shift in responsibility that the state was embracing. As with interwar models of civic buildings there was an implicit understanding that the public needed to be kept informed about how their taxes were being used, particularly in such new and far-reaching ways. Public funds were being spent for the benefit of everyone in society and many of the architectural models of public buildings made during this period were characterised by an expression of the democratic utopianism that accompanied the implementation of the welfare state. With thousands of new schools to build, dozens of new hospitals, and countless police stations, libraries, and government offices, dedicated architects' departments were established in almost every local authority in the country, the state employing more than half of all registered architects by 1957.[46] Drawing the brightest new talent graduating from architectural schools, the architects' departments responsible for creating the buildings integral to the delivery of the welfare state fully embraced the principles of the modern movement,[47] which was seen as the perfect match for the utopian ambitions of the enormous social intervention that was being planned. Following the provision of social housing (as outlined in Chapter 2), the second highest priority of the successive postwar governments that implemented the welfare state was the extension of secondary education.[48] One in five schools in England and Wales had been destroyed or badly damaged during the Second World War,[49] and with postwar birth rates rapidly increasing the government's commitment to secondary education for all until the age of fifteen required an urgent and extensive schools building programme. Between 1945 and 1955 more than two and a half thousand new schools were built,[50] which for secondary schools initially comprised the tripartite system of grammar, technical, and secondary moderns, before later being dominated by the comprehensive school. The question facing many architects working in local authority architects' departments at the time was how they could design 'fresh, imaginative and practical schools… not just for the few but for the many?'[51]

As a result, architectural models of various concepts for new school buildings poured from modelmakers' workshops across the country, including Thorp's. Architects at both local authorities and the Ministry of Education worked with teachers, education specialists, and school administrators to develop school designs based on the concept a central four-storey block of classrooms with specialist rooms such as workshops, laboratories, and halls clustered around it along a central spine,[52] and in 1952 Thorp was commissioned to make a model of a version of this design that demonstrated as much an ideological change to secondary education as it did an architectural one (Figure 5.13). Designed by the architects' department of West Riding County Council, Calder High School in the village of Mytholmroyd near Hebden Bridge was planned to be one of the first comprehensive schools to be built in Britain, replacing the local grammar school to provide

FIGURE 5.13  Model of Calder High School. Architect: West Riding County Council Architects' Department. Made by Thorp, 1952. Courtesy Thorp Archive, AUB.

universal secondary education for all. Adopting a floor plan centred on a quad of classrooms with longitudinal wings enclosing twin playgrounds, Calder made use of its open aspect by incorporating large windows to maximise natural daylight and ventilation, its steel and concrete construction using prefabricated panels as had already been demonstrated so successfully by Hertfordshire County Council's new school programme.[53] In responding to the demands of the dream of comprehensive education as a replacement for the tripartite system, the architects behind the design of Calder High School sought to balance both the technical and humanistic elements of modern architecture by providing a space in which this particularly egalitarian dream could be realised, but as Thorp's model suggests, this was a vision that was struggling to break free from the confines of postwar austerity, built cheaply and resulting in a rather prison-like appearance. The model itself, employing the prewar technique of cladding timber blocks with simply painted card facings, was also cheaply made and its simplistic finish gave little indication of the radical new approach to education that this building was to house.

Following the focus on school buildings, architectural models of hospitals began to appear in Thorp's records once more as architects were tasked with the even greater challenge of reimagining the buildings that would become the backbone of the National Health Service. Initial progress during the 1950s was slow, partly due to materials shortages but mainly because the organisational challenges of integrating thousands of separate institutions into a cohesive national system needed to be addressed first. By the early 1960s a hospital building plan had nevertheless been established that set out a clear vision

**FIGURE 5.14**   Model of Poole Hospital. Client: Wessex Regional Health Authority. Made by
Throp, 1964. Courtesy Thorp Archive, AUB.

that involved the closure of more than one thousand smaller hospitals, the extension of
three hundred and sixty larger ones, and the construction of ninety entirely new hospitals
at the cost of some £500 million.[54] Design work had already begun during the 1950s,
heavily influenced by a Nuffield Provincial Trust study into the function and design of
future hospitals,[55] and central to the overall strategy was the provision of general district
hospitals serving a population of 300,000 people each.[56] Poole Hospital was announced
in 1957 as one of these new district hospitals to replace the earlier Cornelia voluntary
hospital that had been built in the town in 1907. Designed by the in-house architects of
the Wessex Regional Health Authority, Poole incorporated the latest thinking on how
hospitals should be organised with the proposal evolving over time as new guidance was
released from the government, and in 1964 Thorp was commissioned to make a large
model of the hospital site as it was then projected to be realised (Figure 5.14). The overall design of the main hospital building conformed to an emerging template that was to
become a standard layout followed not only across Britain but around the world that
involved the stacking of wards above a two-storey podium that contained the operating
theatres and other diagnostic departments.[57] Pioneered by the Princess Margaret Hospital in Swindon in 1953, this was a future-facing design for hospital care for the masses
that took the principles of modernist architecture and paired them with the clinical and
surgical needs of modern medicine. The wards were to be T-shaped, serving as prototypes
for future hospitals and designed to combine maximum privacy for patients with an ease
of care by using an open plan layout with a central nurses' station containing the latest
diagnostic equipment such as x-ray viewers.

Thorp's model, with the thirteen-storey nursing accommodation block in the foreground and the main hospital building behind, captured both the size and startlingly
modern design of the scheme extremely well. In comparison to the model of Calder High
School, this was evidently an expensive commission, with an impressive amount of detail

included and made using modern model construction methods with painted card and plastic facades covering Perspex cores to better represent the modernist architecture of the design. Photographed against a sky background and lit with prominent and correctly angled shadows matched to the hospital's actual orientation on a summer's day, the model presented a convincing and optimistic vision of the NHS as the central pillar of the community, bright, clean, and an unmissable symbol of significant state investment.

The creation of the welfare state and the continued expansion of both local and central government responsibilities in managing public services during the postwar era also generated a need for additional office space, and while still referring to the traditions of the past through the symbolic nature of their design, postwar civic administrative buildings sought to provide much better facilities for their staff, including spacious canteens and the introduction of open plan offices.[58] The unbuilt proposal for Rochford Rural District Council's new offices, as projected by Thorp's 1965 model (Figure 5.15), while surprisingly large for such a small and sparsely populated community, was typical of such schemes at the time. Designed by Edward Mills, this was an example of the 'slab' approach to civic offices that grew in popularity during the 1960s.[59] Reflecting the dominance of the car during the 1960s as already seen in the earlier chapters on work and leisure, the council's offices were to be relocated to an edge of town location, as while Mills still considered town centres to be the hearts of their communities, in his view

**FIGURE 5.15** Model of an unbuilt proposal for Rochford Rural District Council. Architect: Edward Mills & Partners. Made by Thorp, 1965. Courtesy Thorp Archive, AUB.

building on rural land on the outskirts of towns allowed the design of such facilities to be realised without compromise.[60] The block-like design straddled the entrance roadway on stilts, providing enough space for the functions of the council and the new ways of working that were becoming common in civic offices that included photocopiers, automated telephone systems, typing pools, and even internal document transfer systems.[61] The proposal for Rochford, despite its modernist appearance, was still implicit in the same expression of traditional social structures and the deference to state authority seen in the prewar proposals for both Walthamstow and Bristol, however, with the institution of local government literally looming over its citizens as they arrive underneath and rise up from the entranceway into the elevated offices above.

By the middle of the 1960s, the models of future schools, hospitals, and other public buildings that Thorp was commissioned to make had begun to reflect a period of introspection during which the first postwar generation of such buildings had been tested in practice, which helped to inform further experimentations with different approaches, particularly within the design of schools. Thorp's 1965 model of an early proposal for what eventually became Kelsey Park School in Beckenham clearly shows the change in school design that emerged as a result, particularly when compared to the earlier model of Calder High School (Figure 5.16). The rate of school building following the Second World War was quite extraordinary, with a new school being completed every day between 1950 and 1970.[62] Different approaches, both pedagogical and architectural, were explored through models, largely driven by a major push for comprehensive schools

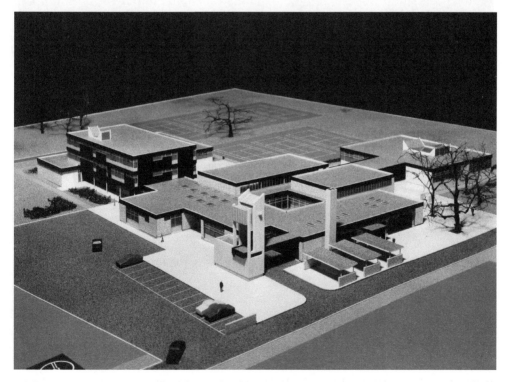

**FIGURE 5.16**   Model of an unbuilt proposal for Kelsey Park School. Architect: unknown. Made by Thorp, 1965. Courtesy Thorp Archive, AUB.

to replace the secondary moderns after it was recognised that comprehensive education offered a more successful integrated learning environment over the segregated tripartite system. The Kelsey Park model reflected these new ideas, although it depicted an unrealised version of the school that was just one of many put forward between 1958 and its eventual completion ten years later. Compared to the model of Calder High School, Kelsey Park was offering a much more architecturally characterful approach to the design of schools, with greater space given over to parking, the inclusion of bike sheds, and a more irregular plan based around the actual projected use of the space rather than an aesthetic symmetry. Close attention was given to bringing natural daylight into every space, either through skylights or the central quad, with the overall layout following the by then proven approach used in both school and hospital design of stacking repetitive elements vertically (in this case classrooms) with the hall, library, workshops, and science laboratories feeding outwards. The model itself, free from the austerity constraints of the immediate postwar era, was also far more inviting, using modern materials and techniques to present a crisp and appealing vision of this future school.

Three years later, further major changes to Britain's education system were evidenced in a stunning timber model outlining the overall masterplan for Southampton University (Figure 5.17), as with the postwar population boom moving its way through the school

**FIGURE 5.17**  Masterplan model of the University of Southampton. Architect: Basil Spence. Made by Thorp, 1968. Courtesy Thorp Archive, AUB.

and towards a university sector in desperate need of additional capacity, new thoughts about the design of university campuses began to emerge. The desire for social equality that lay behind the foundation of the welfare state had been accompanied by an ambition to remove the sense of elitism from higher education[63] and this could only be achieved by massively expanding and broadening the social makeup of the student population.[64] With state funding increasing from £7 million to £157 million a year by 1966, and student numbers rising from 82,000 to 236,000 by 1970,[65] new universities were clearly needed to cope with demand, with Sussex, York, East Anglia, Warwick, Kent, Essex, and Lancaster universities all founded during the 1960s. The creation of entirely new universities gave architects an opportunity to set out a radical new vision of what a university should be in a modern democracy,[66] driven in part by a desire to move away from the 'red brick' image of the Victorian and interwar universities and to build on greenfield sites on the edges of towns and cities.[67] This resulted in a new concept drawn from a merging of existing British and American practices that considered the university as a miniature, idealised town,[68] and Thorp's model of Southampton University reflected this new approach.

Proposals for new and expanded university campuses were invariably accompanied by large architectural models of the kind that had previously outlined the plans for the postwar New Towns and which were made to communicate the passionately modernist and often radical ideas of architects such as Chamberlin, Powell and Bon, Hugh Casson, Alison and Peter Smithson, and Basil Spence, all of whom helped to set the tone for this new imagining of what a university campus should be. It was to Spence, following his work on the new University of Sussex, that the University of Southampton turned to design their own campus masterplan in 1958. Having been granted its royal charter in 1952, Southampton was growing rapidly and keen to compete with the new universities by building its reputation as a nationally important centre of learning. Spence oversaw the design of most of the buildings constructed on the university's Highfield campus over the next ten years, and Thorp's 1968 model outlined Spence's updated plan as it was then envisaged for completion in the late 1970s. Spence's plan cleared two halves of the campus on either side of a main road with more compact buildings arranged in open parkland adjacent to Southampton Common to the west (on the right of the model) and denser areas of more substantial buildings to the east.[69] The 1:500 scale model, as was the fashion at the time, was made entirely from timber, stacked vertically in slices to create an abstract impression of the forms of the buildings. The choice of timber and the dramatic lighting in the photographs of the model suited Spence's brutalist style well, and the model showcased a clear alternative to the traditional civic campus. This was a dream of a dynamic, modern, state-funded university fit for the future, and one that must have seemed utterly revolutionary to most students, academics, and the general public at the time.[70]

As a result of the enormous demand for new universities, schools, council offices, and hospitals during the postwar era, architects were granted an unprecedented opportunity to reimagine the form and function of many different types of public buildings, and in doing so they embraced modernist architecture and an optimism about the future that was expressed through their confident designs. That hopefulness was captured in the architectural models of the time, acting as utopian surrogates for the future they were attempting to build and testaments to the sustained political consensus that had enabled the grand dream of the welfare state to be realised. That consensus was shortly to expire, however, and during the final decades of the twentieth century, the future visions of public buildings captured in Thorp's models shrank in both number and ambition.

## Public Buildings and Private Futures

The collapse of Britain's economy in the mid-1970s did much to temper the construction of new public buildings. With a softening of ambition accompanied by the perhaps inevitable reassessment of the success or otherwise of the modern movement, architects found the public sector's role as the grand patron of postwar architecture coming to an end,[71] which resulted in a wholescale move towards private practice as local authority architects' departments were reduced in size. After thirty years of seemingly endless investment during which 'the welfare state took shape in steel frames and concrete,'[72] a new set of ideas were coming to the fore that consolidated under the political leadership of the Thatcher government from 1978 onwards. 'Denationalisation' became a priority, a softer term for what later became recognised as privatisation,[73] and following the 1983 general election this was pursued with enthusiasm, and while the core elements of the welfare state remained out of bounds, investment in many areas was dramatically curtailed. The final decades of the twentieth century were by no means devoid of new ideas about the future design of public buildings, however, and while the number of models of such buildings that Thorp was commissioned to make drastically fell, replaced by endless models of housing estates and out of town supermarkets, they did still occasionally appear. The audiences that many of these models were aimed at nevertheless shifted as the design of public buildings increasingly became the work of privately employed architects. A change back to internal consumption, with models communicating ideas from an architect to their client and stakeholders, as had been the case during the opening decades of the century, became the norm once more, and models of public buildings were increasingly reduced to acting as sales tools rather than to inform the public about what was planned.

Thorp's 1977 model of the proposed new British Library in London stands as an example not only of the shift towards architects from the private sector dominating the design of public buildings but also the declining political appetite for such large public projects (Figure 5.18). The public library embodied many of the civic values that had shaped postwar Britain,[74] and with the use of libraries peaking in the late 1970s, Thorp's model of the British Library generated much excitement. With St. Pancras Station, George Gilbert Scott's Gothic hotel, and many other buildings surrounding the site rendered in outline only, the library, designed by Colin St John Wilson and M.J. Long, appears to crawl along the ground to dominate the plot without overshadowing its more famous neighbour. This was only the latest of many models of various different visions for the British Library that had been made during its long gestation, however, and it was to the great relief of those involved that this design was finally approved for construction in 1978, although the building was not fully completed until 1997.[75]

The British Library as an organisation had been spun out of the British Museum in 1973, some ten years after the idea to create a dedicated building for the library had first been proposed, and the dream was to bring together the library's dispersed collection which was being stored in at least seven different locations. The initial plans developed

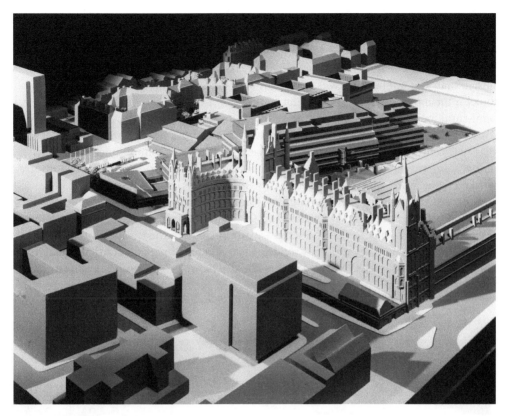

**FIGURE 5.18**   Model of the British Library. Architects: Colin St John Wilson and M.J. Long. Made by Thorp, 1977. Courtesy Thorp Archive, AUB.

by Wilson and Leslie Martin had envisioned the demolition of an entire block of buildings in Bloomsbury directly opposite the British Museum, but under pressure from the Borough Council and the local MP this was rejected by the government in 1967. In 1970 Colin St John Wilson (working with his often uncredited wife, M.J. Long) was invited to put forward another, less ambitious proposal for the same site, but this was ultimately turned down as well. Finally in 1978, Wilson and Long's third design for a less contentious plot of land adjacent to St. Pancras Station was approved. Wilson and Long's design drew from the brick architectural detailing of St. Pancras, Wilson's interest in ships and sailing, and Giles Gilbert Scott's design for Cambridge University Library seen earlier in this chapter. In balancing monumentality and accessibility, this vision of a grand public building to house the library's 170 million books demonstrated the continued power of such schemes to embody the values of public service, but its much-delayed realisation also highlighted the changing political landscape that had begun to slow the progress of all major schemes that were drawing from the public purse.

The political climate of the 1980s had firmly brought into question the role of the state in providing public services and the power and financial influence of local government was severely reduced. The NHS, while not under any existential threat, was not immune from change either, and throughout the 1980s Thorp's order book notably contained far more models of private hospitals than it did public ones. In 1981, Thorp made a model of a proposed Bupa hospital in Cardiff, and while clearly very well made was a relatively inexpensive commission, aimed, as was increasingly common, at the directors of Bupa rather than the public; this was, after all, a private hospital. At first glance the model looks a lot more like one of a budget hotel than a medical facility, benefiting from its semi-rural location on the edge of the city with its ample parking provision (Figure 5.19). This was deliberate, communicating a new vision of how hospitals should be designed that was centred on a whole-patient experience rather than simply medical efficiency,[76] and a shift was underway to incorporate better quality interiors, the inclusion of artworks on the walls, pot plants in the corners of rooms, and a greater overall sense of comfort to create a more welcoming environment. Private hospitals led the way in the adoption of patient-centred approaches to their design, primarily due to the commercial need to make their expensive product more attractive than the free version being offered by the NHS, which by the time this model was made for Bupa, still contained a considerable number of 'pay beds' where patients could pay for private rooms and priority care inside public hospitals.

**FIGURE 5.19** Model of Bupa Cardiff. Architect: unknown. Made by Thorp, 1981. Courtesy Thorp Archive, AUB.

With an increase in models of private hospitals and even private schools in Thorp's order book during the 1980s and 1990s reflecting the increased appetite for private sector alternatives to the provision of costly public services, at the same time one form of public building was undergoing a thorough reimagining that resulted in a number of architectural models of a building type that Thorp had rarely made before: law courts. Changes made to the legal system in 1971 had replaced both the assizes and quarter session courts with the newly created Crown Court which was to permanently sit in seventy-seven locations across England and Wales,[77] creating a need for purpose-built buildings. As a result, more than one hundred new Crown, County, and Magistrates courts were built between 1979 and 1993, providing an opportunity for architects to completely rethink this most imposing of public buildings, models of which duly followed.

As had been the case with the British Library, these large public projects were subject to constant delays and cost overruns, with Croydon's new court building, in particular, taking more than twenty years to be completed. Thorp's 1982 model of the proposal for Croydon Court captured an earlier and more architecturally complex version of what was eventually built (Figure 5.20) and comparing the model to the building today an inevitable process of cost engineering can be seen with the central glass atrium having been omitted, although the overall form was constructed as planned. Croydon Court was designed and built by the Property Services Agency, the government agency that was tasked with building and maintaining state property. The design, internally at least, adhered to a more egalitarian

**FIGURE 5.20**    Model of Croydon Court. Architect: Property Services Agency. Made by Thorp, 1982. Courtesy Thorp Archive, AUB.

notion of how the hierarchies of citizenship should be expressed, such as putting an end to the tradition of elevating the judge above the accused. This was to be a more democratic courtroom, with architects having recognised that the symbolism present in the design of court buildings heavily influenced a community's perception of justice, and that their designs 'should reflect a commitment to legibility, the social importance of the law, respect for dignity and cultural identity, and safety.'[78]

With the Property Services Agency holding an effective monopoly on the design of such buildings, however, in 1981 the government insisted that seventy percent of their work should be contracted to private consultants, leading to their eventual privatisation in 1993. This opening up of the design of government buildings through compulsory competitive tendering gave a much wider pool of architects the opportunity to experiment with new ideas,[79] and in 1990, Thorp was hired to make a timber model of Alistair Sutherland's design of Preston Crown Court, which was one of thirty-three new court buildings designed by private architectural firms.[80] As the model shows, this was a much more open and welcoming vision of a court building, the large expanse of glass along one wall and its softer, less monumental overall form standing in stark contrast to the design of Croydon court (Figure 5.21). With the use of timber in the model forcing an abstraction that focuses attention on the concept of the building's design rather than its

**FIGURE 5.21** Model of Preston Crown Court. Architect: Alistair Sutherland. Made by Thorp, 1990. Courtesy Thorp Archive, AUB.

reality, this was once again a client model, made by Thorp so that the architect could communicate the final design to those that were paying for the building rather than to those who might to use it.

The models of public buildings that Thorp made during the final years of the twentieth century ultimately reflected the ambition of consecutive Conservative governments to redefine the relationship between citizen and state, with the architectural ideas they represented evolving to meet both the changing needs of the people who were interacting with public services and the shifting ideological assumptions behind their provision. With the number of new projects slowing and models of public buildings increasingly being aimed towards private audiences, architectural models nevertheless continued to capture what was proposed, presenting the future dreams of health, education, law, and civic pride in moments of confidence and optimism that symbolised the bold and costly investments made by the institutions of state on the individual's behalf. It would, however, be some years after the election of the New Labour government in 1997 that the demand for architectural models of public buildings would once again become a major line of work for not only Thorp but countless other modelmakers in Britain, fuelled by the consequences of both devolution and a frantic rebuilding of schools and hospitals that echoed the intensity of the postwar era. All of this took place in a different century, however, and remains another history yet to be told.

## Notes

1  Neal Shasore, *Designs on Democracy* (Oxford: Oxford University Press, 2022), 17.
2  Robert Proctor, 'Citizenship: Welfare and the Democratic State in Percy Thomas's Civic Architecture,' In *Reconstruction*, eds. Neal Shasore and Jessica Kelly (London: Bloomsbury, 2023), 275.
3  Colin Cunningham, *Victorian and Edwardian Town Halls* (London: Routledge, 1981), 8.
4  George Boyer, *The Winding Road to the Welfare State* (Princeton: Princeton University Press, 2019), 16.
5  Peter Scott and James Walker, 'Inequality, Living Standards and Welfare Provision,' In *20th Century Britain*, eds. Nichole Robertson, John Singleton, and Avram Taylor (Abingdon: Routledge, 2023), 56.
6  Chris Renwick, *Bread for All: The Origins of the Welfare State* (London: Penguin, 2017), 8.
7  Shasore, *Designs on Democracy*, 20.
8  J.A. Chandler, *Explaining Local Government* (Manchester: Manchester University Press, 2007), 78.
9  Boyer, *The Winding Road*, 169.
10  Harriet Blakeman, 'Sickness: Advances in British Hospital Design after the First World War,' In *Reconstruction*, eds. Neal Shasore and Jessica Kelly (London: Bloomsbury, 2023), 348.
11  Gwendoline Ayres, *England's First State Hospitals 1867–1930* (London: Wellcome Institute, 1971). 31.
12  Derek Stow, 'Transformation in Healthcare Architecture,' In *Changing Hospital Architecture*, ed. Sunad Prasad (London: RIBA, 2008), 15.
13  Stow, 'Transformation in Healthcare Architecture,' 15.
14  Ayres, *England's First State Hospitals*, 281.
15  Elsbeth Heaman, *St Mary's: The History of a Teaching Hospital* (Liverpool: Liverpool University Press, 2003), 24.
16  Blakeman, 'Sickness,' 334.
17  Blakeman, 'Sickness,' 334.
18  Blakeman, 'Sickness,' 342.
19  Blakeman, 'Sickness,' 339–340.
20  Martin Pugh, *We Danced All Night* (London: Vintage, 2009), 42.
21  Juliet Gardiner, *The Thirties: An Intimate History* (London: HarperCollins, 2010), 515,

22 Barry Doyle, 'Democracy, Diversity, Dispersal,' In *Reconstruction*, eds. Neal Shasore and Jessica Kelly (London: Bloomsbury, 2023), 354.
23 David Jeremiah, *Architecture and Design for the Family in Britain, 1900–1970* (Manchester: Manchester University Press, 2000), 30.
24 Davide Deriu, 'Transforming Ideas into Pictures: Model Photography and Modern Architecture,' in *Camera Constructs*, eds. H. Higgott and T. Wray (Abingdon: Routledge, 2012), 159.
25 Proctor, 'Citizenship,' 275.
26 G.A. Bremner, *Building Greater Britain* (London: Paul Mellon Centre for Studies in British Art, 2022), 179.
27 John Stewart, *Twentieth Century Town Halls* (Abingdon: Routledge, 2019), 32.
28 Roethe, 'A Pretty Toy,' 25.
29 Shasore, *Designs on Democracy*, 27.
30 Rodney Lowe, *The Welfare State in Britain since 1945* (Basingstoke: Palgrave, 2005) 21.
31 Jonathan Clarke, 'Development: Speculative Office Development and Public Sector Tenants,' In *Reconstruction*, eds. Neal Shasore and Jessica Kelly (London: Bloomsbury, 2023), 94.
32 Chandler, *Local Government*, 148.
33 Jonathan Roethe, 'A Pretty Toy or Purely Functional?' In *The Architecture of Public Service*, eds. Elain Harwood and Alan Powers (London: Twentieth Century Society, 2017), 32.
34 Roethe, 'A Pretty Toy or Purely Functional?' 27.
35 Shasore, *Designs on Democracy*, 49.
36 Stewart, *Town Halls*, 92.
37 Stewart, *Town Halls*, 31.
38 Roethe, 'A Pretty Toy,' 37.
39 Stewart, *Town Halls*, 31.
40 Gavin Stamp, *Interwar: British Architecture 1919–1939* (London: Profile, 2024), 181.
41 Elain Harwood, *Space Hope and Brutalism: English Architecture 1945–1975* (London: Yale University Press, 2016), 539.
42 Robert Drake, 'Public Libraries in the Twentieth Century,' In *The Architecture of Public Service*, eds. Elain Harwood and Alan Powers (London: Twentieth Century Society, 2017), 115.
43 Stamp, *Interwar*, 12.
44 Anthony Thompson, *Library Buildings of Britain and Europe* (London: Butterworth, 1963), 239.
45 Renwick, *Bread for All*, 1.
46 Nicholas Bullock, *Building the Post-war World: Modern Architecture and Reconstruction in Britain* (London: Routledge, 2002), 219.
47 Stewart, *Town Halls*, 263.
48 Andrew Saint, *Towards a Social Architecture: The Role of School-building in Post War England* (London: Yale University Press, 1987), 36.
49 Elain Harwood, *England's Schools* (Swindon: English Heritage, 2010), 73.
50 Barry Turner, *Beacon for Change* (London: Aurum, 2011), 2.
51 Saint, *Towards a Social Architecture*, 35.
52 Alfred Roth, *New School Building* (London: Thames and Hudson, 1966), 233.
53 Bullock, *Building the Post-war World*, 186.
54 Lowe, *The Welfare State*, 193.
55 Stow, 'Transformation in Healthcare Architecture,' 16.
56 Stow, 'Transformation in Healthcare Architecture,' 19.
57 Stow, 'Transformation in Healthcare Architecture,' 16.
58 Susan O'Connor, 'The Body Politic and the Body Corporate,' In *The Architecture of Public Service*, eds. Elain Harwood and Alan Powers (London: Twentieth Century Society, 2017), 175.
59 O'Connor, 'The Body Politic and the Body Corporate,' 166.
60 David Hutchison, Graham Locke and Natalie Robinson, 'Town Halls, Civic Centres and Municipal Buildings,' In *Planning: Buildings for Administration, Entertainment and Recreation*, ed. Edward Mills (London: Newnes-Butterworths, 1976), 1:9.
61 Hutchison et al., 'Town Halls, Civic Centres and Municipal Buildings,' 167.
62 Saint, *Towards a Social Architecture*, ix.
63 Stefan Muthesius, *The Postwar University: Utopianist Campus and College* (Yale, Yale University Press, 2000). 3:
64 Muthesius, *The Postwar University*, 95.

65 Robert Stevens, *University to Uni: The Politics of Higher Education in England since 1944* (London: Politico's, 2004), 15 and 35.
66 Saint, *Towards a Social Architecture*, 214.
67 Alan Powers, *Britain: Modern Architectures in History* (London: Reaktion, 2007), 149.
68 Muthesius, *The Postwar University*, 1.
69 Harwood, *Space Hope and Brutalism*, 248.
70 Harwood, *Space Hope and Brutalism*, 248.
71 Graham Stewart, *Bang! A History of Britain in the 1980s* (London: Atlantic Books, 2013), 264.
72 Stewart, *Bang!* 264.
73 Richard Vinen, *Thatcher's Britain* (London: Pocket Books, 2010), 192.
74 Owen Hopkins, *Lost Futures: The Disappearing Architecture of Post-War Britain* (London: RCA, 2017), 92.
75 Powers, *Britain*, 204.
76 Sunad Prasad, 'Introduction,' In *Changing Hospital Architecture*, ed. Sunad Prasad (London: RIBA, 2008), 4.
77 Historic England, *Law Courts and Courtrooms: The Buildings of Criminal Law* (London: Historic England, 2016), 3.
78 Linda Mulcahy and Emma Rowden, *The Democratic Courthouse* (Abingdon: Routledge, 2020) 146.
79 Mulcahy and Rowden, *The Democratic Courthouse*, 147.
80 Mulcahy and Rowden, *The Democratic Courthouse*, 149.

# 6

# TRANSPORT

At the 1955 Earls Court Motor Show, the British Road Federation (BRF) devoted its entire stand to a large architectural model that ran around three sides of the booth (Figure 6.1). Made by Thorp, the model was a diagrammatic representation of a concept that the BRF had been promoting for more than a decade, the urban motorway. As an industry body representing road builders, car manufacturers, haulage firms, and oil companies, the BRF had become increasingly concerned about traffic congestion in Britain's largest towns and cities and in 1942 its own exhibition Motorways for Britain, designed by Geoffrey Jellicoe, had called for urgent motorway construction.[1] Thirteen years later, and with no motorways having yet been built, the BRF was focusing its campaign on the potential benefits of building elevated motorways through high-density urban areas, with Thorp's model offering a sanitised vision of what was to come as cities such as London, Manchester, and Birmingham embraced the idea with the construction of multi-lane arterial throughways and ring roads during the 1960s.

Models such as this were a common sight across Britain in the twentieth century, particularly during the postwar era of reconstruction and modernisation, as they were intended to inform and educate the public about grand new transport schemes that would revolutionise how people travelled around the country. The architectural historian Elain Harwood once observed that transport was the greatest area of change during the twentieth century, with the motor car in particular having profoundly influenced Britain's built environment.[2] Through the construction of new roads and motorways, petrol stations, garages, motels, airports, railway stations, bridges, and tunnels, the landscape of Britain was transformed on a scale that was arguably even greater than during the building of the railways in the previous century.[3] Different ideas about how we should move have already been seen shaping the visions put forward in every chapter of this book so far, including the models of Motopia, the prototype New Town, and the driving of a motorway through central Edinburgh in Chapter 1, the suburban housing estate models of Chapter 2, and the models of out-of-town developments in Chapters 3–5; however, this final chapter is dedicated to exploring architectural models specifically relating to the architecture and infrastructure of transport itself such as motorways, railway stations,

DOI: 10.4324/9781032715728-7

FIGURE 6.1    Model of a proposed urban motorway at the BRF stand at the 1955 Earl's Court
Motor Show. Made by Thorp, 1955. Courtesy Thorp Archive, AUB.

bridges, petrol stations, and airports. Almost all of them, as with Thorp's model for the
BRF, were for public display, and in many cases were necessary to explain entirely new
concepts, such was the pace of technological change.

Across the twenty-five models featured in this chapter a range of different and sometimes competing visions of how the future of Britain's transport infrastructure was
imagined provide important insights into how architects and civil engineers responded
to the development of new transport technologies. Transfixed by the possibilities
afforded by the motor car, the electrified railway, the aeroplane, the hovercraft, and
grand engineering projects such as the Channel Tunnel, the public was drawn to models
that offered exciting glimpses of fast, convenient, and above all modern means of transport. Technological change is consequently a core factor that can be seen influencing
the visions portrayed by all of the models in this chapter, as is the sheer scale of mass
movement that developed as the century progressed, with a single transport facility
such as Heathrow Airport handling more than the entire population of England in
just a single year by late 1990s.[4] Global influences also dominate, with both the motor
car and aeroplane imported from the United States, while international connections
through the design of airports and the Channel Tunnel illustrate the need for common
architectural styles and engineering standards. Brian Edwards' description of transport
architecture as 'the story of modernity acted out in ever more daring manifestations
of interior space, light, technology and speed,'[5] rings true in many of the models discussed in this chapter, and in embodying similarly ambitious and utopian ideas as the
planning models featured in Chapter 1, they continue a long tradition of the merging
in miniature of visionary dreams of technology, movement, and progress that was best

exemplified by Norman Bel Geddes' Futurama model that was the centrepiece of the 1939 New York World's Fair. As a 'seductive and propositional vehicle for a utopic automobile-centred future,'[6] Futurama helped entwine the miniature, modernism, and the motor car together, and these themes can be seen in most of the models that this chapter presents.

Inspired by the car to 'produce ever more dramatic schemes that might reshape the world,'[7] by the end of the century Britain's built environment had been redesigned to suit the motorist. Few would have imagined the car's impact at the start of the twentieth century, however, with its place in society rapidly evolving from one of ridicule, then to fascination, before ultimately being seen as a fundamental instrument of civilisation.[8] The changing nature of the transport models recorded in Thorp's archive reflect this remarkable progression, with the tussle between visions of public and private modes of transportation ultimately won by the latter as the car became a symbol of both freedom and private pleasure.[9] As the models that follow evidence, however, the greatest architectural and engineering visions continued to be associated with public transport and by examining different dreams of both public and private modes of movement in Britain as they were put forward, this chapter reveals the common challenge of keeping up with accelerating change.

### The Future Is Already Here

When studying photographs of the very earliest transport models John Thorp made during the first decades of the twentieth century, it can be easy to forget how utterly new and transformative the concepts they represented actually were. The first electrically powered underground railway in London had opened in 1890, the 1896 Motor Act had heralded the arrival of the motor car on Britain's roads, and the Wright brothers first took to the air in the United States in 1903, and yet by the time of John Thorp's passing in 1939, his company had made models of motorways, aircraft factories, and multi-level underground electric railway stations. The rapid development of new transport technologies during the early twentieth century provided Thorp with a steady stream of model commissions with the burgeoning motor industry and the expansion of London's underground railway network driving most of the work. Such was the pace of change at the time that many visions of the future of transportation in Britain were outdated almost as soon as they were proposed.

The impact of the motor car on the landscape was already causing alarm just ten years after its first introduction,[10] and having generated futuristic visions from the start,[11] in 1923 Thorp was commissioned to make a series of models of a daring proposal for the North and Western Motorway, the brainchild of the prominent motoring campaigner John Scott Montagu, Lord Montagu of Beaulieu. As a private proposal in an era in which the notion of a coordinated transport policy had yet to be considered, Montagu had formed a company to build a two hundred mile long motorway linking London, Birmingham, Manchester, and Liverpool.[12] Designed by the engineers Whitley & Carkeet-James[13] and inspired by the 1914 Bronx River Parkway in the United States and the Italian motor expressways that were then under construction,[14] the route was intended to be the first part of a network of long-distance roads built exclusively for motor vehicles. Quite literally a motorway – a road for motors – this was a dream that

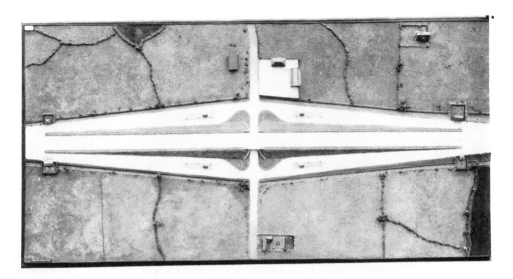

**FIGURE 6.2**    Model of the proposed North and Western Motorway. Client: Lord Montagu.
Made by Thorp, 1923. Courtesy Thorp Archive, AUB.

was shared by many pioneering motorists at the time who were deeply frustrated by the
condition of Britain's existing roads.[15] Thorp's models were made to show different possible junction types that motorists might encounter, including one of a flyover and under-
pass combination (Figure 6.2). As can be seen from the model, this was to be a tolled
roadway with gates and tollbooths controlling the entrances and exits in both directions.
Fully enclosed by high fencing, this was a vision of a purpose-built road solely for the
use of powered vehicles, its fifty-foot wide carriageways designed around a maximum
gradient of one in forty and a minimum curvature of a quarter of a mile to provide an
optimally smooth and safe journey.[16]

Montagu had long campaigned for better roads suitable for motor cars and being
firmly of the view that Britain's existing roads were completely unsuited to heavy vehicles, he had already proposed a 'motor-way' from London to Brighton in 1906.[17] His
later scheme for the North and Western Motorway gained popular favour in the press
and held cross-party support in Parliament, however when the proposal was put forward
as a private members bill in 1923, objections from the railway companies and their sup-
porters began to sour public opinion.[18] With the estimated £15 million cost of construction due to be raised privately, in the end the Ministry of Transport felt the project was
impossible to finance and ruled the proposal out,[19] with Britain having to wait another
thirty-five years before its first motorway was completed.

Models relating to the motor car nevertheless continued to emerge from Thorp's
workshop during the 1920s and 1930s as the number of cars on the road swelled from
one hundred thousand in 1918 to over two million in 1939. In 1938, V.L. Churchill &
Company commissioned a beautifully detailed model of a hypothetical maintenance
garage that reflected an ideal layout of such a facility that included forecourt petrol
pumps, a spacious and airy showroom at the front, and a comprehensive servicing
workshop behind, all wrapped up in fashionable art deco styling with a curved glass

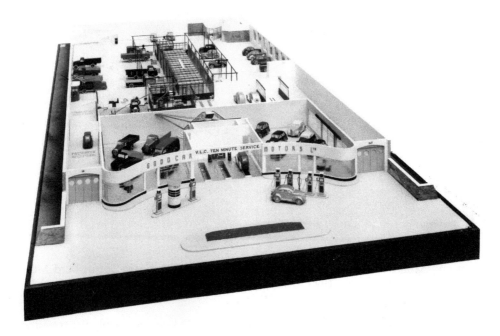

FIGURE 6.3    Model of V.L. Churchill's Ten Minute Service ideal garage layout, made by Thorp, 1938. Courtesy Thorp Archive, AUB.

frontage (Figure 6.3). The model was likely made for Churchill to display at their stand at the 1938 Earls Court Motor Show to promote their V.L.C. Ten Minute Service system, designed to offer lightning-fast maintenance checks to the time-pressed motorist. As a new company providing tools and equipment to the motor trade, Churchill was keen to showcase its concept as at the time just a single garage, Stanhays in Sevenoaks, had adopted it. The idea was that Churchill would sell all the tools necessary for an independent garage to offer the ten-minute service as a complete package, with the V.L.C. branding used to advertise the facility. Thorp's model was designed to illustrate the concept in its very best light, with the architecture of the fictitious Good Car Motors garage presenting a new and appropriately modern vision of what was ostensibly an industrial building in disguise. Dedicated car garages had grown out of engineering workshops and carriage builders without a clear expectation of how they should be designed, and with the car recognised by the 1930s as a central symbol of modernity, garages began to adopt a new form of architecture that blended 'efficiency with elegance.'[20] Thorp's model captured a hypothetical vision that matched the modernity of the automobile with the fresh and visually striking lines of modern architecture to great effect.

The desire to match the architecture of transportation with the increasingly modern technologies they were accompanying was also reflected in a number of models Thorp made for the Underground Electric Railway Company, more readily known as the Underground Group, which at the time owned all of London's major underground lines apart from the Metropolitan. By the 1920s the oldest parts of these railways were sixty years

**FIGURE 6.4**   Model of an alternative design for Hendon Central station. Architect: unknown. Made by Thorp, 1923. Courtesy Thorp Archive, AUB.

old and with the conversion to electric trains and massive expansions into new territory underway, a growing need had arisen to embrace more overtly modern visions of how its stations should be designed. As a result, in 1923 Thorp was commissioned to make a model of one of the latest planned stations, Hendon Central (Figure 6.4). Hendon opened later that year as part of the Charing Cross, Euston and Hampstead Railway's extension from Golders Green to Edgware, part of a move for the deep tube lines to reach out into the countryside surrounding London just as the Metropolitan Railway had in the previous two decades.[21] Thorp's model outlined a striking station building with extensive glazing and a curved roof that would have employed the very latest concrete construction methods, while the facades were to be clad with white ceramic tiles. This is not the station that was actually built, however, and this is where the great mystery of this model begins, as despite being made in the very same year that the station opened, it is of a completely different design.

Hendon station as built was designed by Stanley Heaps, the Underground Group's principal architect and who was responsible for all the stations on the Edgware extension. The same basic plan can be seen in both Thorp's model and Heaps' realised design, but the completed station adopted a neo-classical style inspired by Italian villas using Portland stone, Doric columns, and a tiled pyramid roof that was eventually replaced by a three-storey extension when the station, as had been intended from the start, was incorporated into a much wider parade of shops. Quite who designed the version portrayed in Thorp's model is rather puzzling, with the complex roof construction outwardly similar to the work of John Easton and Howard Robertson, who would later design Loughton station,[22] while the tiled facade recalled Charles Holden's early work on the entrances to Westminster and Bond Street stations that had been commissioned in 1922. It was Holden who effectively took over from Heaps several years later due to Frank Pick, the Underground Group's Assistant Managing Director, becoming increasingly dissatisfied with Heaps' work, and it is likely this dissatisfaction with Heaps' actual designs for the Edgware extension that prompted Thorp's model to be made. Heaps' design for Hendon was already under construction by the time the model was commissioned, meaning the design it represented could never have been more than a thought experiment, the Hendon site perhaps used as the basis for other architects Pick may have been courting to propose their own ideas for how future stations might appear. Pick had certainly wanted stylish stations on the Edgware extension[23] and Heaps' suburban classical offerings were likely a major disappointment given that there was a growing sense that the design of the network's stations no longer reflected the forward-thinking nature of the company,[24] with Pick seeking buildings that were 'modern, efficient, self-respecting and confident.'[25]

Whoever set out the ultimately unsuccessful vision of the future of London's underground stations depicted in the Hendon model, it undoubtedly reflected Frank Pick's search for a new architectural language that Charles Holden ultimately fulfilled, and in 1926 it was one of Holden's designs that prompted John Thorp to make one of the most unusual architectural models of his career, that of the new Piccadilly Circus underground station (Figures 6.5 and 6.6). Thorp himself often spoke of the complexity of the design and how the only way to fully understand what was being built was to study his model, the drawings produced of the site being far too confusing for anyone but an expert to comprehend. The model needed to show how Holden's design for a new circular hall underneath the roundabout would connect through a series of tunnels and escalators to the platforms of the two underground lines that crossed each other at an angle on different levels. Piccadilly station had become hugely overcrowded by the mid-1920s with over one million passengers using it each year and as it was not possible to extend the station entrance at street level, the solution put forward was to move the station concourse itself underground.[26] This was to be the most ambitious station upgrade of its time,[27] and Thorp designed the model in layers that could be removed to allow better visibility of what was happening underneath. With the road surface and subway entrances detached, the grand circular concourse and various connecting tunnels were shown in a rather unusual but strangely effective manner that revealed how they might appear if the solid ground around them was removed. The tiled circular hall that Holden designed offered a radical new concept for a station design that had become necessary to meet the demands of mass transportation on a scale that the original station had been ill-equipped to handle.

With the use of all modes of transport rapidly increasing, the renewal and upgrade of existing transport facilities in this manner would become a common theme of many such models that Thorp produced as the century progressed. As with earlier models of motorways and garages, the Piccadilly model also demonstrated that during the interwar years such visions of the future of transportation in Britain had grown in both ambition and size, a process that was to accelerate almost out of control in the years that followed with the models emerging from Thorp's workshop in the postwar era evidencing an enthusiastic and sometimes frantic response to the evolving demands of mass transportation and rapid technological change.

FIGURE 6.5 Model of Piccadilly Circus underground station with the road level in place. Architect: Charles Holden. Made by Thorp, 1926. Courtesy Thorp Archive, AUB.

FIGURE 6.6 Model of Piccadilly Circus underground station with the road level removed. Architect: Charles Holden. Made by Thorp, 1926. Courtesy Thorp Archive, AUB.

## Modernised Movement

During the postwar era, a re-examination of Britain's transport networks became a key priority. Housing, health, and education, as evidenced by models in previous chapters, were addressed first, but by the middle of the 1950s the state of the country's roads, and more urgently, its railways, were being approached with vigour by both civil engineers and architects in casting new visions of the future of transportation in Britain. The largest and most comprehensive plan put forward was that for the railways. Having been stretched to the extremes during the Second World War, Britain's largely Victorian

**FIGURE 6.7** Demonstration model of the West Coast Mainline electrification project. Client: BICC Ltd. Made by Thorp, 1962. Courtesy Thorp Archive, AUB.

railway infrastructure and steam-powered locomotives seemed almost anachronistic in the new age of jetliners and nuclear power, and in 1955 the British Transport Commission unveiled a £1.2 billion modernisation plan that aimed to completely re-equip the railway network by 1970. The intention was to position the railways to better compete with road transportation in carrying both passengers and freight.[28] An enormous number of architectural models were made as part of the modernisation plan, mostly by the in-house modelmakers working within the architects' departments of British Railways' four regional offices, but in 1962 Thorp was commissioned to make a rather unusual model to illustrate the flagship element of the plan, the electrification of the West Coast Mainline between London, Birmingham, Manchester, and Glasgow (Figure 6.7).

Made for British Insulated Callender's Cables Ltd (BICC), the model was quite different from Thorp's standard architectural models as this was to be a working model railway. The modernisation plan had set an ambition of replacing all steam locomotives with diesel and electric traction within fifteen years by electrifying 1500 miles of railway. A section of the West Coast Mainline between Crewe and Manchester was upgraded as a prototype between 1957 and 1960, and following this work proceeded south towards London, which was reached in 1966, and eventually north to Glasgow in 1974. BICC had won the contract for the work as British Railways lacked the sufficient expertise to complete such a mammoth task and BICC had already gained valuable experience in electrification projects in Europe.[29] Thorp's model, made at 1:76 scale to make use of commercial model railway products such as the trains and the track, was used as part of a massive marketing campaign to inform the public about what was happening on the railways. Showcasing all the different types of masts and portals that BICC were installing to carry the overhead wires, the model attempted to capture the feel of the fully modernised line, complete with brand new station buildings and platforms, signals, and bridges, all of which needed upgrading to accommodate the electrification equipment. With moving trains intended to capture the attention of passers-by, this was a vision of a modern, clean, fast, and regular railway that was fit for the future.

With further railway modernisation models handled by British Railway's own mod-elmakers, Thorp's order book of transport-related projects during the 1950s and 1960s was subsequently dominated by road transportation instead, with the car, the archi-tecture that accompanied it, and the road network itself undergoing its own period of intense modernisation. During the 1950s car ownership doubled to more than nine mil-lion vehicles,[30] which put an enormous pressure on existing facilities such as maintenance garages and petrol stations, with the latter being the focus of two sets of models Thorp made for Shell-Mex/BP between 1952 and 1954 (Figure 6.8). The first set of three mod-els (on the left of the photograph) were produced to illustrate the winning designs of a service station of the future competition that Shell-Mex/BP ran in conjunction with the RIBA. More than five hundred entries were received and the winners were announced using Thorp's models in 1952. The top left model in the photograph was of a petrol sta-tion in a suburban location, the middle one for a motorway service area, and the model at the bottom was designed for a more rural location. In all of the models, developing ideas about which elements of the plot should be covered and where individual build-ings should be located can be seen, with the now ubiquitous flat overall roof starting to emerge in the designs.

Shell-Mex/BP was a joint venture between Shell and BP to jointly market their UK fuel distribution operations and the competition was overseen by BP's chief architect, Denis Birchett, who was keen to identify a modular design for petrol stations that could be rep-licated up and down the country.[31] Following the end of petrol rationing in 1950, the use of 'solus' agreements had begun to change how the fuel retail market was structured by tying independent forecourt operators to single oil companies rather than allowing them to sell a selection of different brands.[32] As part of this change the oil companies wanted to impose their own branding on the petrol stations they supplied, and following American practice began to hire design consultants to develop their corporate images. There was no standard 'look' to British petrol stations at the time and many that had been built before the Second World War had experimented wildly with pitched roofs and neo-Georgian and mock-Tudor styling.[33] The Design and Industries Association was highly critical of such whimsical and picturesque connotations and called for a more standardised design as had been adopted by oil companies in the United States.[34] The three competition models were therefore early attempts to define precisely what a modern petrol station in Britain should be like, and around two years later a further set of three models was commissioned by the company (on the right of the image), and while these were of com-pletely different designs, a close inspection of the models reveals that they were all based on the exact same locations as the 1952 designs, as best seen by the position of the trees and the adjacent house in the bottom two photographs of the rural models. In exploring even more radical forms including circular self-service islands and dramatic glass-fronted buildings, the second set of models suggests that Birchett's department used the same hypothetical sites for at least several years while the company imagined what future

**FIGURE 6.8**   Models of proposed designs for future petrol stations. Client: Shell-Mex/BP. Made by Thorp, 1952–1954. Courtesy Thorp Archive, AUB.

petrol stations should be like in preparation for the era of mass car ownership that was by then looming on the horizon.

By the 1960s Thorp was also making models of proposed motorways once more; however, unlike Lord Montagu's 1923 North and Western Motorway model, these were actually built as Britain embarked on its largest ever road-building programme. Thorp's 1965 model of the then-proposed Lofthouse Interchange between the M1 and the M62 captured the utopian nature of the motorway dream beautifully with its depiction of the M1 passing underneath on the bottom level, the M62 crossing at a right angle above, and the 240 metre wide connecting roundabout elevated on a third tier over them both (Figure 6.9). Designed by the Highways and Bridges Department of West Riding County Council, the Lofthouse Interchange involved the excavation of thousands of tons of soil, the construction of five separate bridges, eight slip roads, and all the associated ground works. Partially opened in 1968, it was not until 1974 that the M62 continued all the way through, after which it became the first motorway junction in Britain with two separate motorways flowing in four different directions. As one of the first three-tier

**FIGURE 6.9**  Model of the Lofthouse Interchange. Engineers: West Riding County Council Highways and Bridges Department. Made by Thorp, 1965. Courtesy Thorp Archive, AUB.

motorway junctions, Lofthouse was hailed as the 'Piccadilly Circus of the north' when unveiled,[35] with Thorp's model projecting a vision of speed, safety, and the established narrative that motorways represented nothing less than 'cutting-edge modernity.'[36] Prime Minister Harold Macmillan identified motorways as symbols of Britain's technological and economic progress,[37] standing as physical adverts for 'affluence and social mobility,'[38] and their expansion across the nation's countryside was astonishingly rapid, with an average of one mile of motorway completed every week during the 1960s, totalling one thousand miles by 1970.[39] The gently curving grassy banks and carefully placed trees on the model also reflected a desire to plan the landscaping of these new roads in great detail, with consultants from Sir Owen Williams and Partners brought in to advise,[40] the effortlessness of Thorp's model conveying an idea of motorways as a form of sculpture, artistically considered as well as engineered.[41]

Motorways also demanded entirely new types of buildings to accompany them and in 1961 Thorp made a model of an unbuilt proposal for the Toddington service area, which was to be the third to open on the M1 (Figure 6.10). Toddington was one of the five original locations for services that had been included in the 1958 design for the M1 and with Newport Pagnell to the south having reached capacity almost immediately upon opening, the Ministry of Transport called for designs for additional services at Toddington to be put forward. Thorp's model was of the Kenning Motor Group's 1961 proposal, and it clearly highlighted the cramped nature of the site with very small car parks on either side of the motorway and individual buildings scattered around. Designed for Kenning by T.P. Bennett, the proposal placed a three-hundred seat restaurant on one side of the complex with a paved seating terrace overlooking the motorway. A connecting overbridge would

FIGURE 6.10 Model of an unbuilt proposal for Toddington motorway services. Architect: T.P. Bennett. Made by Thorp, 1961. Courtesy Thorp Archive, AUB.

have allowed access from the other side of the carriageway, with separate petrol stations, toilet blocks, and haulage cafes provided in both directions.

The haphazard nature of the Kenning proposal for Toddington reflected the challenges facing the designers of Britain's first motorway services as there were no British precedents to draw from, leading to the referencing of American and Italian designs instead.[42] Because no stopping was allowed on the roadside of Britain's new motorways, service areas at regular intervals of approximately twenty-four miles were included in the earliest plans,[43] with the Ministry of transport determining the locations and specifying that they should remain open for twenty-four hours a day, set back from the road and accessed via dedicated slip roads. Tenders were then invited from private operators to build and operate the facilities on fifty-year leases. Neither the Ministry of Transport nor the bidding operators had any experience of what the needs of a motorway traveller might be,[44] other than offering restful and attractive environments in scenic locations.[45] The Kenning Group, for example, owned a chain of one hundred petrol stations but had no experience in hospitality management. Their proposal for Toddington reflected this, as did many others at the time, with few bidders carrying out any meaningful research. The Ministry of Transport had also secured the necessary land for them without considering the possibility of future expansion and this created a significant problem for the early services as they were quickly deemed to be far too small.[46] None of the 1961 bids for Toddington were successful and the tendering process was repeated the following year. Kenning put forward another, slightly larger, design, but Granda's plan for a two-storey complex was deemed the most appropriate and it was this design that was actually built. Thorp's model of the unbuilt Kenning Group proposal nevertheless captured an early

**FIGURE 6.11**    Model of the Oxford Motor Lodge. Client: Forte Group. Made by Thorp, 1964. Courtesy Thorp Archive, AUB.

vision of offering comprehensive facilities to the motorist on Britain's new motorways that included food, maintenance, fuel, entertainment, and relaxation. As entirely new places to explore, motorway services represented the 'optimism of the motorway age,'[47] offering an egalitarian dream where all types of people would eat and rest together and architectural models of these new facilities were vital in informing the public and the press about the new experiences they offered.

Three years later an altogether more polished vision of roadside hospitality was captured in Thorp's model of the proposed Forte Motor Lodge near Oxford just off the A34 (Figure 6.11). This was a grand, almost luxurious concept for a roadside rest stop with the Autogrill restaurant and its distinctive roof shown on the right, a spacious car park which was planned to host the country's first park and ride facility behind, and clustered around the lawn and swimming pool to the left was the Excelsior Motor Lodge, comprising three two-storey blocks with stone cladding, balconies overlooking the lawn, and individual garages underneath. The lodge opened in 1964 as planned and was immediately celebrated for its modern design and welcoming atmosphere, drawing heavily from the American motel tradition. Roadhouses catering for the needs of the long-distance motorist by providing food, entertainment, and overnight rooms had existed since the 1930s, but in the 1960s American-inspired motels had started to spring up, with fifteen in 1961 and seventy five by 1965,[48] of which Forte's Oxford Motor Lodge was certainly one of the most innovative and stylish designs.

Forte's design for Oxford, created by an unknown architect, drew from an earlier design pioneered in Epping in 1962 whereby the bedrooms were raised above internal garages.[49] Adopting modern architectural features such as large windows, integrated bathrooms and kitchens, and shade-forming overhanging rooflines, the Forte Motor Lodge offered a comfortable, low-density vision of roadside accommodation, albeit one that was already becoming out of date as with the number of cars on the roads rapidly increasing, it was clearly not the most efficient use of space. Able to accommodate just thirty families, lodges such as this were soon replaced by motor hotels which followed standard hotel designs with multiple floors and internal corridors situated in the middle of expansive car parks. Oxford nevertheless proved to be a popular resting place and Thorp's model demonstrated yet another attempt to respond to the rapidly changing demands of the age of mass motoring that was by then underway. As Britain's transport infrastructure was modernised following the Second World War, the car was emerging as the clear winner in the battle between public and private transport, but alongside visions of upgraded roads and railways, Britain's architects and engineers were also dreaming of far bolder alternatives in response to additional technological and engineering advances that resulted in some of the most spectacular architectural models of the time.

## Grand Ambitions

As was evidenced by the mass-electrification of Britain's railways outlined by Thorp's model for BICC, the postwar era was gripped by a certainty that technology was the solution to many of the nation's problems and could be used to actively improve society.[50] This was very much the core of modernist thinking and in celebrating the machine age, transportation – particularly the aeroplane – was seen as the ultimate expression of technological achievement.[51] Flight had captured the imagination of modernist architects from the very start as evidenced by Le Corbusier's great passion for aviation. With the arrival of the commercial passenger jet in the 1950s, the world was suddenly opened up and architectural models of grand visions of entirely new ways of connecting people began to emerge from Thorp's workshop.

The Pilkington Glass Age Development Committee, as has already been seen in this book with both the Motopia and Sea City models, was by far the most radical and forward-thinking client that Thorp worked for, interested in stretching the boundaries of both architecture and engineering. As meticulously considered thought experiments, the designs that the Committee produced carefully projected what was just about technically possible at the time into the near future, usually the year 2000. Transport systems played an important part in all of their schemes, but in none more so than their 1957 proposal for Skyport 1, designed for the Committee by James Dartford. Thorp's model of the proposal (seen with the final finishing touches being applied in Figure 6.12) was a relatively small construction when compared to the enormous models for the Committee that would follow, but it clearly outlined Dartford's plan for a five hundred feet tall trio of landing pads held aloft above a combined hotel, office, and parking complex. Glass enclosed lift shafts would carry passengers between the ground level terminal facilities and awaiting intercity helicopter flights that would whisk them to destinations across Britain and Europe.

Planned to be built at St. George's Circus in Southwark, Skyport 1 was a vision of the airport relocated from the edges of the city and brought into its heart. The idea was to use advances in helicopter technology to create point-to-point connections between the centres of major cities, thus removing the need to change to a different mode of transport to get from far-flung airports to city centres. Up to twenty-four landings per hour were envisaged and Dartford's design drew from earlier proposals for similar structures that included John Lloyd Wright's 1926 concept of a three hundred metre high megastructure with airship docking stations in Los Angeles and Charles Glover's 1931 proposal for a

**FIGURE 6.12**    Model of Skyport 1. Architect: James Dartford for the Pilkington Glass Age
Development Committee. Made by Thorp, 1957. Courtesy Thorp Archive, AUB.

ringed airport to be built above Kings Cross station.[52] Thorp's model was widely featured
in publicity materials for the scheme put out by the Glass Age Development Committee,
with all the major architectural journals dedicating articles to what was a highly speculative but much-needed intervention into London's growing traffic problems.

Dartford's vision for Skyport 1 was considered radical at the time and yet in many
ways it completely underestimated the scale of change that air travel would bring in the
postwar era, particularly in terms of the size of the buildings and associated infrastructure

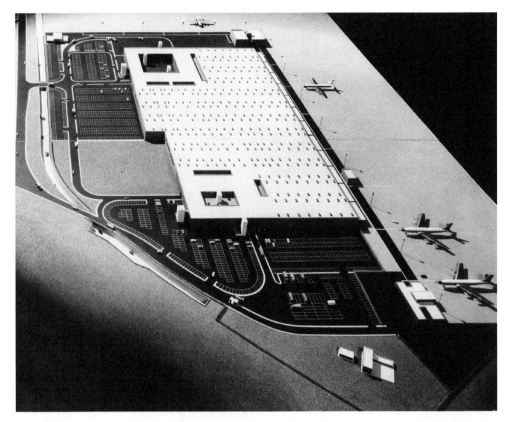

**FIGURE 6.13** Model of Heathrow Cargo Terminal. Engineer: Frederick Snow. Made by Thorp, 1966. Courtesy Thorp Archive, AUB.

that would be called for. Airports remained stubbornly outer-urban affairs, however, spreading over the landscape with increasing confidence. The scale of airport growth during the 1960s was captured by Thorp's 1966 model of the proposed joint BOAC and BEA cargo facility at Heathrow Airport (Figure 6.13). Photographed by Henk Snoek, the enormity of the ten acre building can be seen in comparison to the tiny model cars parked outside. To the bottom left of the model is the entrance to the road tunnel that would provide access from the main airport site on the other side of the southern runways, while the aircraft lined up on the apron demonstrated how up to thirteen separate flights could be accommodated at any one time. As with the model of Southampton docks discussed in Chapter 3, this was a vision that was formed in response to massive changes to how freight was being shipped around the world and an early sign of the importance of globalised trade. Designed by the engineer Sir Frederick Snow, the terminal was planned to incorporate the largest mechanical handling system in Britain and the model itself depicts an early version of the scheme that was slightly modified before completion in 1969.

London's Heathrow airport, only renamed as such in the same year that Thorp's model was made in order to distinguish itself from the growing second airport at Gatwick, had experienced a phenomenal growth in both passenger and freight volumes since the first permanent buildings at the site, designed by Frederick Gibberd, had opened in 1955, with twelve million passengers passing through and a quarter of a million tons of cargo being processed a year, the latter growing at a rate of twenty-five percent per annum. The cargo terminal was therefore designed to cope with future growth and employed light-weight aluminium construction methods that had already been pioneered at Heathrow in the 1950s with the building of aircraft hangers with clear spans of more than two hundred feet.[53] The enormous building and the cargo tunnel connecting the site to the central terminal complex that Thorp's model depicted was a significant undertaking and an unmissable sign of confidence in the future of air transportation.

While jet travel had accelerated the growth of airports and their associated facilities and forced architects and engineers to rapidly respond to their changing needs, airport design had at least been evolving for more than forty years by that point, whereas just one year after the Heathrow model was completed, Thorp was asked to make a model that demonstrated an idea of how to accommodate an entirely new form of transport, the hovercraft. The 1967 model of the proposed Ramsgate International Hoverport (Figure 6.14) was a stunning creation, depicting one hovercraft departing while another refuelled as arriving cars exited down its forward ramp and departing passengers and cars boarded from the rear. Behind, the strikingly modern terminal with its balcony restaurant and cocktail bar, shopping centre, bank, and customs hall dominates the scene. Designed by the Essex-based architects Barnard, Morris, Evans and Partners, Ramsgate

**FIGURE 6.14** Model of Ramsgate International Hoverport. Architects: Barnard, Morris, Evans and Partners. Made by Thorp, 1967. Courtesy Thorp Archive, AUB.

was the world's first purpose-built hoverport, constructed at Pegwell Bay just along the coast from the town. Intended to handle over one million passengers per year, the chosen location was a controversial one, being a site of special scientific interest, and so the low buildings were designed to reduce their visual impact on their surroundings. With no previous designs for such a complex to serve as a guide, the architects, and Hoverlloyd, their newly-formed client, envisaged a facility that was a cross between a ferry terminal and an airport, seeking a smooth and rapid passenger experience that would reflect the high-speed nature of the hovercraft themselves. Using the British Hovercraft Corporation's two hundred ton SRN4 Mountbatten class vehicles that could carry two hundred and fifty passengers and thirty cars, the twenty-eight mile crossing to Boulogne was to be completed in less than thirty five minutes. As an alternative to slower ferry services from Dover, this was a vision of high-speed, convenient, and utterly modern transport, and all just ten years after the first manned hovercraft had been successfully tested.[54] The animation Thorp included in the model, with strolling passengers and the departing hovercraft's whirling propellers depicted by circular disks of Perspex, helped to communicate the efficiency of the design, and while passenger numbers never reached initial projections upon opening in 1968, the vision put forward by the model of Ramsgate nevertheless captured the ambition of the hoverport concept and its architects' idea of an entirely new type of building for an entirely new mode of transport.

The notion of a cross-Channel hovercraft service was almost immediately replaced as a popular vision of the future of transport by an even bolder dream that almost came to fruition just one year after the Ramsgate hoverport opened, and in 1969 Thorp made the first of what would eventually prove to be a long line of models relating to the largest civil engineering project ever undertaken in Britain, the Channel Tunnel (Figure 6.15). Depicting one

**FIGURE 6.15** Sectional model of the proposed Channel Tunnel. Engineer: unknown. Made by Thorp, 1969. Courtesy Thorp Archive, AUB.

of the many proposals put forward by different construction consortia that were lobbying for whatever contracts that might be forthcoming, Thorp's cut-through model outlined the basic premise of the tunnel that had been established in 1961 and which specified twin railway tunnels and a connecting service tunnel between. The desire to find new cross-Channel communication links had become particularly urgent during the 1960s, as evidenced by both the Channel Tunnel and Ramsgate Hoverport models, due to a perception that rapidly increasing volumes of both people and goods would soon overwhelm the capacity of Britain's ferry ports.[55] In 1964, the first tentative agreement between the British and French governments outlined their joint intention to build a tunnel, with a formal declaration made in 1966 following underwater surveys of the seabed to assess the concept's feasibility.[56] The plan was to start construction in 1969 for an estimated completion in 1975, but by 1967 the project had already lost momentum. The issue was that the tunnel was as much a political dream as it was an engineering one, viewed by Prime Minister Harold Wilson as a necessary step to support his desire to take Britain into the European Economic Community.[57] When the French government vetoed Britain's entry into the EEC, combined with growing internal political distractions in both Britain and France, the proposal lost much of its political support and was quietly put on hold.[58]

Thorp continued to build models of proposed Channel crossings for the next thirty years, however, including two 1973 models of what was the most ambitious scheme put forward, the European Common Market Channel Bridge, Industrial City and Port (Figures 6.16 and 6.17). Conceived as a private proposal that would be independently financed, it was developed by the civil engineer Wilem Frischmann, the architect Gordon Lorimer, and the promoter Edgar Detwiler, and positioned as an alternative to the Channel Tunnel that aimed to build not only both physical road and railway links between Britain and France but also a vast island city in the middle of the English Channel that

**FIGURE 6.16** Model of the proposed Common Market Channel Bridge and Industrial City. Engineer: Wilem Frischmann. Made by Thorp, 1973. Courtesy Thorp Archive, AUB.

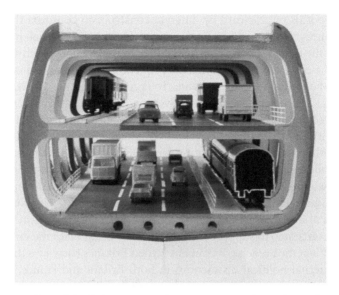

**FIGURE 6.17** Sectional model of the proposed Common Market Channel Bridge. Engineer: Wilem Frischmann. Made by Thorp, 1973. Courtesy Thorp Archive, AUB.

was not too dissimilar to the Sea City concept (see Chapter 1). The larger masterplan model of the scheme showed the three-deck road and rail bridge crossing the Channel between Dover and Calais at a height of more than two hundred metres above sea level, and had it been built, this would have been by far the longest bridge span in the world.[59] In the centre of the model and halfway between the two bridges was the most spectacular element of the proposal, the Common Market City and Port. Closer to the bridge to the north end of the island, the model depicted the outline plan of a city with a marina, shopping centre, parks, cinemas, offices, and a single vast apartment building able to house more than one million people. To the south of the bridge, an enormous industrial complex suitable for oil and chemical plants was imagined, surrounded by forty miles of deep-water ports. Built on reclaimed chalk banks and covering twenty square miles, the island city would have been half the size of Manhattan.

The concept was both preposterous and deeply serious, as with the Channel Tunnel once again in political favour, 1973 became a crucial year for those lobbying for alternatives to make their case heard, with Thorp's models generating much debate. Frischmann had been promoting the scheme since 1971, and Thorp's larger model of the bridge cross-section depicted a refined version of the plan as it stood in 1973, which itself was estimated to cost £1.7 billion, with additional funding required to build the city in full.[60] This was a grand vision that embraced speculative thinking on a scale usually reserved for the Glass Age Development Committee, offering a radical proposal for faster transport links and greater international trade that sought to make Britain's seaports and airports obsolete.[61] With the Channel Tunnel approved for the second time in 1973 only to be abandoned once more in 1975, Frischmann's bridge proposal was largely forgotten, although as will be seen later in this chapter, this was far from the last model relating to the Channel crossing that Thorp was asked to make.

**FIGURE 6.18**   Model of the Humber Bridge. Engineer: Freeman Fox and Partners. Made by Thorp, 1973. Courtesy Thorp Archive, AUB.

Entirely by coincidence, the very next model that Thorp completed in 1973 was also one of a large and vastly challenging bridge project, and which when completed actually did become the longest single-span suspension bridge in the world. The 1:1000 scale model of the Humber Bridge, by then one year into its nine-year build, captured not just the size but also the beauty of the two-kilometre-long structure (Figure 6.18). With cars, trees, and a ship passing underneath providing a quite startling sense of scale, the bridge, designed by the engineers Freeman Fox and Partners, was described at the time as 'a span across the imagination' and a 'creative act of faith and ingenuity.'[62] Based on Freeman Fox's earlier concepts for both the Severn and Bosphorus bridges, this was civil engineering on an enormous scale with the road deck suspended thirty metres above the water, twin one hundred and fifty-five metre tall towers at either end and more than 43,000 miles of steel cable. The project had an unusually long gestation with Sir Douglas Fox having been appointed as the consultant engineer to the project in 1928. The alignment of the bridge was established in 1935 and then in 1955 his company put forward a revised proposal which was submitted to Parliament for approval in 1958. Powers to construct the bridge were granted the following year, although it took until 1972 before work actually began.[63] This was a grand vision that showcased Britain's engineering skills at its very highest level, and which when completed transformed journeys in the area by providing a much lower crossing on the Humber that formed a central part of the area's post-industrial regeneration. It was also notably a road bridge rather than a road and rail bridge as had been proposed for the Channel Bridge, a reminder that despite the era's interest in other forms of transport, the car was already utterly dominating the second half of the twentieth century.

## Public Transport for Tomorrow

The political preference for supporting either public or private means of transportation in Britain, usually reduced to a choice of whether to invest in roads or railways, shifted both ways throughout the twentieth century, although roads generally saw the greatest favour following the Second World War due to an 'unshakable belief in the superiority and inevitability of the car.'[64] By the 1980s, a backlash driven by environmental concerns had begun to swing the pendulum back towards the benefits of public transport once more, however. The models relating to road transportation that Thorp was commissioned to make reflected this, as gone were the grand visions of new motorways and replaced instead by humbler models of supermarket petrol stations. Conversely, the number of railway-related projects Thorp was asked to make saw a steady increase, partly enabled by the demise of British Rail's in-house modelmaking capacity, but more significantly due to a number of ambitious rail-based architectural and civil engineering projects that dominated the final two decades of the century. Amid rising concerns about urban air quality and traffic congestion, public transport had become the future once more.

In 1962, British Railways was given the freedom to develop the enormous swathes of land that it owned for commercial purposes (as seen with the Bishopsgate model in Chapter 1) and by the 1980s Victoria, Charing Cross, and Fenchurch Street stations had been redeveloped to incorporate large shopping and office complexes.[65] The largest of these projects was Liverpool Street station, and in 1983 Thorp made the last in a series of models the company had been commissioned to make to illustrate an ultimately unsuccessful proposal for the station's redevelopment designed by Fitzroy Robinson for the British Rail Property Board (Figure 6.19). With the Victorian roof spanning the right-hand side of the station still visible, the model makes it very clear that the site was to be dominated by a bulky office development. Using a stacked glass cube motif to highlight the various entrances into the complex, Fitzroy Robinson's design involved the complete demolition of the neighbouring Broad Street station, the raised approach to which can still be seen as a roadway heading towards the main office building from the top left of the model, with the idea being to make the best use of the station's prime location on the edge of the City of London by building commercial office space and using the funds raised from this to take an ageing Victorian station and make it fit for the twenty first century.

Fitzroy Robinson's first proposal for the station, outlined in 1975, had been even more dramatic, envisioning a startlingly large megastructure that involved the complete demolition of both stations and replacing them with a high-rise office complex of hexagonal towers that was reminiscent of the New Barbican proposal described in Chapter 1. The intention was to build 'a new city within a city'[66] with the station platforms underneath, but the plans generated a particularly fierce reaction. The Department for the Environment placed an emergency listing on several parts of Liverpool Street station and after

**FIGURE 6.19**   Model of an unbuilt proposal for the redevelopment of Liverpool Street station. Architect: Fitzroy Robinson. Made by Thorp, 1983. Courtesy Thorp Archive, AUB.

a public enquiry that identified which areas could be demolished and which had to be preserved, the architects were sent back to the drawing board.[67] A revised plan that kept more of the existing Liverpool Street station and focused the office development onto the Broad Street site was given planning approval in 1979, with Thorp producing models of the scheme in both 1981 and 1983 as the details were finalised. By the time of Thorp's last model, however, this early attempt to create a successful private-public partnership was struggling to secure a financial backer, and just a few months later British Rail decided to split off the Broad Street location for redevelopment first, with Peter Foggo's Broadgate complex put forward to occupy the site, and Fitzroy Robinson's plan for Liverpool Street was dropped in favour of an in-house design by British Rail's Nick Derbyshire which was ultimately a far more sensitive solution that preserved and even enhanced the existing architecture.

Six years later, an altogether different vision of public transport was put forward by a model of Briway's Advanced Guided Transit System that demonstrated the opposite end of the scale from the redevelopment of one of London's busiest stations (Figure 6.20). Emblematic of the popularity of light rail and guided busways at the time, Thorp's 1989 model outlined Briway's concept for a low-cost urban transit system that would run on an elevated trackway above existing streets. Showing the patriotically liveried vehicles running down the central reservation of an urban dual carriageway, the model presented a clear picture of what Briway was hoping to achieve, a means of bypassing the traffic below and moving people around a town or city centre with ease. The system was essentially a guided busway with the vehicles fitted with tyred wheels and running between guard rails. Electrically powered, each unit could carry twenty passengers at a time. Thorp's model was likely prepared as part of Briway's submission to a competition set up by Southampton City Council for proposals that would meet the requirements

**FIGURE 6.20** Model of the proposed Briway Advanced Guided Transit System. Developer: Briway Transit Systems. Made by Thorp, 1989. Courtesy Thorp Archive, AUB.

of its Rapid Transit Initiative, a plan to build a three-mile-long elevated transit system through the city centre.[68] Briway won the contract and by 1990 was already working with at least three other cities and two major airports that were similarly keen on introducing the concept.

Briway offered a means of efficiently installing a new public transport system within an existing urban landscape cheaply and with minimal disruption. Described as a 'horizontal passenger lift,'[69] Briway was developed by the helicopter entrepreneur Alan Bristow, who invested £8 million of his own money into the project, although after a televised crash on the demonstration track at his home in 1991, all orders fell away and the Southampton scheme was abandoned. The proposal nevertheless reflected a period in which interest in light rail and rapid transit systems was increasing, with work to build new tramlines already underway in Manchester, Birmingham, and Leeds, while thirty seven other towns and cities were actively exploring similar schemes.[70] Following the success of the Tyne and Wear Metro and the Docklands Light Railway, rapid transit schemes such as Briway were positioned as the solution to Britain's urban transport problems. Offering smaller vehicles, cheaper and faster construction, and lower operating costs than standard railways,[71] rapid transit had the potential to revolutionise public transport in busy towns and cities, and Southampton's plan for Briway sought to link the railway station and the city's shopping and leisure destinations together with a fast and frequent service, extending a dream of integrated and environmentally conscious transport that, in Briway's case at least, was never realised.[72]

At precisely the same time that Thorp was making the Briway model, the company's modelmakers were also busy making their next series of models relating to the Channel Tunnel, this time to outline the plans for the Channel Tunnel Rail Link. Construction of the tunnel itself had begun in 1988 with France already building the TGV Nord line to link their side of the tunnel to Paris. British Rail had been considering a similar line through Kent to London since the 1970s, but with the tunnel now a certainty detailed planning had begun as to precisely which route the line should take, but the publication of various options in 1988 proved to be a public relations disaster that resulted in more than ten thousand people protesting in Maidstone.[73] The following year, British Rail identified a single preferred route which was to head south from London in a tunnel from a new underground station between Kings Cross and St. Pancras stations before turning east and heading towards the Channel Tunnel portals at Cheriton. Thorp was hired to make a series of detailed 1:1000 scale models of various sections of the route, including one of South Darenth (Figure 6.21) and one of Detling (Figure 6.22). The South Darenth model showed the new high-speed line following the alignment of an existing railway as it passed the edge of the village on a short viaduct before descending into a cut-and-cover tunnel, while the Detling model demonstrated how the line would skirt Maidstone by following the route of the M2 motorway, emerging from a tunnel portal to the north-west and heading through a woodland close to the village in a deep cutting. Both models attempted to emphasise the carefully considered landscaping that would help to minimise the new railway line's visual impact, although the scenes captured in both, with mature trees seemingly unaffected by the enormous construction work, would clearly not exist for many years after the line's completion.

Thorp's models nevertheless projected a vision of a fast, direct railway line built to continental standards that aimed to realise a journey time between London and Paris as close to two hours as was possible. This was to be a massive investment in the nation's infrastructure and Britain's first new mainline railway in nearly a century. The proximity to housing in both locations caused further alarm, however, and with even larger protests following, the models did little to calm the flames and if anything they may have made the situation worse. British Rail was subsequently forced to launch a £3 million public relations campaign to repair the damage inflicted by their poorly handled announcement of the route,[74] and by 1991 an alternative alignment put forward by Ove Arup had been adopted that shifted the north-western section of the railway away

FIGURE 6.21   Model of the proposed Channel Tunnel Rail Link at South Darenth, Kent. Engineer: British Rail. Made by Thorp, 1989. Courtesy Thorp Archive, AUB.

from South Darenth to follow the A2 dual carriageway, although the Detling model was very close to what was finally constructed, with the first section of the line from Cheriton to a junction with the existing railway network near Gravesend and onwards to the interim terminus at Waterloo, opening in 1998, some four years after the Channel Tunnel was completed.

Further models of the Channel Tunnel Rail Link continued to provide a lucrative line of business for Thorp throughout the 1990s, particularly as plans for the envisaged permanent terminus in the Kings Cross area were developed. British Rail established Union Railways in 1992 to develop the project,[75] and in 1993 Thorp was commissioned by the company to build a large masterplan model to outline their latest thinking for the site (Figure 6.23). By this time, the route of the second phase of the line into London had changed to an easterly approach through Stratford, thus requiring a northerly facing station in the Kings Cross area rather than the originally planned southern orientation. This opened up the possibility of using either the existing Kings Cross or St. Pancras stations, and Union Railways was asked to put forward proposals for both. Thorp's model of the St. Pancras option showed the new high-speed line running alongside the existing North London Line on a viaduct at the bottom left before curving southwards into a massively expanded St. Pancras station. Although a concept model only, the clear potential for the redevelopment of the Kings Cross railway lands in the middle of the scene would have

**FIGURE 6.22** Model of the proposed Channel Tunnel Rail Link at Detling, Kent. Engineer: British Rail. Made by Thorp, 1989. Courtesy Thorp Archive, AUB.

been impossible to ignore, while the scale of the extension required at St. Pancras outlined the architectural challenges ahead. The route as built closely followed the approach shown by the model, although the line was eventually constructed in a tunnel underneath the North London Line rather than alongside it.

With the St. Pancras option approved, the following year Thorp produced a 1:500 scale model of an early outline of the proposed layout of the station itself (Figure 6.24). The model was made to represent an impression of the scheme only, with detailed design work yet to begin. As the proposal involved the modification of the Grade I Listed station building, parliamentary approval was required and so a basic reference design had to be drawn up to show MPs and other stakeholders what was planned.[76] The design outlined by Thorp's model was therefore just a concept, never intended to be built as shown. The overall plan was clear, however, and the model presented a new vision of an entirely novel concept for Britain, an international railway station complete with passport and customs control. In order to accommodate the four-hundred-metre-long Eurostar trains a large extension to the north was required, and at this early stage, it was envisaged that both the Eurostar platforms, shown in blue, and the Midland Mainline platforms, in yellow, would extend all the way back into the existing Barlow trainshed, with the Kent high-speed services only using the extension on the far left. To the right of the trainshed on the western side of

**FIGURE 6.23**  Model of the proposed Channel Tunnel Rail Link terminus at St. Pancras. Client: Union Railways. Made by Thorp, 1993. Courtesy Thorp Archive, AUB.

the station, the model showed the proposed international departure suite, from which Eurostar passengers would reach the central international platforms via an overbridge. The original concept was by Nick Derbyshire, with Alistair Lansley later taking over as the detailed design work progressed, during which the Midland services were moved out of the trainshed to open up the undercroft for use as retail and circulation space.

The St. Pancras model was one of the last major transport projects that Thorp worked on during the twentieth century, with the station itself not opening until 2007. St. Pancras International, as it became known, was instantly hailed as an architectural masterpiece and the entire Channel Tunnel Rail Link (later rebranded as High Speed 1) stands as a symbol of the resurgence of interest in public transport as a means of providing a much-needed alternative to Britain's increasingly congested roads by using the latest engineering and transport technologies. Throughout the twentieth century, as all the models featured in this chapter have highlighted, architects and civil engineers were constantly forced to respond to dramatic changes to both transport use and transport technology, extending dreams of the first motorways, inventing entirely new facilities such as service areas and hoverports, and imagining and then realising the vast engineering achievement of crossing the Channel. Inspired by the possibilities of new technologies such as the motor car, hovercraft, electrified railways, and the aeroplane, the projects captured here in model form illustrate the scale of influence that the desire of people to move swiftly and efficiently had on Britain's built environment during a century of profound change.

**FIGURE 6.24**    Model of an early proposal for St. Pancras International Station. Client: Union Railways. Made by Thorp, 1994. Courtesy Thorp Archive, AUB.

## Notes

1  Kathryn Morrison and John Minnis, *Carscapes: The Motor Car, Architecture and Landscape in England* (London: Yale University Press, 2012), 258.
2  Elain Harwood, *Space Hope and Brutalism: English Architecture 1945–1975* (London: Yale University Press, 2016), 299.
3  David Edgerton, *The Rise and Fall of the British Nation* (London: Penguin, 2019), 299.

4 Brian Edwards, 'Introduction,' In *The Architecture of British Transport in the Twentieth Century*, eds. Julian Holder and Steven Parissien (London: Yale, 2004), 7.
5 Edwards, 'Introduction,' 1.
6 Thea Brejzek and Lawrence Wallen, *The Model as Performance* (London: Bloomsbury, 2018), 7.
7 Morrison and Minnis, *Carscapes*, 91.
8 Martin Pugh, *We Danced All Night* (London: Vintage, 2009), 251.
9 Edwards, 'Introduction,' 18.
10 David Jeremiah, *Architecture and Design for the Family in Britain, 1900–1970* (Manchester: Manchester University Press, 2000), 34.
11 Morrison and Minnis, *Carscapes*, 383.
12 Peter Thorold, *The Motoring Age: The Automobile and Britain 1896–1939* (London: Profile, 2003), 195.
13 Morrison and Minnis, *Carscapes*, 241.
14 Harwood, *Space Hope and Brutalism*, 316.
15 Morrison and Minnis, *Carscapes*, 239.
16 David Bayliss, *What Went Wrong? British Highway Development before the Motorways* (London: RAC Foundation, 2008), 13.
17 George Charlesworth, *A History of British Motorways* (London: Thomas Telford, 1984), 1.
18 Morrison and Minnis, *Carscapes*, 240.
19 William Plowden, *The Motor Car and Politics in Britain* (London: Penguin, 1973), 190.
20 Jeremiah, *Architecture and Design for the Family*, 161.
21 Christian Wolmar, *The Subterranean Railway* (London: Atlantic, 2005), 221.
22 David Leboff, correspondence with the author, January 2024.
23 Wolmar, *Subterranean Railway*, 222.
24 David Lawrence, *Underground Architecture* (Harrow: Capital Transport, 1994), 50.
25 Sheila Taylor and Oliver Green, *The Moving Metropolis* (London: Lawrence King, 2001) 179.
26 Taylor and Green, *The Moving Metropolis*, 196.
27 Wolmar, *Subterranean Railway*, 231.
28 Christian Wolmar, *Fire & Steam* (London: Atlantic, 2007), 227.
29 Christian Wolmar, *British Rail* (London: Penguin, 2023), 8.
30 Otto Saumarez Smith, *Boom Cities* (Oxford: Oxford University Press, 2020), 16.
31 Harwood, *Space Hope and Brutalism*, 313.
32 Morrison and Minnis, *Carscapes*, 152.
33 Nick Evans, *Fuelling the Motoring Age* (Cheltenham: The History Press, 2019), 12.
34 Morrison and Minnis, *Carscapes*, 149.
35 Joe Moran, *On Roads* (London: Profile, 2010), 49.
36 Moran, *On Roads*, 24.
37 David Lawrence, *Always a Welcome: A Glove Compartment History of the Motorway Service Area* (Twickenham: Between Books, 1999), 14.
38 Moran, *On Roads*, 26.
39 Charlesworth, *British Motorways*, 50.
40 Charlesworth, *British Motorways*, 41.
41 James Drake, *Motorways* (London: Faber and Faber, 1969), 25.
42 Morrison and Minnis, *Carscapes*, 312.
43 Harwood, *Space Hope and Brutalism*, 316.
44 Lawrence, *Always a Welcome*, 15.
45 Harwood, *Space Hope and Brutalism*, 316.
46 Lawrence, *Always a Welcome*, 105.
47 Morrison and Minnis, *Carscapes*, 314.
48 Morrison and Minnis, *Carscapes*, 306.
49 Morrison and Minnis, *Carscapes*, 306.
50 Jeremiah, *Architecture and Design for the Family*, 174.
51 Hugh Pearman, *Airports: A Century of Architecture* (London: Lawrence King, 2004), 79.
52 Pearman, *Airports*, 89.
53 Harwood, *Space Hope and Brutalism*, 327.
54 Angela Croome, *Hovercraft* (Leicester: Brockhampton Press, 1971), 87.

55 Nicholas Comfort, *The Channel Tunnel and its High Speed Links* (Usk: Oakwood Press, 2006), 11.
56 David Hunt, *The Tunnel: The Story of the Channel Tunnel, 1802–1994* (Upton-upon-Severn: Images, 1994), 109.
57 Hunt, *The Tunnel*, 113.
58 Nicholas Faith, *The History of the Channel Tunnel* (Barnsley: Pen and Sword, 2018), 27.
59 Louis Edgar Detwiler and Wilem Frischmann, *Proposed European Common Market Channel Bridge, Industrial City and Port Project* (London: Channel Project Management Corporation, 1972), 9.
60 Detwiler and Frischmann, *Proposed European Common Market Channel Bridge, Industrial City and Port Project*, 11.
61 Detwiler and Frischmann, *Proposed European Common Market Channel Bridge, Industrial City and Port Project*, 2.
62 George Wilkinson, *Bridging the Humber* (York: Cerialis Press, 1981), 1.
63 Wilkinson, *Bridging the Humber*, 5.
64 Morrison and Minnis, *Carscapes*, 345.
65 Wolmar, *British Rail*, 237.
66 David Lawrence, *British Rail Architecture 1948–97* (Manchester: Crecy, 2018), 196.
67 Nick Derbyshire, *Liverpool Street: A Station for the Twenty-first Century* (Cambridge: Granta, 1991), 43.
68 M.R. Taplin, 'Light Transit Proposals in British Cities: A Review,' In *Light Transit Systems*, ed. B.H. North (London: Thomas Telford, 1990), 12.
69 S.M. Keys, 'Moving People within Urban Centres,' In *Light Transit Systems*, ed. B.H. North (London: Thomas Telford, 1990), 125.
70 Taplin, *Light Transit Proposals*, 17.
71 Taplin, *Light Transit Proposals*, 5.
72 Keys, *Moving People*, 121.
73 Keys, *Moving People*, 217–219.
74 Comfort, *The Channel Tunnel*, 169.
75 Hunt, *The Tunnel*, 246.
76 Alastair Lansley, *The Transformation of St Pancras Station* (London: Lawrence King, 2008), 54.

# CONCLUSION

## Model Futures

Through this book's examination of just some of the many thousands of architectural models Thorp made during the twentieth century, the optimistic and hopeful ideas that lay behind them have been described, but of the 120 models featured, only half of the projects they represented were actually built as planned. Even for those models, the future visions they put forward were never entirely realised, however, as sullied by the ongoing effects of the weather, litter, graffiti, traffic, and the more fundamental issues of inadequate, unsympathetic, or simply inappropriate design choices, reality is forever unable to match the promises that pristine and utopian architectural models extend. Across the previous six chapters it has therefore been possible to see not only the inherent optimism and hopefulness of architectural models but also their fallacy. As the architectural critic John Chisholm lamented in his polemic about the dangers of architectural models in 1969, 'perhaps one of the saddest experiences of present-day city life is to see a prestige model on display in the glass-fronted reception area of a large redevelopment project, as pristine and bright as the day it was proudly unveiled…while about it the all-too-familiar reality of the dream stands – stained and tatty.'[1] From a certain perspective, Chisholm was right, although the problem he was addressing at the time was perhaps less that architectural models were so idealised but rather that the designs put forward and the building materials used during the rebuilding of postwar Britain were incapable of living up to what had been promised (Figure 7.1). His attack on the fictitious nature of Model Britain nevertheless highlights the gap between the visions that architectural models portrayed and what was actually built, and with even the models of projects that were completed so distanced from actual reality in this manner, what then has been the value of examining them?

As the models featured in this book have demonstrated, architectural models are depictions of ideas that allow us to bypass the constraints of reality to gain important insights that go beyond an understanding of what was built to reveal what was imagined. Chisholm, in comparing models to reality, was looking in the wrong direction, as architectural models have always been much closer to the realm of hopes and dreams than the day-to-day world we experience around us, and they remain crucial in this regard

DOI: 10.4324/9781032715728-8

**FIGURE 7.1**   An unrealistic depiction of the future? A pristine model of a prefabricated concrete residential tower block. Architect: Beryl Hope Associates. Made by Thorp, 1964. Courtesy Thorp Archive, AUB.

even today. The role of an architectural model is to communicate, and often to sell, an individual dream, presenting proposals in their best light, and not just to whoever might commission the projects they outline, but also to the architects, planners, and engineers who created them. The intrinsic appeal of models can be highly seductive, creating a fantasy that encourages a belief that the ideas they contain are achievable when in practice they may be far from possible, and it is clear that some of the models featured in this book were not just a means of communicating ideas to others but were also acting as surrogates through which their dreamers could indulge in their false realities. The historical value of such models is that they provide visibility of those realities and the dreams that shaped them, allowing us to access a future horizon that was always in a constant state of becoming.

In recognising this, this book has examined the rich body of evidence that such architectural models provide in order to understand how the future of Britain's built environment was imagined during the twentieth century, and by using the records of Thorp Modelmakers it has been able to put forward a history of just some of the ideas behind yesterday's dreams of tomorrow. The intention was to illustrate the breadth of ideas that were put forward, whether ideologically or commercially driven and how architectural models were used as an important means of communicating those dreams to the public. In doing so, this book has contributed to the wider understanding of the history of Britain's built environment in the twentieth century by presenting a parallel history of Model Britain, the imaginary, miniature realm in which visions of both the built and unbuilt can be examined alongside in order to gain insights into how the past thought about tomorrow. Through its recognition of the importance of anticipatory practices as a means of enriching historical studies,[2] this book has sought to bring to life some of the ambitions of the past to explore the imaginative and visionary processes involved in formulating possible futures during a century of radical change. Beyond the direct knowledge that this investigation provides, this book also set out to encourage the use of architectural models as a form of historical evidence, recognising that in serving as a means of recording such anticipatory practices, historic models, and their photographic echoes, remain the most revealing and evocative medium in which the future horizons of the past can be seen. Today we can use architectural models to revisit moments of conviction, imagination, and optimism, unaffected by the passing of time, and by entering Model Britain we have been able to witness not just the past, but the past's own future, expressed through visions very much of their time and which can tell us a great deal about the contemporary concerns they were attempting to resolve.

Throughout the twentieth century, tens of thousands of architectural models were made by dedicated modelmakers such as those working at Thorp alongside countless more made by architects themselves, with the immediate postwar decades standing as a high point in the history of the architectural model where it utterly dominated the expression of architectural ideas. The complex reasons as to why this was the case is another story yet to be told, but with models acting as gateways into alternate worlds, throughout the whole of the twentieth century people were able to access the visions they held in a multitude of ways – in an estate agent's window or a developer's marketing suite, at a public exhibition or planning consultation, as photographs in magazines and newspapers, or in a professional context as a client or financial stakeholder. As this book has demonstrated, the miniature world of Model Britain was and still is an attractive place to explore, providing an opportunity to look down on models of the future, their scale granting us a command over the world that we so often lack in reality. As manifested dreams laid out so convincingly, during the twentieth century architectural models provided a safe landscape in which huge changes could be considered in response to the political, economic, technological, and social influences of the time. Their value was recognised in their ability to fix the multitude of possibilities into a single, conviction-driven path. While many of the visions they contained were never realised, and even those that were could never match the idealised perfection of the model world, the certainty that architectural models provided was necessary in order to summon the confidence to make any changes at all, and whether history regards those visions as successes or failures, the optimism and hopefulness visible in the models used to communicate those dreams cannot be ignored.

Through this book's positioning of architectural models as evidence of the changing ideas relating to the future of place, home, work, leisure, citizenship, and transport put forward during the twentieth century, it has been clear that Britain's architects, planners, and civil engineers were driven by an overriding desire to forge a future in which the standards of daily life were improved. The models of different visions of place highlighted the strength of ideological conviction behind plans to correct the perceived failures of the nineteenth century in rethinking the fundamental layout and composition of Britain's towns and cities, while the models of home similarly showcased the same imposition of new ideas about where and how people should live. In both chapters, a genuine desire to use the built environment to improve people's lives was seen to have often overridden the ambitions of the people who would be affected, while many models have also evidenced the contrast between state-approved and privately funded visions of the future. In terms of work, and offices and industrial buildings in particular, Thorp's models have demonstrated just how rapidly the social, economic, and technological changes of the twentieth century forced the nation's architects to reimagine the buildings in which Britain's workforce was accommodated, and the same influences were also seen in the models of leisure that followed, with increased affluence and the commercialisation of free time driving changes in terms of both building design and the overall planning of the built environment. In the chapter dedicated to visions of citizenship, the desire to raise standards of healthcare that eventually led to the creation of the welfare state, and the rise and fall of civic pride, were both reflected in the changing nature of the models Thorp was commissioned to make, and through the models of transport infrastructure that followed, it has been possible to see the dramatic influence of the car and other new forms of transport in radically shifting how the future of Britain's built environment was envisaged.

The impact of the car has been particularly prevalent in this book, whether in models outlining the growth of suburbia, predicting out-of-town development, or showcasing plans for hotels and leisure centres with plentiful underground parking, while the demand to keep up with rapid technological change can be seen across the entire collection of models described, accompanied by the increased influence of commercial motivations in place of ideological concerns. Modernism, despite its lofty position in the historiography of British architecture between the wars, is almost entirely absent in Thorp's models until the 1950s, an indication of how limited modernism's physical impact on the built environment actually was compared to the enormous numbers of neo-classical or Tudorbethan buildings that were constructed during the same period. Across many of the chapters the influence of the property developer has also been seen, with the sales role of many of the models featured emphasising the commercial intentions of the projects they represented. The relationships between the individuals creating the visions of the future that the models captured and those who would live or work in them also stand out as a recurring theme, with the humbler and more practical wishes of ordinary people so often subsumed by the ideologically driven will of an architect or planner. Regardless of their motivations, however, what all the models presented in this book have ultimately demonstrated is an unwavering belief in the ideas being put forward, embracing a conviction and optimism that each individual vision of the future was absolutely the right one. In an uncertain and constantly changing world, architectural models provided a reassuringly confident prediction of what was to come, and it is that certainty above all else that unifies the different dreams of the future that the models described in this book were made to convey.

Fundamentally, the continued use of architectural models as a means of exploring and communicating different ideas about what the future of Britain's built environment should be like was a result of their bringing what was imagined into a tangible, if miniaturised, form. Models of projects that were never built such as Sea City, the Phoenix development, or Lutyens' Liverpool Cathedral were as real as their ideas ever became, existing for brief periods of time as physical manifestations of the futures they proposed that their designers, clients, the press, and the public could walk around and examine. For models of projects that were actually built, such as St. James's Grove, Ramsgate Hoverport, and the Plymouth Holiday Inn, for example, these existed in far more pristine and utopian states than their full-sized counterparts could ever maintain, and in both cases it was through the models themselves that the futures they contained were accessed, and while decisions were rarely made based on models alone, they formed an important element of the pitch, acting as persuasive devices that held far greater power than a drawing, diagram, or planning application could ever hope to muster. That power continues to fuel their use today, despite the prevalence of alternative digital means of communicating architectural designs, and with no end in sight of the defiantly analogue architectural model, perhaps in another seventy five years a similar volume to this one but dedicated to the future visions of Britain put forward by architectural models during the twenty first century will make the same observations.

This book, in using architectural models drawn solely from Thorp's admittedly comprehensive catalogue of work, has only been able to provide a glimpse of the totality of miniature visions put forward relating to the future of Britain's built environment during the twentieth century, and even in terms of the Thorp Archive the models included here amount to little more than one percent of the total number the company made. This study has therefore only explored a tiny fraction of Model Britain and further work is needed to fully capture the insights of Thorp's work alone, and given how many other twentieth century modelmaking firms have seemingly disappeared without trace it is also tempting to wonder what the records of McCutchon Studio, Partridge's Models, Cockade, and other major modelmakers of the previous century might also reveal should they be found. Through its introductory tour of Model Britain, this book has nevertheless extended an examination of the ideas, values, and assumptions that lay behind the architectural models it describes and in seeking to reveal yesterday's dreams of a better tomorrow as captured in miniature form, it has been able to cast a new light on some of the bold visions of the future that architectural models of twentieth century Britain contain and the dreams of the architects, planners, and engineers who imagined them.

**Notes**

1  John Chisholm, 'Rehearsal for Reality,' *The Architect and Building News*, February 27, 1969, 24.
2  Zoltan Boldizsar Simon and Marek Tamm, 'Historical Futures,' *History and Theory* 60, no 1, 2021, 3.

# BIBLIOGRAPHY

Ashby, Madeline. 'Prediction Fiction.' *RSA Journal* 1, 2023, 10–15.

Ayres, Gwendoline. *England's First State Hospitals 1867–1930*. London: Wellcome Institute, 1971.

Barrett, Helen, and Phillips, John. *Suburban Style*. London: MacDonald Orbis, 1987.

Bayliss, David. *What Went Wrong? British Highway Development before the Motorways*. London: RAC Foundation, 2008.

Beanland, Christopher. *Unbuilt*. London: Batsford, 2021.

Beattie, Susan. *A Revolution in Housing*. London: The Architectural Press, 1980.

Blakeman, Harriet. 'Sickness: Advances in British Hospital Design after the First World War.' In Neal Shasore and Jessica Kelly (eds.). *Reconstruction: Architecture, Society and the Aftermath of the First World War*. London: Bloomsbury, 2023, 335–352.

Blanchet, Elizabeth, and Zhuravlyova, Sonia, *Prefabs: A Social and Architectural History*. Swindon: Historic England, 2018.

Blunt Alison, and Dowling, Robyn. *Home*. Abingdon: Routledge, 2006.

Borer, Mary Cathcart. *The British Hotel through the Ages*. Cambridge: Lutterworth Press, 1972.

Borsay, Peter. *A History of Leisure*. Basingstoke: Palgrave Macmillan, 2006.

Boughton, John. *Municipal Dreams: The Rise and Fall of Council Housing*. London: Verso, 2019.

Boyer, George. *The Winding Road to the Welfare State*. Princeton: Princeton University Press, 2019.

Brejzek, Thea, and Wallen, Lawrence. *The Model as Performance*. London: Bloomsbury, 2018.

Bremner, G.A. *Building Greater Britain*. London: Paul Mellon Centre for Studies in British Art, 2022. https://yalebooks.co.uk/book/9781913107314/

Brodie, Allan. *The Seafront*. Swindon: Historic England, 2018.

Bullock, Nicholas. *Building the Post-War World: Modern Architecture and Reconstruction in Britain*. London: Routledge, 2002.

Bunting, Madeline. *The Seaside*. London: Granta, 2023.

Burnett, John. *A Social History of Housing 1815–1985*. London: Methuen, 1986.

Burns, Wilfred. *British Shopping Centres*. London: Leonard Hill, 1959.

Chance, Helena. *The Factory in a Garden*. Manchester: Manchester University Press, 2017.

Chandler, J. A. *Explaining Local Government*. Manchester: Manchester University Press, 2007. https://manchesteruniversitypress.co.uk/9780719067075/#:~:text=By%20J.,Chandler& text=Explaining%20local%20government%2C%20available%20at,1800%20until%20 the%20present%20day.

Chanin, Eileen. 'The New London.' In Neal Shasore and Jessica Kelly (eds.). *Reconstruction: Architecture, Society and the Aftermath of the First World War*. London: Bloomsbury, 2023, 59–86.

Charlesworth, George. *A History of British Motorways*. London: Thomas Telford, 1984.

Chisholm, John. 'Rehearsal for Reality.' *The Architect and Building News*, February 27, 1969, 21–27.

Clarke, Jonathan. 'Development: Speculative Office Development and Public Sector Tenants.' In Neal Shasore and Jessica Kelly (eds.). *Reconstruction: Architecture, Society and the Aftermath of the First World War*. London: Bloomsbury, 2023, 87–112.

Cleve Barr, Albert William. *Public Authority Housing*. London: Batsford, 1958.

Coleman, Nathaniel. *Utopias and Architecture*. London: Routledge, 2005.

Comfort, Nicholas. *Surrender: How British Industry Gave Up the Ghost 1952–2012*. London: Biteback, 2012.

Comfort, Nicholas. *The Channel Tunnel and its High Speed Links*. Usk: Oakwood Press, 2006.

Crawford, David. *A Decade of British Housing 1963–1973*. London: The Architectural Press, 1975.

Cresswell, Tim. *Place: An Introduction*. Oxford: Blackwell, 2015.

Croft, Catherine. 'David Rock: Architecture Is the Land of Green Ginder, or Form Follows Culture.' In Elain Harwood and Alan Powers (eds.). *The Seventies*. London: The Twentieth Century Society, 2012, 65–73.

Croome, Angela. *Hovercraft*. Leicester: Brockhampton Press, 1971.

Cullingworth, Barry, and Nadin, Vincent. *Town and Country Planning in the UK*, 15th Edition. Abingdon: Routledge, 2006.

Cunningham, Colin. *Victorian and Edwardian Town Halls*. London: Routledge, 1981.

Dahinden, Justus. *Urban Structures for the Future*. London: Pall Mall Press, 1972.

Dean, David. *The Thirties: Recalling the English Architectural Scene*. London: Trefoil books, 1983.

Delgado, Alan. *The Enormous File: A Social History of the Office*. London: John Murray, 1979.

Derbyshire, Nick. *Liverpool Street: A Station for the Twenty-first Century*. Cambridge: Granta, 1991.

Deriu, Davide. 'Transforming Ideas into Pictures: Model Photography and Modern Architecture.' In H. Higgott and T. Wray (eds.). *Camera Constructs*. Abingdon: Routledge, 2012, 159–178.

Detwiler, Louis Edgar. and Frischmann, Wilem. *Proposed European Common Market Channel Bridge, Industrial City and Port Project*. London: Channel Project Management Corporation, 1972.

Doury, Natalie. 'Successfully Integrating Cinemas into Retail and Leisure Complexes: An Operator's Perspective.' *Journal of Leisure Property* 1, no. 2, 2001, 119–126.

Downton, Peter. 'Temporality, Representation and Machinic Behaviours.' In Peter Downton, Andrea Mina, Mark Burry, Michael J. Ostwald (eds.). *Homo Faber: Modelling Architecture*. Sydney: Archadia Press, 2007, 42–49.

Doyle, Barry. 'Democracy, Diversity, Dispersal.' In Neal Shasore and Jessica Kelly (eds.). *Reconstruction: Architecture, Society and the Aftermath of the First World War*. London: Bloomsbury, 2023, 353–373.

Drake, James. *Motorways*. London: Faber and Faber, 1969.

Drake, Robert. 'Public Libraries in the Twentieth Century.' In Elain Harwood and Alan Powers (eds.). *The Architecture of Public Service*. London: Twentieth Century Society, 2017.

Drexler, Arthur. 'Engineers Architecture: Truth and its Consequences.' In Arthur Drexler (ed.). *The Architecture of the Ecole des Beaux-Arts*. London: Secker and Warburg, 1977, 13–59.

Dunn, Nick, and Cureton, Paul. *Future Cities: A Visual Guide*. London: Bloomsbury, 2020.

Edwards, Brian. 'Introduction.' In Julian Holder and Steven Parissien (eds.). *The Architecture of British Transport in the Twentieth Century*. London: Yale, 2004, 1–19.

Ellard, Patrick. 'New Ash Green: Span's Latter 20th Century Village in Kent.' In Barbara Simms (ed.). *Eric Lyons and Span*. London: RIBA, 2006.

Emerson, Giles. *Sainsbury's: The Record Years, 1950–1992*. London: Haggerston Press, 2006.

Engerman, David. 'Introduction: Histories of the Future and Futures of History.' *The American Historical Review* 117, no. 5, December 2012, 1402–1410.

'English Housing Survey 2014 to 2015: Housing Stock Report.' Ministry of Housing, Communities & Local Government, 2015, https://www.gov.uk/government/statistics/english-housing-survey-2014-to-2015-headline-report.

Esche, J. 'Architecture in Miniature.' In Marg Von Gerkan and Partner (eds.). *Idea and Model.* Berlin: Ernst and Son, 1994, 22–30.

Esher, Lionel. *A Broken Wave: The Rebuilding of England 1940–1980.* London: Allen Lane, 1981.

Evans, Nick. *Fuelling the Motoring Age.* Cheltenham: The History Press, 2019.

Faith, Nicholas. *The History of the Channel Tunnel.* Barnsley: Pen and Sword, 2018.

Ferry, Kathryn. *Holiday Camps.* Oxford: Shire, 2010.

Ferry, Kathryn. *The British Seaside Holiday.* Oxford: Shire, 2009.

Fishman, Robert. *Bourgeois Utopias: The Rise and Fall of Suburbia.* London: Basic Books, 1982.

Forsyth, Alastair. *Buildings for the Age: New Building Types 1900–1939.* London: HM Stationery Office, 1982.

Franklin, Geraint, and Harwood, Elain. *Post-Modern Buildings in Britain.* London: Batsford, 2017.

Freeman, Joshua B. *Behemoth: The History of the Factory and the Making of the Modern World.* New York: W.W. Norton, 2019.

Gardiner, Juliet. *The Thirties: An Intimate History.* London: Harper Press, 2010.

Gazeley, Ian, and Newell, Andrew. 'Introduction.' In Nicholas Crafts, Ian Gazeley and Andrew Newell (eds.). *Work and Pay in 20th Century Britain.* Oxford: Oxford University Press, 2007.

Gerrewey, Christian. '"What are Rocks to Men and Mountains?" The Architectural Models of OMA/Rem Koolhaas.' *OASE* 84, 2011, 31–36.

Gibberd, Frederick. *Town Design.* London: The Architectural Press, 1962.

Girouard, Mark. *Robert Smythson and the Architecture of the Elizabethan Era.* Chicago: University of Michigan Press, 1966.

Glendenning, Miles, and Muthesius, Stefan. *Tower Block: Modern Public Housing in England, Scotland, Wales, and Northern Ireland.* London: Yale University Press, 1993.

Gloag, John. *The Englishman's Castle.* London: Eyre & Spottiswoode, 1945.

Goobey, Alastair. *Bricks and Mortals.* London: Century Business, 1992.

Goss, Anthony. *British Industry & Town Planning.* London: Fountain Press, 1962.

Gray, Fred. *Designing the Seaside.* London: Reaktion, 2006.

Grindrod, John. *Concreteopia.* Brecon: Old Street, 2013.

Grindrod, John. *Iconicon.* London: Faber and Faber, 2022.

Hall, Peter. *Cities of Tomorrow.* Oxford: Blackwell, 2002.

Hall, Tony. *Nuclear Politics.* London: Pelican, 1986.

Harvie, Christopher. *Fool's Gold.* London: Hamish Hamilton, 1994.

Harwood, Elain. 'Building for Span and the Public Sector.' In Barbara Simms (ed.). *Eric Lyons and Span.* London: RIBA, 2006, 53–71.

Harwood, Elain. *England's Schools.* Swindon: English Heritage, 2010.

Harwood, Elain. 'Markets, Arcades, Precincts and Shopping Centres.' In Susannah Charlton and Elain Harwood (eds.). *100 20th Century Shops.* London: Batsford, 2023, 32–38.

Harwood, Elain. *Space Hope and Brutalism: English Architecture 1945–1975.* London: Yale University Press, 2016.

Harwood, Elain, and Powers, Alan. 'From Downturn to Diversity, Revisiting the 1970s.' In Elain Harwood and Alan Powers (eds.). *The Seventies.* London: The Twentieth Century Society, 2012, 9–35.

Heaman, Elsbeth. *St Mary's: The History of a Teaching Hospital.* Liverpool: Liverpool University Press, 2003.

Hendrick, Thomas. *Model Making as a Career.* London: Percival Marshall, 1952.

Hill, Jeffey. *Sport, Leisure and Culture in Twentieth-Century Britain.* Basingstoke: Palgrave, 2002.

Hillier, John, and Blythe, Martin. *Poole's Pride Regained, 1964–1974*. Poole: Poole Historical Trust, 1996.

Historic England. *Law Courts and Courtrooms: The Buildings of Criminal Law*. London: Historic England, 2016.

Hobbs, Edward. *House Modelling for Builders and Estate Agents*. London: The Architectural Press, 1937.

Hobbs, Edward. *Pictorial House Modelling*. London: Crosby, Lockward and Son, 1926.

Hohl, Reinhold. *Office Buildings: An International Survey*. London: The Architectural Press, 1968.

Hopkins, Owen. *Lost Futures: The Disappearing Architecture of Post-War Britain*. London: RCA, 2017.

Howard, Ebernezer. *Garden Cities of Tomorrow*. London: Faber and Faber, 1945.

HRH The Prince of Wales. *A Vision of Britain: A Personal View on Architecture*. London: Doubleday, 1989.

Huggett, Frank E. *Factory Life & Work*. London: Harrap, 1973.

Hunt, David. *The Tunnel: The Story of the Channel Tunnel, 1802–1994*. Upton-upon-Severn: Images, 1994.

Hutchinson, Maxwell. *The Prince of Wales: Right or Wrong? An Architect Replies*. London: Faber and Faber, 1989.

Hutchison, David, Locke, Graham, and Robinson, Natalie. 'Town Halls, Civic Centres and Municipal Buildings.' In Edward Mills (ed.). *Planning: Buildings for Administration, Entertainment and Recreation*. London: Newnes-Butterworths, 1976, 1:1–1:9.

Jellicoe, Geoffrey. *A Comprehensive Plan for the Central Area of the City of Gloucester*. London: Jellicoe, Ballantyne and Coleridge, 1961.

Jellicoe, Geoffrey. *Motopia*. London: Studio Books, 1961.

Jeremiah, David. *Architecture and Design for the Family in Britain, 1900–70*. Manchester: Manchester University Press, 2000.

Jones, Edgar. *Industrial Architecture in Britain 1750–1939*. London: Batsford, 1985.

Jones, Stephen. *Workers at Play: A Social and Economic History of Leisure, 1918–1939*. London: Kegan Paul, 1986.

Kefford, Alistair. 'The Arndale Property Company and the Transformation of Urban Britain, 1950–2000.' *Journal of British Studies*, 61, no. 3, 2022, 563–598.

Keys, S.M. 'Moving People within Urban Centres.' In B.H. North (ed.). *Light Transit Systems*. London: Thomas Telford, 1990, 119–133.

Kirby, Andrew. 'The Architectural Design of UK Supermarkets: 1950–2006.' PhD diss., UAL, 2008.

Koselleck, Reinhart. *Futures Past: On the Semantics of Historical Time*. New York: Columbia University Press, 2004.

Kynaston, David. *Austerity Britain*. London: Bloomsbury, 2008.

Kynaston, David. *Family Britain*. London: Bloomsbury, 2010.

Kynaston, David. *Modernity Britain*. London: Bloomsbury, 2015.

Lahti, Markku. 'The Magical World of Models.' In Jari Jetsonen (ed.). *Little Big Houses*. (Helsinki: Building Information Ltd, 2000.

Laing, Andrew. 'New Patterns of Work: The Design of the Office.' In John Worthington (ed.). *Reinventing the Workplace*. London: The Architectural Press, 1997, 23–38.

Lansley, Alastair. *The Transformation of St Pancras Station*. London: Lawrence King, 2008.

Lawrence, David. *Always a Welcome: A Glove Compartment History of the Motorway Service Area*. Twickenham: Between Books, 1999.

Lawrence, David. *British Rail Architecture 1948–97*. Manchester: Crecy, 2018.

Lawrence, David. *Underground Architecture*. Harrow: Capital Transport, 1994.

Leboff, David. Correspondence with the author, January 2024.

Lethbridge, Lucy. *Tourists*. London: Bloomsbury, 2022.

Lowe, Rodney. *The Welfare State in Britain since 1945*. Basingstoke: Palgrave, 2005.

Lowenfeld, Jonah. 'Estate Regeneration in Practice: The Mozart Estate, Westminster, 1985–2004.' In Elain Harwood and Alan Powers (eds.). *Housing the Twentieth Century Nation*. London: The Twentieth Century Society, 2008.

Lund, David. *A History of Architectural Modelmaking in Britain: The Unseen Masters of Scale and Vision*. Abingdon: Routledge, 2022.

Manning, Peter. *Office Design: A study of Environment*. Liverpool: Department of Building Science, Liverpool University, 1965.

Marr, Andrew. *A History of Modern Britain*. London: Macmillan, 2007.

Marr, Andrew. *The Making of Modern Britain*. London: Macmillan, 2010.

Martin, Craig. *Shipping Container*. London: Bloomsbury, 2016.

McColdrick, Peter, and Thompson, Mark. *Regional Shopping Centres*. Aldershot: Avebury, 1992.

McIvor, Arthur. *A History of Work in Britain, 1880–1950*. Basingstoke: Palgrave, 2001.

Metropolitan Railway. *Metro-Land: British Empire Exhibition Number*. London: Metropolitan Railway, 1924.

Millar, Laura. *Archives: Principles and Practices*. London, Facet, 2017.

Moon, Karen. *Modelling Messages*. New York: Monacelli Press, 2005.

Moran, Joe. *On Roads*. London: Profile, 2010.

Morrison, Kathryn. *English Shops and Shopping*. London: Yale University Press, 2003.

Morrison, Kathryn, and Minnis, John. *Carscapes: The Motor Car, Architecture and Landscape in England*. London: Yale University Press, 2012.

Mulcahy, Linda, and Rowden, Emma. *The Democratic Courthouse*. Abingdon: Routledge, 2020.

Munce, James F. *Industrial Architecture*. London: Iliffe books, 1961.

Muthesius, Stefan. *The Postwar University: Utopianist Campus and College*. Yale: Yale University Press, 2000.

Newell, Andrew. 'Structural Change.' In Nicholas Crafts, Ian Gazeley and Andrew Newell (eds.). *Work and Pay in 20th Century Britain*. Oxford: Oxford University Press, 2007, 35–54.

Newton, Matthew. *Shopping Mall*. London: Bloomsbury, 2017.

O'Connor, Susan. 'The Body Politic and the Body Corporate.' In Elain Harwood and Alan Powers (eds.). *The Architecture of Public Service*. London: Twentieth Century Society, 2017, 163–175.

Oliver, Paul, Davis, Ian, and Bentley, Ian. *Dunroamin: The Suburban Semi and its Enemies*. London: Barrie and Jenkins, 1981.

Osborn, Frederick, and Whittick, Arnold. *The New Towns: The Answer to Megalopolis*. London: Leonard Hill, 1969.

Papadakis, Andreas. *Paternoster Square and the New Classical Tradition*. London: Academy Editions, 1992.

Parry-Jones, David. *Taff's Acre: A History and Celebration of Cardiff Arms Park*. London: Willow Books, 1984.

Pearman, Hugh. *Airports: A Century of Architecture*. London: Lawrence King, 2004.

Perrin, Gerald. 'Sports Centres and Swimming Pools.' In Edward Mills (ed.). *Planning: Buildings for Administration, Entertainment and Recreation*. London: Newnes-Butterworths, 1976, 6:1–6:32.

Pinder, David. *Visions of the City*. New York: Routledge, 2011.

Pipe, Paulette. 'Great Expectations.' *DR: The Fashion Business*, November 24, 1990, 58–59.

Pleydell-Bouverie, M. *The Daily Mail Book of Post-War Homes*. London: Associated Newspapers, 1944.

Plowden, William. *The Motor Car and Politics in Britain*. London: Penguin, 1973.

Powers, Alan. *Britain: Modern Architectures in History*. London: Reaktion, 2007.

Prasad, Sunad. 'Introduction.' In Sunad Prasad (ed.). *Changing Hospital Architecture*. London: RIBA, 2008.

Proctor, Robert. 'Citizenship: Welfare and the Democratic State in Percy Thomas's Civic Architecture.' In Neal Shasore and Jessica Kelly (eds.). *Reconstruction: Architecture, Society and the Aftermath of the First World War*. London: Bloomsbury, 2023, 267–294.

Pugh, Martin. *We Danced All Night*. London: Vintage, 2009.

Rabbitts, Paul. *Bandstands*. Swindon: Historic England, 2018.

Rappaport, Erika Diane. *Shopping for Pleasure*. Princeton: Princeton University Press, 2001.

Raymond, Santa, and Cunliffe, Roger. *Tomorrow's Office*. London: E&FN Spon, 1997.

Reiwoldt, Otto. *New Office Design*. London: Lawrence King, 1994.

Renwick, Chris. *Bread for All: The Origins of the Welfare State*. London: Penguin, 2017.

Roethe, Jonathan. 'A Pretty Toy or Purely Functional?' In Elain Harwood and Alan Powers (eds.). *The Architecture of Public Service*. London: Twentieth Century Society, 2017, 25–40.

Roth, Alfred. *New School Building*. London: Thames and Hudson, 1966.

Ruston, Phil. *Out of Town Shopping: The Future of Retailing*. London: The British Library, 1999.

Ryan, Deborah. *Ideal Homes 1918–39: Domestic Design and Suburban Modernism*. Manchester: Manchester University Press, 2018.

Ryan, Deborah Sugg. *The Ideal Home Through the 20th Century*. London: Hazar, 1997.

Rykwert, Joseph. *The Seduction of Place*. Oxford: Oxford University Press, 2000.

Ryle, Sarah. *The Making of Tesco*. London: Bantam Press, 2013.

Saint, Andrew. *Towards a Social Architecture: The Role of School-Building in Post War England*. London: Yale University Press, 1987.

Schilling, Alexander. *Architecture and Model Building*. Basel: Burkhauser, 2018.

Scott, Peter. 'Leisure, Consumption and Consumerism.' In Nichole Robertson, John Singleton and Avram Taylor (eds.). *20th Century Britain*. Abingdon: Routledge, 2023, 113–129.

Scott, Peter. *The Making of the Modern British Home*. Oxford: Oxford University Press, 2013.

Scott, Peter, and Walker, James. 'Inequality, Living Standards and Welfare Provision.' In Nichole Robertson, John Singleton and Avram Taylor (eds.). *20th Century Britain*. Abingdon: Routledge, 2023, 46–65.

Sea City, directed by H.G. Casparius. Pilkington Glass Age Development Committee, 1968.

Sharples, Joseph. *Liverpool*. London: Yale University Press, 2004.

Shasore, Neal. *Designs on Democracy*. Oxford: Oxford University Press, 2022.

Silverstone, Roger. 'Introduction.' In Roger Silverstone (ed.). *Visions of Suburbia*. Abbingdon: Routledge, 1997, 1–25.

Simms, Barbara. 'Community and Common Space.' In Barbara Simms (ed.). *Eric Lyons and Span*. London: RIBA, 2006, 97–113.

Simon, Zoltan Boldizsar, and Tamm, Marek. 'Historical Futures.' *History and Theory* 60, no. 1, 2021, 3–11.

Singleton, John. 'The British Economy.' In Nichole Robertson, John Singleton and Avram Taylor (eds.). *20th Century Britain: Economic, Cultural and Social Change*. Abingdon: Routledge, 2023, 29–45.

Smith, Otto Saumarez. *Boom Cities*. Oxford: Oxford University Press, 2020.

Smith, Otto Saumarez. 'The Lost World of the British Leisure Centre.' *History Workshop Journal*. 88, Autumn 2019, 180–203.

Stamp, Gavin. *Interwar: British Architecture 1919–39*. London: Profile, 2024.

Stevens, Robert. *University to Uni: The Politics of Higher Education in England since 1944*. London: Politico's, 2004.

Stewart, Graham. *Bang! A History of Britain in the 1980s*. London: Atlantic Books, 2013.

Stewart, John. *Twentieth Century Town Halls*. Abingdon: Routledge, 2019.

Stobart, John. *Spend Spend Spend: A History of Shopping*. Stroud: The History Press, 2008.

Stourton, James. *Heritage*. London: Head of Zeus, 2022.

Stow, Derek. 'Transformation in Healthcare Architecture.' In Sunad Prasad (ed.). *Changing Hospital Architecture*. London: RIBA, 2008, 13–48.

Sudjic, Deyan. *The 100 Mile City*. London: HarperCollins, 1993.

Swenarton, Mark. *Homes for Heroes*. London: Heinemann, 1981.

Tallon, Andrew. *Urban Regeneration in the UK*, 2nd Edition. Abingdon: Routledge, 2013.

Taplin, M.R. 'Light Transit Proposals in British Cities: A Review.' In B.H. North (ed.). *Light Transit Systems*. London: Thomas Telford, 1990.

Taylor, Norman. *Architectural Modelling and Visual Planning*. London: Cassell, 1959.

Taylor, Sheila, and Green, Oliver. *The Moving Metropolis*. London: Lawrence King, 2001.

'The Fascination of Models.' *The Building News*, March 28, 1924, specially reprinted copy of the original article made by John Thorp, Thorp Modelmaking Archive.

Thompson, Anthony. *Library Buildings of Britain and Europe*. London: Butterworth, 1963.

Thorold, Peter. *The Motoring Age: The Automobile and Britain 1896–1939*. London: Profile, 2003.

Thorp, John. *Models of Buildings, Estates, Works, etc. For Exhibitions or Law Cases*. London: John. B. Thorp, 1913.

Topalovic, Milica. 'Models and Other Spaces.' *OASE* 84, 2011, 37–45.

Turner, Barry. *Beacon for Change*. London: Aurum, 2011.

Vinen, Richard. *Thatcher's Britain*. London: Pocket Books, 2010.

Weatherell, Sam. *Foundations: How the Built Environment Made Twentieth-Century Britain*. Princeton: Princeton University Press, 2023.

Weaver, Lawrence. *Exhibitions and the Arts of Display*. London: Country Life, 1925.

Wellings, Fred. *British Housebuilders: History & Analysis*. Oxford: Blackwell, 2006.

Wilkinson, George. *Bridging the Humber*. York: Cerialis Press, 1981.

Wilson, John F. 'Big Business and Management in Britain.' In Nichole Robertson, John Singleton and Avram Taylor (eds.). *20th Century Britain: Economic, Cultural and Social Change*. Abingdon: Routledge, 2023, 143–157.

Winter, John. *Industrial Architecture*. London: Studio Vista, 1970.

Wolmar, Christian. *British Rail*. London: Penguin, 2023.

Wolmar, Christian. *Fire & Steam*. London: Atlantic, 2007.

Wolmar, Christian. *The Subterranean Railway*. London: Atlantic, 2005.

Woudstra, Jan. 'Landscape First and Last.' In Barbara Simms (ed.). *Eric Lyons and Span*. London: RIBA, 2006.

Wright, Lance. 'Hotels.' *The Architectural Review*, 152, no. 907, September 1972, 131–142.

Wrigley, Chris. 'Work, the Labour Market and Trade Unions.' In Nichole Robertson, John Singleton and Avram Taylor (eds.). *20th Century Britain: Economic, Cultural and Social Change*. Abingdon: Routledge, 2023, 98–112.

Wylson, Anthony. *Design for Leisure and Entertainment*. London: Newnes-Butterworths, 1980.

# INDEX

T - #0027 - 091024 - C57 - 246/174/11 - PB - 9781032715094 - Matt Lamination